THE NUMBER WE
END UP WITH

ALSO BY BETH GOLDNER

Wake

THE NUMBER WE END UP WITH

a novel

BETH GOLDNER

COUNTERPOINT

A MEMBER OF THE PERSEUS BOOKS GROUP

NEW YORK

JUL 2 7 2005

Copyright © 2005 by Beth Goldner

Published by Counterpoint
A Member of the Perseus Books Group

Selection from "The Nude Swim" reprinted by permission of SLL/Sterling Lord Literistic, Inc. Copyright by Anne Sexton.

"One Bright Day" courtesy of the British Columbia Folklore Society.

Books published by Counterpoint are available at special discounts for bulk purchases in the United States by corporations, institutions, and other organizations. For more information, please contact the Special Markets Department at the Perseus Books Group, 11 Cambridge Center, Cambridge, MA 02142, or call (617) 252-5298 or (800) 255-1514, or e-mail special.markets@perseusbooks.com.

A CIP catalog record for this book is available from the Library of Congress

ISBN-13 978-1-58243-270-0
ISBN 1-58243-270-8

07 06 05   10 9 8 7 6 5 4 3 2 1

To Mom

Thanks to my toile de Jouy sister,
to the usual suspects (JLC), Paul, MH, Khadijah,
and to Rich, for his help with the baby.

We found a little unknown grotto
where no people were and we
entered it completely
and let our bodies lose all
their loneliness.

—from "The Nude Swim,"
Anne Sexton

THE NUMBER WE
END UP WITH

1

PEMBROKE AVENUE

I CALL MY FATHER for the twenty-third time in six weeks. I finally have a cell phone. Since Quinn died, I have ended my boycott of technology. I now have a computer at home, wireless connection to e-mail, and videophone features. I bought a microwave, a Palm Pilot that I lost already, an MP3 player that I don't know how to work, and a DVD player I know I'll never use. I went to Circuit City on a Tuesday morning and asked a salesman, a pleasant boy with freckles and short red hair, to help me get wired. I feel the desire to be connected.

My father's phone rings seven times. He does not have an answering machine or voice mail. Sometimes it rings thirty times before I give up. On the eighth ring he picks up, says *Hello* in an aged and unsteady voice. I hang up. It's really not a hang-up. It's the press of a red button that says *End*. Cell phones are unsatisfying. You can't hang up on somebody with a brash physical disconnection, dramatic and certain. I turn the phone off; I have not set up my voice mail. It will just ring and ring if my father presses *69. This way he will not know it is me. At least this is what I tell myself. The evening that Quinn left, three days before he died, I began calling my father. I hear his voice. It is a voice I have not heard in more than seventeen years. Every time he picks up, he says the same thing, *Hello.* Even now, twenty-three hang-ups later, he still has not started saying, *Who's there?*

I have an unending need to count. It is not pathological. I am not obsessive-compulsive. This has been confirmed by a well-schooled and articulate psychiatrist, a handsome man named David who is thirty-two years old. I asked him his age the first time I visited him. He would not tell me where he lives—I asked him that, too. He has confirmed that you will not find me in the *Diagnostic and Statistical Manual of Mental Disorders.* My house is a mess, my shower stall almost always moldy, and I am notorious for leaving the stove, the coffee pot, and sometimes the iron on without ever thinking to check if I have turned off these appliances. Quinn used to say that fires await me. I have no desire to control my environment and certainly not the people around me. I wash my car when the spirit moves me, and the backseat is a potpourri—apple cores and peach pits and orange peels discarded while driving somewhere in a rush. I am plagued by only your garden-variety neurosis, but I have a thing about numbers: I see the world around me according to numbers.

I am a forensic accountant. I work for a large firm in Center City, Philadelphia. Being a forensic accountant requires an investigative nature, the ability to look deep into the numbers to find the real story. My projects vary: digging around to find hidden assets in nasty divorce battles, sniffing out the questionable practices behind mergers and acquisitions, and serving as an expert witness for legal disputes surrounding the ever-desired and frequently mishandled almighty dollar. I am knee-deep in numbers, but I am paid to tune in to the numerical drama and point out the perimeter and questionable core of transactions and decisions. There is always something—some emotion—behind the decision to lie or cheat. I like to bring these secrets to light, not to judgment. I do not wave a moral wand at the numbers I calculate, the lives behind them. I am just as guilty as the next person, maybe not to the same tally, but I have sinned enough in what I have added and subtracted in my life.

I felt no need to truly develop my career, to take it to new heights or become *something*. I settled—quite comfortably—by taking the quiet and simple route for me, this numeric path. This career did not seize my soul or feel emotionally fulfilling in any sense of the word beyond a moderately impressive salary, a healthy 401(k), a generous vacation and holiday schedule, and a postage-stamp twin home in Glyn Neath, a time-encapsulated hamlet outside Philadelphia. But it felt natural, and there's something to be said for that. After Quinn died, I was fired from this well-paying and secure job. Now I am an enumerator, part-time and temporary, for the 2000 United States Census. And that is why I'm standing here on Pembroke Avenue, on the north side of the railroad tracks in my small town.

221 Pembroke Avenue

I am not a people person, and I never will be. According to my sister Stella, this is another reason my decision to be an enumerator is problematic. But even though I am not a people person, Glyn Neath is a people town.

This home on Pembroke is towering—with spires and nooks and outcroppings like something right out of a Brothers Grimm fairy tale. I ring the doorbell twice, and finally, after several minutes, a man opens the door. He is tall, with hair a shade between blond and brown, short and messy with clumps sticking up and out and to the left and right. He is very good looking, in a rumpled and unassuming way. His eyes are a supernatural blue, vampire-radiant. I think of the Blue Grotto and how his eyes may be made of glass from an old bottle that is perched on the window of an old house like his. He has a scar above his left eyebrow in the shape of a wishbone. I am struck by the urge to trace my finger across it. I love scars.

His is the fourth home on this block that failed to submit a completed Census form by the April 1st deadline. He and his neighbors have been available, courteous, and welcoming of the Census process. Glyn Neath believes in responsibility. Furthermore, the 2000 Census Short Form is far from intrusive. It asks the most basic questions—number of household occupants, their names and ages, how they are related to the owner or lease holder, and the category of the home—whether it is a single-family dwelling, an apartment, or even a mobile home. The form does address race, but Glyn Neath residents do not seem to have a problem with a topic that often causes controversy.

The numbers are going backward: He is the seventh person I am counting today, after I walk off his porch this will probably be the sixth time I cry today (I can feel the swallow in my throat), and this is the fifth day in a row that I have contemplated setting my neighbor Glenn's house on fire. Glenn lives on my street, and it hasn't been until this week that I have actually hated him: He tries to join me when I'm walking my dog in the early morning hours. He wants us to be dog-walking pals. I'm not looking for pals, nor is my dog, Lurch. He has no sense of boundaries. I'm not a fan of having acquaintances, let alone chatting with them before the sun is up. Glenn knows that Quinn is dead, yet this has not stopped him from his attempts to join me. Lately I have been crying on my walks, making Glenn's attempts to be neighborly—a fair thing to do in this town—more than infuriating.

"Good afternoon," I say. "My name is Anjou Lovett and I'm from the United States Census."

I hold up my laminated Census identification card that I wear on a government-issued string around my neck.

"I'm here today because a Census form was not completed for your residence. I was wondering if you have a few minutes so I can ask you some questions."

He smiles at me, and I know that if it were three years ago, he is exactly the type of guy I would be interested in. I would go home, knock on Kip's door, and tell him I have a crush on some guy on Pembroke Avenue. He answers all of the questions—this is a single-family dwelling and he lives here with his wife, Caroline, who is thirty-six, and his son, Nathan, who is six, and his name is Tom.

When he is done and shuts the door, I stand on the porch of this home and cry for a full three minutes. I cry quietly, but my nose is running and there is a blood-thick sadness I imagine that only old people and the physically feeble know. Quinn only seems dead when I am outside, or in the Rite Aid, or pumping gas, or buying fruit at Acme. Quinn is dead when I am at a traffic light, my windows down now that spring is birthing up from the ground. He is dead when I am surrounded by strangers. He is dead even when I count.

I have not shed a single tear in my house, my old creaky and dusty and perfect tiny house. I can cry on the sidewalk in front of the health foods store on King Edward's Avenue, Glyn Neath's main street. Sometimes I cry in front of Kip's house, my neighbor and friend who lives directly across the street, standing there with Lurch at my side. Lurch is a border collie with a mood disorder—he is often cranky, frequently sullen, and occasionally unpredictably bursting with joy. He is small for a border collie, scruffy and dusty like an old rug, with remarkably bright eyes and a large black spot on his tongue. His coat has more black than white, a metaphor for his psyche. I adopted him from the Knauss couple three houses behind mine, who, pregnant with triplets, were moving to a large house in the open-spaced section of West Chester. I loved Lurch immediately, moods and all. Half of his left ear is missing from an infraction with another dog or a squirrel or a raccoon. Lurch doesn't take to many people, but when he does, it is with an immeasurable depth of love and loyalty. I know this because he did not take to me for a long time, but when he did, we became intrinsically dependent on each other. I anthropomorphize my dog, and I think, were he a human, he'd eat steak and potatoes every day, watch late-night television, speak kindly to and of his wife, adore his grandkids with fervor, be partial to strawberry ice cream, and favor single-malt scotch.

Since Quinn died, the three of us often go on nocturnal strolls through the narrow, winding streets of our neighborhood. I always stop crying when Kip comes out, but he knows that I've been crying. I cry at Commerce Bank, where this morning I deposited a check. Patty is my regular teller and she pretended everything was okay as my shoulders heaved and strange sounds came out of me. Patty knows about Quinn, and after the initial condolences she has not attempted to intrude on my unabashedly public display of my private grief.

The first month after Quinn died, I patronized stores and commercial businesses in a serial manner. I went to five Walgreen's pharmacies and eight Acme supermarkets across two counties. Gas stations were easy. They appear on every block and my visits were brief. Men at the pump next to me who saw me crying—tears and snot down my face, both of my hands on the gas pump—met this vision with almost frightened stares, men and women who for the most part remained silent. A few would say something to me: *You okay? Is everything all right?* Strangers were walking toward me to see if I was okay and some were staring oddly at me and walking away quickly. Crying while shopping or pumping gas or picking up your dry cleaning or depositing your paycheck is unnerving to the masses. Yelling at your child or bickering with your husband is more socially acceptable than public grief.

I am already relieved by how easy it will be to enumerate in Glyn Neath, this town full of the compliant, scattered, scarred, and comfortable, this town that is branded by a 1950s sentiment, this town that annoys me but is safe to me. In very small, very old towns, we have decorum. We comply with government processes. We don't raise a fuss or make a lot of noise. People are only secretive in their unease and quiet in their anger. Noise comes in the form of dogs barking in frenzied joy and the fire engines calling to disasters in neighboring towns. Noise is a block party or a fourteen-year-old playing his drums. Noise is the Amtrak flying along the tracks in a painful roar and windstorm, and the commuter line, the R8, which rattles slowly to the station. At night the only noise I hear are my new neighbors on the left side of our twin. I hear them making love; rather, I hear Mavis, the young wife from Scotland, when they make love. Tuesdays, Thursdays, Sundays, and an occasional bonus Friday. People do not lash out or argue aloud or slam doors or slap their kids. They rely on tornadoes—a rare, but very real, occurrence here— to do their screaming and raging.

Kip, a middle-aged, suburban warrior of sorts who was born and bred in Glyn Neath, has always liked our nocturnal strolls—our evening constitutionals. Kip is fifty-seven years old, four times divorced, and known for dalliances with women half his age. He is handsome, with a chiseled square jawline, a bald head he shaves daily, a crooked nose, and a wry smile. He's a retired high school principal and now works part-time at Yeardsley Hardware, mostly because he likes the tool belt he gets to wear and the discount on home improvement supplies. Not that he can fix anything. Quinn was Kip's handyman, and Kip was so possessive of his clean unused tools that Quinn would have to bring over his own. Kip is short and wiry and, despite drinking like a fish, in top-notch shape. He rides his bike everywhere, drives to Ocean City, New Jersey, twice a month and year round to surf with a group of long-haired underemployed twenty-somethings.

Kip is a friendly, assuming but not expectant, hands-on, in-your-face-with-a-beer-and-a-dirty-joke, neighborly kind of neighbor who, after enough conversations and cocktail hours and borrowed cups of milk, on one unknown day stopped being a neighbor and became a friend. He is a talker, a charmer, a teddy bear. He always shows up at my house unannounced; he even has a key that Quinn and I never quite knew how he acquired.

Kip is a devout Catholic, but with a smorgasbord approach to the Church's doctrine. He and I go to the same church—St. Theresa's—on Berriedale Avenue, and we argue over our differing beliefs. I always tell him we should never discuss politics and religion, but he is intolerant of the word *never*.

"You're not supposed to take communion without going to confession first," he told me.

"Says who?"

"The Church," he replied.

"If the Bible says not to take communion, fine, I won't. If the Church says it, then that's just doctrine."

"You don't even read the Bible," he said.

"That's not true. I read some of it."

"Only Ecclesiastes and Psalms. You told me so yourself."

"I like King David's son. He sums it all up, *Everything is meaningless*. I like that sentiment. It's useful for a faith-ambivalent person like me."

"Why do you bother with going to church if you're not sure you believe in God?"

"It beats going to the gym."

Kip rolled his eyes at me and said he was thankful that at least I'm not a Mormon.

One thing Quinn and I always agreed on was Kip. That he was ours. His front yard is filled with a menagerie of decorative paraphernalia: three Pittsburgh Steelers helmets lined up like the stars of Orion, four black-painted wood silhouettes of ducks, a requisite pair of pink flamingoes, three bushes strung with lights in the shape of red peppers, two stuffed peacocks that he keeps on either side of the porch steps under the awning, a laminated wedding photo of his grandparents nailed to a telephone pole on the side of the house, yellow construction boots worn at the heel filled with blossoming pansies under his oak tree. His yard is envied and revered. Quinn's favorite lawn ornament was a school desk-and-chair set, the kind where the chair is attached to the desk, solid wood with the seat like a booth and an arm of steel connecting it to the desk top, something out of a 1920s one-room schoolhouse. Kip placed it next to a sweeping Japanese maple on the side of his house. In the summertime Quinn and I would stand in Kip's driveway drinking cold beers and gossiping about our neighbors, and Quinn would try to sit at the desk, squashing himself into the seat, sending Kip and me into hysterics as he carefully articulated his theory that our ninety-one-year-old neighbor Opal was growing marijuana in her basement.

There is an underbelly in Glyn Neath, as there is in all suburbs. This town and the other charming old towns nearby have seen the occasional murder of a wife by a crazed husband who spent far too much of the household income on cocaine, the tragic suicide pact that left three teenagers face down on a garage floor, the family minivan running, the bodies limp and futures catastrophically halted. The standard affairs are in order—husbands cheating on wives and wives cheating on husbands—and the veneer of solidarity well maintained during cocktail parties and cookouts and Fourth of July parades. The same decisions—good and bad—are made, no matter how much a person's house cost.

Glyn Neath is more of a hamlet than a town, distinctive for factors both physical and cosmic. It is significantly smaller than the other nearby impossibly old boroughs, and notoriously difficult to get in and out of. One wrong turn leads to a ride through a labyrinth of narrow roads and one-way streets peppered with Glyn Neath's hodgepodge of homes—Cape Cods, towering three-story homes from the late 1800s, some of them with sweeping porches and spires shaped like witches' hats, a few Victorians, old stone colonials, A-frames with slate roofs, neo-Georgians, Arts and Crafts bungalows with all squares and triangles, countless styles and shapes of twin homes, and row homes lined up like Legos. Glyn Neath's population is homogeneous, but the homes are a diverse lot—they are architectural snowflakes, not even the twins are identical. But many houses here in Glyn Neath cannot be categorized by type or style. They are simply old—telling and solid, imposing and inviting at the same time. They speak out: I am here. I have been. I always will be.

In Glyn Neath, adhering to the 25-mph speed limit is a matter of moral accountability. The politics are mixed: socially liberal, economically conservative for some blocks and vice versa for others. Diversity is not a strong suit, although religious affiliations cross the board—there are Methodists and Unitarians and Catholics and Jews and plenty of agnostics and vocal atheists. Although houses aren't cheap, the prices pale in comparison to the real estate of neighboring suburbs of quaint distinction. At the northernmost point of this stop-time town is a working-class enclave—mostly tidy row homes filled with Irish families whose great-great-grandparents settled Glyn Neath and helped build not just the town but also the rail line that cross-sects its narrow berth.

Glyn Neath is so quiet that people have simply forgotten about it. This has kept it from being overtaken by anything corporate, franchised, or otherwise mass-produced. Artistic inclinations are encouraged, *dieting* is not a word that is spoken aloud—the croissants and brioche at the French bakery, owned by a warm French couple, sell out daily. Year-round people stand in their front yards talking to their neighbors. It is Mayberry. It is Americana. It is Stepford. It is Brooklyn. It is Baltimore. It is downtown Philadelphia, and it is the quiet proclivities of the Midwest. This town is a lot of things—provincial, open-minded to the point of being close-minded, overeducated—but it is old, very old, and it is never indifferent. There is a real power to this lack of indifference. People will always talk, and people will always reach out, and people will preserve its history.

Glyn Neath is so small—population 3,024 according to the 1990 Census, my boss, Thadius, tells me—that the commercial center is only two blocks in length. There is a family-run supermarket and four dry cleaners, a hardware store, a cheese shop, a pizza place, and a family-owned triumvirate of stores—St. Asaph's Card Shop, St. Asaph's Five and Dime, St. Asaph's Toys—all within 500 feet of each other. They are dusty, with a mishmash of affordable inventory of exactly what you need at that moment (hair dryers, composition notebooks, candy, bath mats).

I started counting people, here in my town, in Glyn Neath, because of love. Because one love left, and then died. And an old love, a man I could never count on, needs to be let back in. It is April 7 and I leave on May 28 for the island of Capri. I am going to swim in the Blue Grotto. I am going to fulfill a prophecy I resent. I am going because of my father. I am going because of a song-poem about the Blue Grotto that he made up, that he sang to us as kids, that was a love letter to our mother. I am going because of my mother. I am going because of my best friend, Liz, whom I swam in a cave with years ago when we were sixteen, in a cave with her cousins, in a cave with sharks. (We think. We will never know for sure. But something big, something unknown, touched her.) I am going to swim in a cave in the Tyrrhenian Sea. I will float on my back, end this history, and live out the one my mother dreamed of.

I was conceived under a pear tree in Valley Forge Park in 1965 while a half-moon glowed in the August night. My parents named me Anjou. The name was my father's idea, and the only honest gesture he managed during my childhood. Five years later my sister was born. They named her Stella. This name was my mother's idea. Her favorite play was *A Streetcar Named Desire*. But Stella turned out, minus the violent streak, more like Stanley: loud, forthright, unflinching, and willful.

I like to imagine my parents at that time in their lives, in the beginning, young and passionate, smug and confident in their display
of this marriage. That gripping awareness: reveling in the self-
righteous belief that they were different than all of the other cou-
ples, that they had captured a love that surely nobody else could
understand or relate to, seeing the other across the room doing
something as inane as taking a fork from the silverware drawer or
getting up to turn the station on the television set, thinking *He's
mine, She's mine.* I have no pictures of my parents that show me
their start or where my history was launched. I have no evidence of
their courtship, no wedding photos or saved copies of their invita-
tions. Only now, at the age of thirty-five, during a year where things
are lost and gone and hopefully regained, have I learned how my
parents met. Stella told me. She has been talking to my father for
seven years now, and he told her how our parents met, the week
after I started calling him.

My parents met at Vincenzo's Pizzeria on 16th and Sansom
Streets. My father said it was a crisp and windy January night.
Vincenzo's windows were moist with steam, the crowd of young
people was lively, the mood jubilant. My father was working as an
actuary for Endy & DelGrego in the Penn Mutual Building at 5th
and Walnut Streets in downtown Philadelphia. He sat with three
friends at the back of the restaurant in the last booth. My mother
was working as a secretary at the *Ladies' Home Journal* in the
Public Ledger Building, catty-corner from my father's building.
They may have even passed each other on the street, not knowing
they would eventually be together. My mother was in the second-
to-last booth with her cousin, Meredith. My mother stood up
from the booth to go to the ladies' room and she turned—with the
force and determination that anybody going anywhere turns. My
father, wanting to buy a pack of Camels from the machine in the

opposite direction, stood and turned around with that same kind of force, his body twisting to the right. They turned. They collided. They fell to the ground, and then in love and toward their future.

Growing up, I had no knowledge of their beginning, where they went on dates, when they went steady, and when they knew the other was the one with whom they wanted to cement their years. I knew better than to ask. Their middle and forecasted end told me plenty when I reached the age of curiosity about anything that didn't have to do with myself. Stella was more insightful, and braver. She would ask my parents for details of their lives before she came along, masking her deliberation and pointed agenda with a posed innocence and naïveté. The only question Stella really wanted an answer to was how our parents had met. Her friend Gillian's parents had met on a sailboat, and Stella thought this was exotic. She'd press my mother, who would respond with a silence shrouded in sadness; she would literally walk away. If Stella asked our father, he'd always say the same thing: *I met your mother on the moon, married her on a star, and then you see, we went to Capri, to eat gelato and swim in the grotto.* He'd recite this in a manner that was a cross between a poem and a song, reaching for Stella, lifting her high in the air. Stella kept asking, and our father kept saying the same thing. It seemed like a hundred times I heard it: the moon, the star, Capri, the grotto.

The grotto was a rhyme, but my father loved much more than a marriage of words. He loved poetry and could recite lines from both Brownings, Keats, Shakespeare, and Yeats. In private moments that I rarely witnessed, he drank the words of Rilke and Rossetti and Shelley. My mother once told me that my father rhymed because he wanted to, but he read poetry because he had to. My father, a charming and lyrical and larger-than-life spectacle, sought out the stanzas, the unrhyming and unnerving and heart-jolting verse, of the known and unknown, the poets lost and dead and always (or never) read.

My mother told me one piece of their history. She told me about my name, how it came to be, about the pear tree. In an unexplainable burst of openness—one I would later find out was motivated by our father's whispered promise that yes, one day, eventually, they could try to have another baby—my mother's words spilled out. I was twelve. I was standing in the kitchen, damp in August's hazy and humid heat. I asked my mother, *Where did you come up with the name Anjou?* It sounded silly to me, fancy. My mother was at the kitchen sink scrubbing a brownie pan. Her fair, heart-shaped face was grimacing, and her small hand clutched a Brillo pad. She told me that under a pear tree, I was conceived. She told me how the crickets were deafening, how there was no wind and only a heavy stillness in the summer air. In her fourth month of carrying me, my father put his hand on her just-round belly and boastfully claimed that it was a girl in there. That the girl was perfect. That she should be named after her beginning. He said that I would be called Anjou. He smiled at my mother when the lilting, whispery-soft name came to him.

"Anjou?" my mother asked.

"Yes, Anjou," my father said.

"I thought the pears were called D'Anjou."

"They are, but our beautiful baby girl should not have an apostrophe in her name," he said.

"But I think the pear tree we were under was just an ornamental."

"In spirit it was fruitful though, wasn't it? Look what's inside you."

"How do you know it's a girl, Jack?"

"Because I know."

"That's like saying you know why the sky is blue and the grass is green."

"I'll tell you why I know. But only if you remember that I love you more than peach cobbler. Okay?"

My mother said she squinted at him.

"You see," my father continued, "when a woman is carrying a girl, the baby sucks the beauty out of the mother. The baby needs it, this mother's beauty, something of which you have plenty to spare."

My mother said she started to cry, feeling insulted. My father hugged her and laughed, tickled her under her arms, told her he was teasing. Weak from morning sickness that would plague her until her eighth month, my mother said she later realized there was a bit of truth to his joke, that she was gray and blotchy and frail throughout the pregnancy. My father, in his usual grand gesture, picked her up in his arms and kissed her forehead and told her how he couldn't wait to meet their lovely pear. He carried my mother in his arms and walked outside and left the house with the front door open, and placed her in the passenger seat, and pulled out of the driveway. Driving down Beidler Road he made up the first of many poem-songs to come. He sang, *Anjou, Anjou, we're adoring fans of you,* driving them to Minella's Diner in Wayne for chicken-noodle soup, the only thing my mother's stomach could tolerate.

My mother paused, stopped scrubbing the pan, a lock of her blond hair curling on her forehead. She blew at it and looked out the window above the sink, staring at our willow tree. I imagined that her mind was traveling to years gone by, flipping like calendar pages stroked by a sudden breeze.

"That's how you were named," she said moments later, snapping back to our kitchen, to her hands in the soapy-warm sink water.

Had our parents not conceived me under that tree in the oppressive summer heat, I would be named something else and maybe would have become someone different altogether—perhaps not so prone to bruising, not so soft. I guess the same could be said for Stella. What if my mother's favorite story had been *The Scarlet Letter?* What if she had named my baby sister Hester? But it didn't happen that way. *A Streetcar Named Desire* was the story she probably related to the most: a man, a woman, a child on its way—a family—and the fragility of all of those bonds. How could Stella ever be named Hester? My mother would never cling to *The Scarlet Letter.* There was no A to brandish on her child. Stella was not the adulterer in our family.

And it would be a half-moon—not in the sky above the pear tree—that brought another adulterer into my life, one whom I would love with the same intensity, the same recklessness, with which I imagine our mother loved our father. This half-moon was on the top of my hand, in the soft spot between the thumb and forefinger, wine-colored and permanent, a dime-size birthmark that became my own constellation that was unwavering with the shifting tides. Quinn saw this half-moon of mine when I would walk down the aisle of the second car on the 8:18 A.M. R8 commuter train, the same car I sat in, day after day.

A different set of boundaries exist on the R8 train into Philadelphia, for you are in the middle of the world and removed from it at the same time. You can safely become the person you always wanted to be, or the person you were always scared you'd become. The R8 is everything: a beauty pageant, a board of directors meeting, the PTA, a singles-only book club. In the wee early-morning hours it is a movie theater, for it is understood that you should never talk. The R8 is a meat market, a chance encounter, a quiet desperate collection of stale and exhausted marriages and the pounding loneliness of the unmarried.

And in this social microcosm, Quinn and I noticed each other. More accurately, Quinn noticed my half-moon. He'd be sitting two rows back, in the aisle seat, and my hands would be holding up a paper and I could feel his eyes staring at my mark. I loved my half-moon. It was a beautiful piece of jewelry, a wedding ring to myself. Because of it, Quinn and I were more than strangers. That's what happens when you get on the same train car at the same time every day, day in and day out. You don't know these people and then you do. You are in their presence for a longer time every week than you are with your sister who lives up the street or your best friend who lives in Connecticut. So I knew Quinn before we knew each other, and he knew me. For weeks? For months? You can never calculate how long the other person had been there, part of your morning, remotely part of your life. And that was where we began.

I picked up the train in Glyn Neath, and Quinn picked it up one town later, Llanfair. He sat next to me one cool June morning and, in a quiet tone, asked me how I got my scar.

"It's not a scar," I said, feeling warm and scared.

"I'm sure it is, though," he said.

I was thirty-one years old, and that June morning Quinn and I collided without touching, creating a union that was always meant to be doomed; these things simply are. At the time we met, he was a thirty-six-year-old, very handsome, and very married linguistics professor. Tenured, firm with stature, engaging, social and distinguished and tailored—nothing like my stereotypical image of a corduroyed frayed-collared academic with greasy hair and questionable breath. Quinn looked like any of the other well-paid professionals on the train. Quinn collected people: friends and coworkers and students and postdocs and third-tier acquaintances and hangers-on. These people gravitated to him, wanting his opinions, glad that they could be in the steamy mist that surrounded him. I'd eventually learn that the women he pursued while with me were not nubile and eager students easily charmed by his good looks and the sweeping, gentle cadence of his voice. All of that was entirely too obvious for Quinn. He preferred transgressions outside the expected avenue for his position in life.

I was more than willing to be collected by him, for a reason that came long before I loved him: With Quinn, I was freed from counting. Unintentionally—and unnoticeable even to me, at first—I stopped cataloging what passed through my life, what had yet to happen or repeatedly did happen. Through my ups and downs with him, time became a fluid, incalculable theory. And from the moment he touched my half-moon mark, I stopped counting. I did not balance my checkbook (and nothing bounced). I stopped timing my thrice-weekly runs. Professionally, I still counted—I performed well at my job, documenting incomes and deductions, detecting the liars and thieves. But when I left work every night, knowing that somehow and some way I'd be in the three-dimensional presence of Quinn's spiraling and buzzing mind (and his body, smooth and giving and demanding and warm), I didn't need numbers. I ignored how I tallied my past: how many months it had been since I had seen my father (168), how many years since Stella had moved to Newfoundland with her husband (8), how many men I had categorically loved, wholeheartedly and desperately (2), how many close friends I had (3, including my dog).

I told my psychiatrist, David, months into the affair, that all of this was good, this wrongness was right. I had stopped counting! A feat! A breakthrough! A success! But David wasn't as enthusiastic, and with a delicate hand he asked me, *What do you want, Anjou?* Of course, of course, of course I wasn't getting what I wanted. But the world I had always known was now layered and sharper and deeper. I finally saw the world in the angles that I knew Stella had—by her birthright she saw them. She didn't need to fall in love with a married man to see the complexities of our choices, what to give or take in the name of love. The price for this thicker world seemed irrelevant; love is devastating by nature.

Quinn and his wife were childless, by design, the two of them convinced the world was overpopulated. Lily was fluent in Latin, born and raised in Detroit, and was blind in one eye. She was a lawyer. For a long time that was all I knew about her. He said nothing derogatory about her, nothing like she was a caustic bitch or a needy hag or a cold, cold woman. Before he moved in with me, her name was frequently mentioned—but always in context. If he was telling me about two weeks spent in Argentina or the purchase of a leather couch or his first year in graduate school, her name would come up in a neutral and unobtrusive way. I didn't ask, because this was my way. I didn't want the answers. Who he was when he was with me was enough. His history was of little use. Because it didn't matter what those truths were anyway: I knew the first time he touched the half-moon on my hand that I could love him.

He was a self-professed mixed breed, and hated golden retrievers because of it. His Greek mother met his Austrian father on the island of Corfu on the Adriatic Sea and married him two weeks later. His parents immigrated to the States after their first child was born; his father worked in the steel mills, and his mother was a seamstress. He was the only son and fifth-youngest of seven. He grew up in a modest house in Bethlehem and, although his parents were close to poor and far from educated, they were determined to change this for their children. Quinn was their dream realized: Yale undergrad, Stanford for his master's, and Berkeley for his Ph.D.

Quinn was tall and lithe, with the supple frame of a runner, his body a stereotypical model of his Austrian heritage. He had an acute beauty: a thick head of near-midnight hair, waves of gray sprouting at his temples, an angular nose with a swift bump at its bridge, a wide mouth that cased straight teeth save his left front tooth overlapping the right one. His Austrian blood gave him eyes of crystalline blue. It hurt to stare at him, his angles and depths of colors. I loved looking at him in the dark, the world softening around his features. He didn't tell me he was married until two weeks after he asked about my half-moon mark. He had already kissed me by then, standing at my car in the parking lot of the Rose Ferry Café in West Chester. We had driven there separately to meet in the woodsy outskirts for drinks and oysters on the half-shell. With salty, beer-coated mouth, he took my half-mooned hand in both of his and kissed me. It was unnerving, nothing romantic or sweet. It was a strangling burn, like getting electrocuted—how the victim can't let go of the live wire even though they want to, how they know they are screwed, positively screwed.

He only told me about his wife, Lily, because he had to.

"How was the Shore?" I asked him on a Monday morning. Mornings were brief and measured. I had nine minutes with Quinn—Llanfair to 30th Street Station was the fastest and deepest nine minutes I could ever remember. It felt like such an important pocket of time.

He had spent the weekend at Long Beach Island, telling me the previous Friday that he was going cell-phone free, disconnected completely to spend the weekend with former college roommates. He leaned back in the train seat, sun-kissed and loose.

"Are you going to have lunch with me today? I don't have any classes until 2 o'clock."

"I can't. I'm going for a run on my lunch hour. So how was the Shore?" I repeated.

"Why do you call it the Shore?"

"'Cause that's what it is," I said.

"I thought it was called the beach," he said with a grin.

"Not if you're from Philadelphia."

"We can run over the Benjamin Franklin Bridge. Have you ever done that?"

"Why aren't you answering my question?" I prodded, feeling chilly, a ghost entering my atmosphere.

"What question?"

"About the Shore. I've asked you twice how the Shore was."

"It was fine," he finally answered, showing nothing. No tales of escapades or parties. In the very short time I had known him, he always had something to say.

"So can I join you on your run?"

I don't know where it came from—do we ever know where big answers come from? How discoveries rise to the surface? Is it a smirk or lack thereof? An unanswered question? A glance away? The bricks came: Heavy bursts of clay flew at every angle, dusty and with force, interrupting the electrical current that rested— unrestfully—between us.

"Quinn," I said slowly.

"Yes," he replied slowly, the corners of his mouth moving upward and, with his black hair and widow's peak, he was, for just a moment, a devil, the sound of serpents under my seat.

"Were you at the Shore with your girlfriend, your fiancée, or your wife?"

I wanted him to laugh and put his face close to my cheek and whisper *Neither, neither, neither.* Instead, he looked out the window.

"Can we please run across the bridge today? You cross states. Don't you want to go to Jersey? Everybody wants to go to Jersey."

"Answer my question, Quinn."

"I'll answer you when we run to Jersey."

He stared at me, waiting for what I imagined was a chance to step backward, or forward, or somewhere that wasn't in the second car of the R8 being asked about his marital status. And I knew right then and there what I had known when the first brick hit and blood ran to my head: that nothing good could come of this. Hours later, we ran on the footpath of the Benjamin Franklin Bridge, the gray waters of the Delaware River below us. We were halfway across its expanse, moving east toward Camden. On our left, cars below sped by on the hot macadam of the bridge. My father loved bridges, would roll down the weather regardless of rain, shine, or cold when driving across them, calling to the gods and hollering over the rushing air to Stella and me, telling us to swallow the air, that bridges invade unclaimable space.

"I have a wife," Quinn finally said to me.

"A wife," I repeated, like it was something small to contemplate.

I quickened my pace listening to our breaths and the swooshing cars. I tried to will myself to turn around, to head west, back to my office, back to my life, but I could only move forward on the bridge, heading down its arc, the wind blowing dusty fumes and grit. I couldn't turn around, simply because I didn't know how. We should never blame our parents for our mistakes and bad choices. But what I knew of love I learned from my parents, and what I learned from my parents was that love is illogical, executed at high stakes, and always most realized in impossible circumstances.

By profession, Quinn was obsessed with language, its history, its nuances. With words—how they came to be, how they are used, even how to pronounce them—the anatomical machinations of talking, of language. The way numbers crept into all of my thoughts, words—new ones and old ones and used ones and obsolete ones—compelled Quinn. He once told me that words never disappeared for him, they weighed too much, that even if they left his mouth or entered his ears or were picked up from his eyes, an imprint of them stayed and stuck to him, took up space, living in neat compartments that opened doors to each other.

"Why didn't you become a writer?" I asked Quinn.

"For all of that work, there's no money in it," he said.

"That's not true. What about people who are best-sellers?"

"Fifty-nine thousand, four-hundred and thirty-two books were published in 1999. Of those, less than half of one-half percent were best-sellers. I read this. Statistics. Do the math, my dear. There's no money in writing books. Not that professors make a lot, but we have great perks."

"But you should do what you love. You know, *Do what you love and the money will follow.*"

His head flew back with a hearty and showy laugh, his hands reaching for my arms.

"I don't know who told you that, but that, my precious one, is bullshit."

c/w

232 Pembroke Avenue

A woman with silver hair answers the door. It is April 8. She is dressed in a neatly pressed chambray skirt, a white oxford shirt, and a pink cardigan. High cheekbones, full lips, pert nose, and deep-set hazel eyes, a beauty that is lasting. She is polished: nothing like her house, a small stone house with a slanted slate roof. The house is not wide, but it stretches long to the backyard. The grass needs to be mowed, the tree branches trimmed. There are boxes on the front porch.

"Hello, my name is Anjou Lovett, and I'm from the United States Census. Our records indicate you did not complete the Census form mailed to you last month," I say, flashing my Census identification. "I'd like to ask you a few questions. It won't take very long."

She nods and touches her hair briefly, indicating for me to proceed.

"I need the name of all of the people who reside in this house, starting with an adult, preferably the homeowner," I said.

"Well, that would be me—the homeowner, that is. Actually, I *almost* own the home," she says, with a territorial tone that she seems unaccustomed to using. "My name is Harriet Finley."

"Okay," I say, writing it down.

"I almost own this home," she repeats, tasting her words.

She stands poised, although her neck begins to redden.

"Is there anybody else who lives here, or anybody who usually lives here but is away on a trip or in the hospital?" I ask, reading off the list of questions on the United States Census Short Form.

"My husband is away on a trip," she says.

"But he lives here?" I ask.

"No, actually," she says slowly and firmly.

"Is he in Capri?" I ask.

Both of us look surprised. I have so many questions—particularly for a woman named Grace, a woman who did not show up for Quinn's memorial service, a woman whom I wrote five questions for. I also have questions for my father; that list is building slowly. For now, the phone calls are enough. The questions feel endless and now one simply came out.

"Excuse me?" the woman asks.

"Is he in Capri?" I say with more confidence.

"No," she says, eyeing me slowly. "No, he is not in Capri. My husband hates Italy. He thinks it's too obvious. Why on earth did you ask me that question, Ms. Lovett?"

"I was curious."

"I don't believe you," she says, crossing her arms across her chest.

"It's probably a good idea not to," I say.

"He went to Turks and Caicos," she says, almost yelling at me. As if I have freed her, too.

"I've never been there," I say.

"Me neither."

I still need to ask her how old she is. This is something I should have done as part of the first question.

"Turks and Caicos is really just a day trip, actually. The bigger trip is his midlife trip."

She is staring off behind me, shaking her head. I am secretly thrilled.

"Some people call it a midlife crisis," she continues, "but he is having entirely too much fun for it to be considered a crisis. I'm the one that is having the crisis—because of his trip."

I keep nodding.

"Do you want to know who he's on the trip with?"

"Yes," I whisper.

"He is with a twenty-three-year-old woman named Tifani— and that's spelled with one *f* and one *n* and two *i*'s. And that, when you really think about it, is quite a trip."

"God, that sucks."

She stares at me for a moment.

"It does, doesn't it?"

She and I stare at each other for a long time. Her eyes are puffy and I know that in the home that is almost hers she cries. She finally nods toward my clipboard, where I still have eight questions on the Census Short Form to ask. It is time to get back to business.

2

1965 TO 1975

By WEEK EIGHT IN THE WOMB, the spinal cord has extended the length of the vertebral canal. My mother did nothing to affect the development of my spinal cord; she didn't sand lead paint from the walls or drink too many whiskey sours while I nestled in the warm amniotic fluid. As a child, I stood up straight. I jumped rope. I ran through woods and backyards. I withstood falls and tumbles and somersaults and learned how to jump a perfect back handspring. Anatomically, my spine seemed correct. Physiologically, it had fortitude. Or so I thought.

As I discovered love and all my body and heart had for receiving and taking and hurting and bursting with unquestionable happiness, I simultaneously discovered that my spine was actually soft, that disks had slipped. It was not apparent to the naked eye, but I was hunched over. And because I was hunched over, I chose men blindly. I couldn't see the men I was looking at, I couldn't notice what I was walking into.

I inherited this trait from my mother. Stella was spared from this defect. I believe my mother unconsciously decided to never pass on this trait again. My mother's spine was already in disrepair the day she lay there in the delivery room at Hahnemann University Hospital giving birth to me. Our father was there holding her hand and looking her in the eye, telling my frail, sweating, and pain-ridden mother that she could do it, that it would be okay, that he loved her. In the waiting room my Aunt Vicky, our mother's only and younger sister who wore tight bell-bottom pants and too much makeup, sat chain-smoking Arctic Lights.

"C'mon, Ida," my father said as my mother's face contorted from the contractions. It wasn't the norm in 1966 for a father to be in the delivery room, but our dad was there, out of guilt more than anything.

My mother couldn't look at him. As much as she loved him and needed him, as much as the searing pain of me shoving myself through her body and into the world made it clear to her that she was simply not cut out to raise her child alone, she could not look our father in the eye because she knew that even though my father was there with her, in that moment that should be pain-for-joy, he was not with the other woman he loved, the woman our father loved, although not more wholly and in a holy way, still, he loved another. That woman was standing on a sidewalk several blocks away at Rittenhouse Square Park, watching a Cinco de Mayo parade pass. My mother squeezed my father's hand in fear and upset and anger, but she clung to him.

Five years later, when my mother was five weeks from giving birth to Stella, our father left for the first time. My mother, with

her matted blond hair, sat there round and swollen in the July
heat, stared at him from her shrunken position on our couch in
the living room of our three-bedroom split-level in Gulph Mills. I
was in the kitchen eating a bowl of Cheerios in thick milk. It was
evening, but still light. My parents calmly instructed me to go upstairs and play in my bedroom. My mother couldn't even stand
up in her frustration. I look back to this memory and wonder if it
was because she was so pregnant and swollen, or because her
spine was so decomposed.

I sat upstairs listening through the air duct that led from my
bedroom to the living room. The scent of the new baby's freshly
painted room lingered in mine. My mother had let me take home
the paint swatches from Sears that she and my father had studied
one Saturday afternoon. They agreed that the new baby's room
would be yellow. I played with the swatches and listened.

"You can't leave," my mother said in an exhausted voice.

"I can't stay," my father said.

"You have to. In case you haven't noticed, you've got a five-
year-old and a second one on the way."

My mother said this with the calmness of a Buddhist monk, no
sarcasm or wit or anger—all of this simply *was*.

"Ida, I'm sorry."

I pictured my mother staring at him in defeat, wrapping her
hands around her belly. Their conversation was like one at a dinner
table over roast beef and mashed potatoes, like they were contemplating the purchase of a new refrigerator or a car. Momentarily, in
a flash of childhood wisdom and hope, I consoled myself with the
thought that even if there were only two of us after our father left,
the head count would be raised after the new baby came.

"Don't worry about money," my father said.

"This isn't about money," she replied flatly.

Although words had not triggered the same kinetic reaction that they had in my parents—both of them voracious readers—I was compelled by and adept at numbers, beyond my years. I saw my family in terms of digits, explained in math: *Three take away one makes two and then plus one makes three.* My dad's departure and the baby's arrival would bring the number to a stable spot.

"Where are you going to stay?" my mother asked him.

"In a hotel for now, but you can always reach me at work," he said.

"Babies don't necessarily come between the hours of 9 and 5, Jack."

My father's departure was a spineless act. My mother's calm acceptance, her refusal to even raise her voice or at least threaten to divorce him and take him to the bank in alimony and child support, made her spineless. My parents were perfect for each other and they never even realized it. Our father made good on his promise of money, which arrived every Tuesday in a check in a white envelope bearing the letterhead of Endy & DelGrego, the actuary firm where he worked. We were two, almost three, soon to be three, maybe four. My mom. Me. My father, who was living twelve miles away on the 18th floor of the Drake building in Center City Philadelphia, with the other woman he loved. And the baby, resting contentedly in my mother's womb.

My mother's water broke at 2:30 in the morning on September 8, 1971. I heard her come down the hallway, calling me loudly. She was visibly scared, standing in the brightly lit hallway. Her feet were sticking to the clean hardwood floors. Her eyes were wide open, her frayed blue cotton nightgown clung to her belly and pendulous breasts, her calves wet from amniotic fluid. She sat on the hallway floor and muttered out her instructions: *Call your Aunt Vicky.*

Aunt Vicky arrived minutes later. She lived a few miles away in Wayne. Aunt Vicky maneuvered our mother down the stairs and into her garnet-red Ford Fairlane. I climbed into the backseat, practically holding my breath as Aunt Vicky drove and sang the Beatles' "Hey Jude" to my mother. My mother moaned, not singing, Aunt Vicky sang loudly and moved her head back and forth, no radio on. I chimed in—feeling like I was finally helping— when Aunt Vicky got to the *Nah nah nah nah nah nah* part.

Aunt Vicky stayed with my mother in the delivery room but would come out occasionally, trying to reach my father. We finally reached him at his office at 8:00 that morning, approximately two and half hours after his second daughter, Stella Kathryn Lovett, burst into the world. And on the morning Stella came into this world, our father begged to come back into ours.

Our father walked into the recovery room after missing every-thing, saw our mother, Stella on her chest, and then Stella started to scrunch up, her face contorting, getting ready in her newness to the overstimulating world to cry. Our father leaned over our mother, and Stella started wiggling on our mother's chest, right there between our father's hushed whispers to our mother (prom-ises that the woman he loved didn't matter, that it was over, really, over for real, no more, done). There in her newborn wisdom, from the spring of primordial and visceral perception, Stella knew—she sensed the pounding of my mother's heart (love for her, love for our father), and so Stella worked herself up, because she heard how the thump of our father's heart moved back and forth. Our fa-ther leaned over our mother and Stella lay there between them screaming. Stella knew—even though she could not know anything like you think of knowing—she knew that our father was trying to convince himself that he could walk away from the other woman he loved, the woman who did not wear his gold ring inscribed with the word *Endless.*

After Stella was born and our father came home, a pattern began that lasted for the next eleven years, a pattern that defined our family, distinguished it on the block of suburbia, a bedroom community in its infancy, long before strip malls or convenience stores were planted. Tupperware parties and block parties were the social epicenter for the women. The men simply didn't socialize. There was no exercise camaraderie—no rollerblades or bicycle groups or yoga circles. The running craze was in its infancy, and the only runner in the neighborhood was our next-door neighbor Mr. Snyder, who made circles around the block in flat white basketball sneakers and khaki shorts. Our family cycle, until I was sixteen years old and our mother died, went like this: Our father would leave, and then our father would come back, then our soft-spined mother would say *Yes,* then Stella would scream.

He'd live with us, as our father, as our mother's husband, and then after four or five months—or sometimes six or seven or eight months—he'd leave. We would come home from school and make a snack of peanut butter and crackers, go outside and play kickball with the next-door neighbors—but when the time came for him to pull his Volkswagen into our driveway after work, it wouldn't happen. He would be gone just like that—people do this, just like that—and our mother would behave as if he'd always been gone. *Four minus one equals three,* I'd think, certain we'd get back up to four at some point.

I knew her name: Maggie. It was never actually spoken aloud to me directly or overheard or even written down. It was discovered in a song. Long after the radio had stopped playing Rod Stewart's "Maggie May" every hour on the hour, I sometimes would happen upon my father singing it to himself. He was always alone when he was singing it, and he would stop if he noticed that I had walked into the room.

The first time I heard him singing it, I was thirteen. He had been home for five days after staying at her house for seven weeks. He was in the mudroom, pulling towels and sheets out of the dryer and putting them in our wicker hamper, a small gesture toward mending what I imagined were unclosable wounds. He didn't know I was standing in the kitchen watching him.

Oh Maggie, I wish I'd never seen your face.

I knew by the slump of his shoulders—how he was at once saddened but consoled by these words—that Maggie was the name of my father's lover. It would have been easy for Stella and me to draw together our forces, to revolt, to force the third party to be named and discussed and screamed about and explained. It would have been so easy to call both of our parents on their charade. But we didn't. Our parents loved each other abundantly, despite Maggie, despite my father's desertions, despite my mother's reckless passivity. When our father was home, he was ours. Our property, our life force. He loved us with abandon, with exaggeration, with passion and volume. He was grandiose, and it was infectious and sedating. He followed you across the room with his eyes and plagued you with questions you were hoping he would ask. His love swelled through us.

When I grew into my teens, the resentment grew deeper than the charisma could make up for. But before that time it was really all I knew, this committed hopscotch of a marriage, and it often, so often, felt very, very good. When he was home, we were his world. Between the time my mother died and I met Quinn, I could not find such texture in my life, that exciting thrill of pain and pleasure and consistency of inconsistency. As an adult, Stella would seek out the opposite of what we knew. She woke up long before me.

The first few nights after our father would leave, our mother would be very even, without emotion. Our mother typically exuded an understated type of warmth; she quietly gave, enjoyed other people's successes, was easily enveloped in the natural joy and humor of the people around her. She was gracious, in a way that I have known few people to be. She preferred listening to talking. But during those first few days, that quiet love disappeared. Stella would start waking up in the middle of the night; her screams were wordless, rising deep from a young but wise soul. I said nothing—I was very literal about my world, and I wasn't accustomed to pushing through things to get what I wanted or the answers I needed. Eventually it would all settle; Stella stopped screaming, our mother became warm again, and I kept counting.

When he'd come back, there would be no phone call or letter to announce his impending return. He would simply arrive after work, like any other day. He'd walk in the front door and go right upstairs into our parents' bedroom. Our mother would follow. She was usually in the kitchen making tuna-noodle casserole or chicken breast or flank steak. She would have barely heard the car coming in the driveway, which came up to the right wall of the living room instead of the left wall of the kitchen. Our parents bought the house as new construction and the contractors built the driveway on the wrong side of the house.

I never knew what went on in their bedroom each time he came home. Did they sit together on the bed, hands separate from each other and folded on individual laps? Did they talk, negotiate his return? Did he make promises that were just words in the wind that could not land on anything substantive, that made everything in the room light as papier-mâché? Did they simply stare at each other for a few moments before forging forward for another undetermined period of domesticity? Did she slowly remove her dress and whisper in his ear and quietly make love to him?

Eventually our parents would emerge from their bedroom and come downstairs looking much like our parents: our mother in her fitted dresses—she never wore pants—that accentuated her still-slim body. Our mother was petite and lovely and ageless like Audrey Hepburn, with her cornstalk hair and her askew nose that she had broken when she was first pregnant with me, walking into a sliding glass door. Our father would follow her, looking calm, unfazed. He was a lean man, with dark brown eyes and crooked teeth and a head of thick dishwater-blond hair that curled into tight coils. Our mother would go into the kitchen and put away whatever she had been making for dinner—she'd toss the thawing square of creamed spinach back into the freezer, the ground meat back into the fridge, the unopened jar of spaghetti sauce back into the pantry. If something was already cooking, she'd turn off the oven or stove and throw the food out. Eventually, we took over this task for our mother.

"Stella, go turn off the oven," I would say an hour into our father's arrival back home.

"You go turn it off," she'd reply as we sat side by side on the couch watching television.

Usually we were watching our favorite game show, *Joker's Wild*, a modified version of gambling that involved giant cards, answering trivia questions, and an MC whose name was our father's name—Jack. *Joker, Joker, Joker,* Jack the MC with too much hairspray and whose lit cigarette would be behind the podium but with the smoke coming up would say as cards came up on a slot-machine prop. A bet would be placed: "I'll take science for $150, Jack."

"I'll take *How long will Dad stay?* for *$275, Jack,*" Stella would crack sarcastically.

"Stella! The oven!"

Stella would ignore me a few minutes longer, predicting the second before I would burst again, before she'd get up to turn off the oven. Then our father would come downstairs and sit on the couch with Stella and me and watch the *Joker's Wild* with us.

"Dad, that's so wrong. George Washington was not a prime minister of England," Stella would say.

"Well it's called the *Joker's* Wild—get it, joker," he would say, tickling Stella.

And she'd cave, she'd laugh, loving how he'd respond to easy questions with intentionally wrong answers.

⁓

I never felt any shame about our father's departures and homecomings. It was all we knew and, like our misplaced driveway, it still functioned. This changed in the fourth grade, when I was washing the blackboards with Alexis Saunders. I'm not sure if she actually taught me shame; maybe she was just the first person to ever help me let it out of its cage. The tide-like absence and presence of our father had become quiet ebbs and flows. It was our *normal*. What Alexis informed me, with a bold frankness beyond her years, was that the rest of the neighborhood didn't feel the same way.

Alexis was chubby and soft, with dull mouse-colored curly hair and off-putting precociousness. We were inside our classroom washing the blackboard—a misnomer that irked me since it was actually green. The rest of our classmates were outside for recess. The shrieks that came into the classroom soothed me. I loved the sound of recess more than recess itself.

"Your father cheats," Alexis blurted out on that sunny April day.

"What?" I asked, stunned into coldness, chalky water trickling down my wrist from the porous sponges we used.

"Your dad cheats. He has a girlfriend. It's who he stays with when he's gone."

"That's a lie," I lied, trying not to shake.

"It's not a lie," Alexis continued nonchalantly.

"My father is away a lot for business. That's why he is gone so long."

"I don't think so," she said, meticulously moving the wet sponge across her side of the board in neat horizontal rows.

"He goes everywhere, to Australia, Spain, Portugal, Italy. Even Sri Lanka."

Alexis put her sponge down and turned around on the wide step stool she was standing on to look at me. I was caught: because of *Sri Lanka.* Brainy fifth graders who have poor social skills and blurt out inappropriate comments know where Sri Lanka is. They also know Sri Lanka's population, the gross national product, and the colors of the country's flag. But people like me, average students quieted by pains and absences and unanswered questions but simultaneously consumed by the standard fare—the playground, rope swings in the woods, fifty-cent pizza slices at Primo's, and too much television—kids like that, like I was, are too average to know anything about Sri Lanka. We certainly don't know it's a pendant-shaped island off the coast of India.

I only knew that the country existed because I had practiced walking across the living room with the *S* book of the new edition of *Encyclopedia Britannica* balanced on my head. I wanted to see if I could learn to have better posture. Each time the book would fall from my head, it would fall on its spine open to the page on Sri Lanka. Seventeen book falls. Seventeen Sri Lankas.

"Sri Lanka?" Alexis asked, a predatory ring to her voice.

"Sri Lanka," I stated firmly.

"Where is Sri Lanka?" she asked with a feigned curiosity. "I've heard of it, but I don't know where it is."

And neither did I. Because even though the encyclopedia kept opening to the same Sri Lanka page, it had the pronunciation, but it wasn't the Sri Lanka page with the map on it.

"It's next to Spain," I said, relying strictly on an illogical world of alphabetical order.

I cleaned a blackboard that wasn't black. I had a family that wasn't always a family. I had a mother with no spine but who could stand on two feet. And that day, extending an offering of mercy, Alexis agreed that Sri Lanka was next to Spain.

3

TORNADOES

"I'M JUST HAVING FUN."

"You don't know how to just have fun," my best friend, Liz, said solemnly.

This was weeks after I met Quinn. Liz and I have been friends since we were twelve years old. When we met, she lived on General Steuben Road; Stella and I lived on General Muehlenburg Road. We shared the same bus stop and, freakishly, we were the only two kids at that bus stop. For one week at the start of junior high, we said nothing to each other. Not even a hello. *Generally speaking, we're probably somewhat alike,* she finally said with a detached but witty candor. Liz is outgoing and fun with people she knows well, but deep down inside she is a loner. This bonded us instantly before we were even aware of it. I have very few friendships, and those I have are pathologically tight. I do not have the assertiveness or aggressiveness needed for a large social network. This is not a bad thing. I have adapted. I have found ways to get what I want and what I need, and to give and share with equal depth. There of course is room for self-improvement, as Stella delicately and always lovingly reminds me. But self-improvement is a waste, really, at least to me. It's just a distraction from accepting the parts of yourself you are stuck with. Liz understands this.

Liz and I slowly made our way toward being inseparable: I'd bring an extra piece of piece of peanut-butter toast with me each morning and, for a long time, we said very little to each other, munching away on toast. One morning she reciprocated, bringing me a piece of matzo with cream cheese spread on it. *We're not Jewish, but my mom likes crunchy food,* she said. We went from sharing breakfast to watching soap operas after school, to sleepovers, to her being unfazed by the unpredictability of my father's presence. Her family treated me like one of their own even when Liz and I were in the thick of fighting. For an entire five months during our senior year in high school, Liz and I stopped talking to each other. We'd still sit at the same lunch table among all of our friends whom we liked but didn't love, and nothing but silence between Liz and me. Our friends were attuned to the discord, and they navigated a system of communicating with both of us at the same table while respecting the disdain that Liz and I had for each other. Liz and I loved each other in the impenetrable bubble of silence. There was never a question of whether we would speak again, just a question of when. Liz started the silent treatment for an infraction that to this day I cannot remember, but she was unwilling to pander to me or my emotional neediness because of my mother's death and my father's abandonment. Liz was compassionate and thoughtful—loyal to the end—but a fight is a fight, and so during that silent five months with her across from me at the table or passing me in the hall or even sitting next to me on the bus ride home, I never worried. We knew each other to that deepest part of the bone, and this was why she knew that Quinn was not about fun. I wanted pleasure and love and excitement or even pain, but fun left me with a bland ambivalence.

"Stella is going to kick your ass," Liz said, enunciating the second half of her statement as if every word was an individual sentence.

"Stella lives in Newfoundland. She's too far away to kick my ass."

"She'll get on a plane and come here and kick your ass. And then she'll get back on the plane and go home."

"Not if I don't tell her."

"Right. Like that's going to happen," Liz said.

Liz was almost married at the time. She didn't know this fact, but I did. Her boyfriend, Andy, had taken me to Jeweler's Row in the city to help him pick out an engagement ring for her. Andy looked relieved, wanting only to please her, not to prove anything to her. He is a tousle-haired absent-minded computer programmer, entirely too smart for his own good, good-natured, generous to a fault, and quiet, and he loved Liz in that exact way—a steady and quiet way. Liz is his tousle-haired equivalent, great big auburn rings splayed out like Medusa. She is short and voluptuous, with stubby feet and fiery eyes. She has flawless skin and bites her nails to the quick. Liz was working as a financial analyst at the time, tracking high-tech companies and, self-professedly, making entirely too many decisions about entirely too much money. Andy would ask her to marry him that very weekend after I told her that Quinn and I were just having fun.

"Listen, I know that what Quinn is doing is wrong," I said.

"What you are doing is wrong, too."

"It's not *as* wrong," I offered up.

"You just keep telling yourself that, Anjou."

"It's not like you haven't made your share of questionable choices," I snapped at her.

"Well, at least you recognize you're making a bad choice."

"I said questionable."

"Whatever, Anjou. I don't want to hear this I'm-having-fun bullshit. You are walking into a mess. He is married. And he is not going to leave his wife—"

"You don't know that, Liz."

"So you're going to wait around to see? Anjou, even if he leaves his wife one day, he'll be a different person when he gets to the other side of a divorce. He'll be someone else altogether."

That was the one thing I'd discover Liz was completely wrong about.

⁓

Although Stella, according to societal norms, is designated as the person I should be doling out advice to, my younger sister flipped everything upside down and instead has served as my refuge of wisdom, my protector, my reminder, my mentor, my barometer, and always my compass. Stella was made long before me—souls like hers usually are.

Stella is the beautiful one in our family: a combination of captivating features and a willful personality that literally forces other people to see the complex core of her commitment to living in a world her way, a world with unmatched compassion, brutal frankness, and an ability to interpret every angle of a situation. She favors our mother: lithe and petite, with sea-green eyes and hair the color of pine wood, a bright light brown with layers of darker woodsy streaks. She has long legs and hands that show her every vein. Her eyes are set unevenly, the left one a little higher than the right, and when you stare at her you feel a slope to your gaze. I am a different creature altogether. I have none of her bravado. I don't have her capacity to wrap myself around the dynamics of the world. For a long time, I envied her this trait. But she reminded me that we are stuck with each other, and thus we can't be too alike, that we need to complement each other instead of compete. I have never been called beautiful or gorgeous or lovely. Quinn called me fantastically pleasing. I have long brown hair the color of muddy river water, wavy and loose. I have a farmer's body—solid, with wide feet and a full face and child-bearing hips. I am short but not thin—never will be—but there is nothing loose about my body. Strong legs. Full mouth. Large eyes like copper pennies. And I have my half-moon mark.

Stella makes history—she crochets blankets and scarves for friends and strangers, knits mittens for friends' babies. She married an enormous-hearted and jolly man named Bruce, and they have a beautiful baby girl named Merry. Stella and Bruce live in Clarenville, a town on the east coast of Newfoundland. Before she had the baby, she worked as a constable, their version of a local police officer. She funds Third World relief projects with money she and her husband can sorely spare, and she tells nobody about these generous acts. She calls me, every day, without fail, just to check in. I collect history. I pile up the years in the most mundane of ways. My crowning jewels are postcards. Since I was seventeen years old, I have been collecting antique postcards, as well as mint-condition ones and discarded ones and dog-eared moldy ones. I have stolen them from people's cubicles at work and boyfriends' parents' refrigerators. I will collect only cards that have been sent, that have a postmark. After traveling in Europe for a summer with Liz, I made Stella, our Aunt Vicky, and my boyfriend at the time, a tall quiet man named Luke, give me all the postcards I had sent to them. *They're mine, really,* I said, leaving them dumbfounded.

I make greeting cards by affixing the postcard to expensive card stock with four-corner tabs, the postcard fitted in like a framed picture. The postcard's original message can be read by popping it out of the tabs, a second message, really, in addition to the more recent message between two totally different people. It's a cross-section of history, and I leave it to the recipient to decide which message is more important or more poignant. I make small boxes of postcard cards for coworkers and Liz and neighbors, often by theme—ten cards of different angles of the Leaning Tower of Pisa, diners along Route 66, cheesy tourist postcards that are completely black save for a white announcement: *San Diego at Night* or *New Orleans at Night* or *Miami at Night.* The message on the postcard really doesn't matter. It's nice, but it's not terribly important. Really, it's just the gesture itself–a card with a message without an envelope, words for all to see.

When we were in high school, I found my first treasure: a Holiday Inn postcard from the 1950s. Three women in a pool wearing modest bathing suits, with fleshy full figures and heavily coiffed hair, smiling widely with a coy sexuality oozing from their sloped shoulders; in the background was the square-edged low-rise motel in shades of yellow and aqua. *We're with you at every mile,* it read along the bottom in fat block letters. Stella was on the junior high track team, readying herself for the 800-meter relay against the Methacton team the day I gave it to her. Our mother was dead, our father was gone. Aunt Vicky was always there at Stella's meets, as was I. A promise on an old card. I knew she would love it. *Riotous!* she said to me, her favorite word that year. I hung postcards on mirrors and wallpapered the bathroom of my first apartment with them.

Stella and I—glaringly different in looks and personality—talk to each other as if we are twins, finishing sentences, understanding each other's hurts and triumphs, even those far from our individual realm of understanding and experience. Stella is a natural giver. I marvel at her complete disregard for the sense of ownership. Everything that is hers she quite literally believes is mine. Clothes, cars, jewelry, books, money—anything. She is never taken advantage of for this generosity, and it is she who inspired me to give 10 percent of my income to the Catholic Church where I am a member. I told Stella I'm not 100 percent convinced that I agree with God, so why I should I give him 10 percent of my paycheck? *God doesn't need your money, Anjou. Giving up what you think you really need forces you to trust in something bigger than yourself.*

Stella is a Lutheran, a fitting denomination that matches her natural stoicism. She believes in God but talks very little about Him. She addressed her silence on the topic only once and in a tone that was a mixture of annoyance and exasperation: *God is the one topic in which only my actions should do the talking.* I still don't trust God, but I trust Stella and that's enough reason to hand over this money every week to acne-riddled ushers in red robes.

Stella curses like a truck driver and yells at telemarketers. She drives too fast, always. She has a warrant for her arrest in several provinces of Canada. She is overly opinionated all the time, even when she knows she's wrong. She is self-admittedly wasteful: she refuses to keep leftovers, she doesn't recycle, she replaces handbags just because they are not completely in style. She is a firm believer in the necessity of lies. She is intolerant of stupidity. *There is nothing blissful about ignorance when it costs me time and money.* She never, not for one second, has done anything to make me think she's a saint. But her capacity to love, and to give, and to be loyal and protective pushes her close to such status. She's the smartest person I know, this baby sister of mine, and I can't imagine anyone not having one of those—the smartest person they know.

I tell Stella everything. I tell her about all of my failures. I tell her things I can't even tell a God who confuses me. I tell her she should start billing me for her time. So I told her about Quinn right away, the evening after he asked me about my half-moon mark.

"You shouldn't be meeting people on the train," she said.

"Talk about a buzz kill, Stella. I may actually get a date out of this. Not necessarily a horrible thing, is it?"

"No. No. No. I didn't mean it like that. I'm just skeptical about a stranger coming up to you on a train."

"It's not a Hitchcock movie. Nobody on that train is a stranger."

"What do you mean?"

"You have to commute for a while to understand the concept. But in a way you see people for a long time that you didn't know you were seeing."

I called Stella the night after Quinn and I ran on the Benjamin Franklin Bridge.

"Okay, run like hell," she said.

"I know," I said flatly.

"You don't sound convinced."

"He's unhappy. He said his marriage is not well."

"Not well? He said his marriage is not well? Does it need a fucking antibiotic? What kind of line is that?"

"You have to know him, Stella. He uses different words."

"I bet he does," she barked. "He'll tell you anything, Anjou. Don't listen to what he says. Listen to what he does."

"I know," I said.

"You can't see him again," she said.

"He's on the same train as me."

"Give me a break, Anjou. Take a different train."

"I know."

"Stop saying that. You don't know."

"What do you mean?"

"I mean that if you were 100 percent certain that you were never going to look that man in the eye again, this conversation would not be going on as long as it has."

"I know."

∽

I fell in love with Quinn the night of the tornado, three months after we met. It rained for hours that day, starting in the morning with a violent storm, water shooting from the sky in a sideways torrent, coercing the wind into its spectacular rampage of thunder-cracking lightning. Later that day, when the R8 deposited me back in Glyn Neath, the rain had stopped, the skies taking a breath. *The storm is over,* I thought.

The atmosphere was purple and metallic, leaves blowing backward. When I opened my door I found Lurch pacing and whining, circling me in an agitated state. I went upstairs to my bedroom and put towels on the puddles of rain on my hardwood floor, cursing myself for not closing the windows that morning. I cringed looking up, unsurprised but still dismayed at the Raphael-like cloud of wetness spread across my ceiling.

"Doesn't look good, Lurch," I said, and Lurch looked up, too, his tail still and tense.

I went downstairs to feed Lurch and the phone rang.

"This is Anjou," I said, a horrible habit of answering my home phone like I was still at work.

"Where are you?" Quinn said.

"Where am I?" I laughed. "If you haven't noticed, you called me at home."

"But where are *you*?"

"I have no idea, Quinn. I really don't."

Lurch was at my feet, his tail wagging, trying to cheer me up. He saw me shaking my head and staring at my feet. Quinn was quiet, and I imagined he sensed the unshakable regret that I was willing to live with just to be with him.

"Where are you?" I asked, wanting to place him physically.

"Well, I'm stuck, Anjou."

"The train's stuck?"

"Yes, among other things," he said.

"Is somebody sitting next to you, or are you alone?" I asked.

"I'm never alone," he said.

"Well, I am," I said with a cynical laugh.

"No, you're not."

The wind rattled my living room windows, which were mottled and wavy, original to the house, which was built in 1910. The electricity surged, a dim-bright-dim effect, and I peered out to the backyard, where the purple sky had turned to black.

"I gotta go, Quinn. We're gonna lose power, and I need to make sure all of the windows are closed."

"Leave one open," he said.

"Why?"

"For me."

"What?"

"Leave the window open for me. You promise?"

"I promise," I said, the wind rattling the window in the small dining room I never used. Quinn always told me I should use that room more often, that I shouldn't let any space go stale, that we should live in everything that's available.

Glyn Neath is a town that does not have tornadoes. It is not Kansas. No ruby slippers, no rainbows and getting over them. It had been a brutal fall, an odd transfer of seasons, with more bruising from Mother Nature than we were accustomed to. It started in August, when an unexpected cold front hovered over the region and cast a prehistoric shell along our landscape. On Labor Day weekend we had our first frost. We were used to life-sucking humidity from May to September, sometimes hanging on through the first few days of October, followed by a month of nirvana with dry cool air and leaves in colors that made you weep.

I stood in my bedroom with Lurch, folding laundry as the rain began again. The silence of a house when the power is out is overwhelming, welcome and serene, eerie. The room was dusk-like and gray, and I was lulled by the repetition of folding towels. The water-stain cloud I had discovered on the ceiling didn't matter. The food soon to be rotting in my refrigerator didn't matter. Quinn mattered. And downstairs, in the kitchen, for reasons that made perfect sense at the time—because he had asked—I left a window open.

He's mine, I thought.

I started to hear a sound, unnameable and ripe. I kept folding towels, thinking about the ones that Quinn had used, had touched. Yellow towel, yes. Red towel, no. Blue towel, yes. Another red towel, no. Green towel, yes. And he had touched my toothpaste and my shower curtain, my hand soap and my bed. He had touched my brush but not my comb.

The sound—it was a train, I was sure—got louder.

I folded another towel. Blue again, yes.

The sound was closer than the R8's rattle-and-whistle-and-brakes that I heard day and night from the tracks just a block away. The train was outside and all of that joy—of Quinn wanting to know where I was, of the window I left open for him even though it would soak my kitchen floor, the towels he touched—all of it disappeared. Because I pulled up my blinds and saw nothing outside but the swirl of purple and black, and the sound of a train that pushed at my window—*The train, this train, will hit my house.* I heard a cluster of gods and noises pass, and I was sure, then and there, that I was being warned. Lurch was barking, a high-pitched painful cough and whinny—and the train lingered, moving but hovering, and then it passed and a vacuum escape of sound trailed along. The street was still. Tree branches lined the yards and driveways. Wires hung precariously from utility poles. One of Kip's pink flamingoes was on my car.

My neighbors slowly emerged from their homes, all of us looking tentatively to the left and right while stepping out. War stories were quickly built: overlapping raised voices explaining where we were standing when it hit, what we thought it was when we first heard the sound (a train collision, a house that imploded). We listened to the sirens, shook our heads at the wreckage, watched the emergency vehicles. A radio was found and turned on: an F-1 tornado had touched down, with winds that reached 110 miles per hour.

I came inside and walked to the kitchen, ready to see a tree branch in my sink or six inches of water across the floor. Quinn was standing next to the refrigerator that, for the first time in years, was not humming. Lurch sat by his side.

"How did you get here? When did you get here?" I asked, flummoxed and confused. "Did you see the tornado? Where were you?"

"Thank you," he said, standing in a puddle of water, brown streaks spreading out from his muddy shoes. He was drenched, unfazed.

"What? How could I have not seen you?"

"Thank you, my honeysuckle, my tulip, my love, my perfection, my time, my flower."

"For what?" I laughed, holding tight to every word, thinking already about what towel I would get for him—a red one, one he hadn't touched yet.

Three weeks after Quinn moved in with me, we went to Paros, in the Cyclades Islands on the Aegean Sea. His grandmother had lived there, although she had died years before. It was the second week in February, and he came home from the university and walked straight into the kitchen, opening cabinets and drawers. He was almost no longer married. Lily did not come at me, or him, with loud cries or demands. I expected the end of his marriage to be different: I expected him to talk about Lily, about his pain or her pain or the pain we caused. Very few topics were off limits until he left Lily. He faced his divorce with a cool and untouchable demeanor, and it unnerved me. I got everything I wanted—him, his life in mine, his body in my house—but Lily became more present after he left her than when he was still married. I finally wanted to know about her: She and Quinn had a very literal history and I want to know about people's histories. The night before Quinn and I had had our first fight—not the first ever—but the first as the two of us, in a house that was mine but that we shared. I had cried, begging him to talk about Lily, to say anything, and he had become more and more silent, listening to me all the while, shutting down, but not shutting me out.

"Is she okay? I mean, what's going to happen?"

"That remains to be seen, Anjou."

"What do you mean?"

"I mean, that remains to be seen."

"I don't get it."

"Well, the end result of Lily and me is still undetermined. We'll divorce. That's understood. But in a way we're still tethered. That happens when you're married. I'm not trying to be patronizing, but it's the truth. Even when it's over, there's an invisible cord."

I had started to cry. He was in my house, putting things in my drawers, staking claim, posting territory the exact way I wanted him to—he was being assuming. We had just made love on the floor, quiet and almost sad, our initiation of his arrival. He had whispered how I was his half-moon over and over, stroking my marked hand.

Quinn was slamming cabinets and peering into the refrigerator.

"Do we have lime juice?" he asked, walking back into the living room where I sat with Lurch reading the paper.

He put his briefcase down, loosened his tie, kissed Lurch on the mouth, and patted my head.

"Very funny," I said. Lurch growled an affectionate sound.

"Lime juice," he repeated.

Quinn was serious when you shouldn't be and not serious when you should be, but then he would somersault all of this, raising his language and tone to the occasion. It was a lyrical twist of perspective that captivated me, caught me, and left me to my own devices. I couldn't figure him out and then just when my frustration or insecurity peaked, he came toward me with a brilliant force of need and laid out his desire in a straightforward and singular manner: few words, strong eye contact. He would tell me that he needed me at the moment I needed to hear it—not when I asked for it or in a stereotypical moment of lovemaking or reunions or departures. He was magical. So few people are these days.

"It's too cold for gin and tonics. That's a summer drink. You should know this, you went to Yale," I said, looking outside the window where frozen snow clung to the outside window sills of Kip's house.

"Yes, I went to Yale, but I grew up in a lower-middle-class, blue-collar home where we drank Mythos beer that my Uncle Nick lugged over from Athens twice a year. Now, dear, lime juice?"

"No. We don't have any lime juice," I said.

"Then I'll go get some," he said, kissing me on the forehead and heading toward the door.

"Where are you going? What do you need lime juice for?"

"Pie."

"Pie?"

"Key lime pie."

Quinn hated everything about Florida, the weather, the landscape, the bugs. He particularly hated the people. He complained that they were either too old, bad drivers, uneducated, or all three. But he loved key lime pie.

"It's February, Quinn. It's 29 degrees outside. Key lime pie is cold," I said, shaking my head.

"I want key lime pie."

"You don't even know how to make it."

"Get out the *Joy of Cooking*. We'll learn how to do this together. C'mon. I want something to remind me of the warm weather. I always think of sunshine when I eat key lime pie."

"But you hate Florida."

"Of course I do."

"You're missing the point," I said.

"You don't have a point. And I do. I want key lime pie because I want to think of the sun and the sand. Can you look it up in the *Joy of Cooking* while I go to the store to buy some lime juice?"

"Fine," I said, walking to the bookshelf as he headed out the door, closing it softly.

I pulled out my weathered and swollen copy of the *Joy of Cooking*, copyright 1962. It was my mother's copy. I loved its sticky pages with brown and yellow and fading red blotches and splatters of soups and sauces and mixes. My mother's handwritten notes—*Substitute olive oil for butter, Three eggs for cakey brownies, Don't preheat oven or will burn.* My father gave my mother this book on their first anniversary, and buried in the index under *Sweet Potatoes,* my father scratched in red ink, *You are my, page 519,* their wedding date being May 19th.

I flipped to the index, looked up Pies, and scanned down to find *lime, Key, page 657.* When I turned to it, the page opened naturally, and there was an envelope where the recipe was. I didn't hear the door open again as I pulled out plane tickets. Confused, I turned around and Quinn handed me a seashell, smooth and sand-pounded.

"I need for things to be warm," he whispered, pulling me close to him and telling me, in Greek, a language he spoke fluently, about the island we were going to the next week, his words foreign and certain, telling me something I would never understand.

It was far from warm—the temperature only topping at 52 degrees. We walked past the house his mother had grown up in. It was a small island home, built of rock into rock. He pointed to the whitewashed balcony, explaining how his parents, visiting his grandparents with his four sisters, had conceived him on that balcony on a windy night in June.

"They told you this?"

"My mother said that after they made love they whispered prayers in their respective languages, praying for a boy. When my mother found out she was pregnant, she said the baby's name would be Quinn—it's Greek for 'fifth born.' She never questioned that I'd be anybody else."

4

CARDIGAN AVENUE

"Jack knows it's you that's been calling," Stella says.

Stella rarely needs confessions or admissions. She senses things. When we were children, Stella would beg my parents to take her to Cassadega, Florida, a town famous for having the most psychics per capita in America. Stella was not interested in Mickey Mouse or the Space Mountain roller coaster. She wanted to meet the sages and prophets of the world. She wanted to watch them read tarot cards and look in crystal balls and examine the palms of nervous women. Stella wrote to the chamber of commerce and was sent brochures on Cassadega's commercial and residential offerings. She memorized the names of the psychic centers, the Cards Tell All and Crystal Ball Hall and Palms Away. She wrote to the manager of the Psychic Warehouse and asked if they had an apprentice program for high school graduates, because even though she was only ten years old, she already felt the calling to the "psychic ministry." Her letter went unanswered. *They were too busy to write back. I sense it,* she said. But her zeal for the supernatural was undeterred. Stella believed she could read my mind. And eventually I believed she could, too, which is precisely why I feel both incredibly safe and frighteningly vulnerable in my relationship with her.

"Sorry, Anjou. But you and I both know that Jack knows it's you."

"What do you want me to say?"

I am on my cell phone, standing at the corner of St. David's and Cardigan Avenues. I am surprised how crackly and unclear the connections are on my expensive cell phone, this express technology that can take pictures and send e-mail and pay your bills from a device smaller than my hand. The reception is horrible, no matter where I am standing.

"I don't want you to say anything to me—but perhaps you could say something to Jack when he picks up the phone. Okay?"

"Listen, Stella—"

"There's nothing to listen to, Anjou. You need to decide which way you're going to go with Jack. If you want to tell him off and move on with your life, then do it. If you want to tell him off and let him back into your life, then do that. If you want status quo, fine. I know you are in the middle of hell right now. I know that losing Quinn is painful and confusing in ways I'll never understand. I would do anything, and you know anything, to relieve you somehow, but I can't. I can't get past Quinn for you. But, honey, this thing you're doing with Jack, doing it this way, this is not going to make you feel any better."

"I know what I'm doing."

"No, you don't. If you did, you would say something to him when he answers. Why don't you just say something?"

"I want him to say something."

"Well, he's not a mind reader. If you want to know anything, just ask."

"I don't know how."

⌒ℳ⌒

343 Cardigan Avenue

A man with a bushy salt-and-pepper beard answers the door. His house is a small, one-floor A-frame with a sun room in the front. Tiny windows surround the room, and he walks through it to come outside. He is wearing overalls and a gray tee-shirt, and he nods at me warmly. It is April 10. The sun cannot make a decision, but has finally made a brief visit.

"Good afternoon, my name is—"

"You're Anjou."

"How do you—"

"We met," he says coolly, reaching out to shake my hand.

"We did?"

"Last September. You had a bee problem."

And then I recognize him, remembering this exact demeanor. How he almost floated in the space, relaxed in a way I could only dream of.

"I can't believe you remember my bees."

"I pay attention to details," he says. "Part of the job."

Last fall, I came home from work to find bees in the bedroom Quinn and I shared. There were only a few, and they moved slowly, drunk with honey and season-changing expectations. They were easy to kill because of this suspended nature of their flight. For two weeks it was the same every day: two or three or sometimes four bees. I would kill them, flush them down the toilet, and pat Lurch on the head as he looked on with a worried expression. On the fifth day of the bee infestation, I came home to find the bedroom full of countless slow-moving bees. I shut the door and went to the kitchen, calling Quinn in a panic, catching him in his office.

"You need a bee guy," Quinn said.

The night before, we had been lying in bed when he straddled me and pinned my arms down, laughing wildly and singing, *You are bee-sieged by the bees near your bed. They besiege you every day in your head. The bees bee-siege the pear of my life, buzzing about and causing honey-filled strife.* I had laughed at him and told him his imitation of Dr. Seuss was lousy.

"What the hell is a bee guy?"

"There are lots of bee guys in western Pennsylvania. They take care of bee's nests getting in unwanted places. They eliminate bee problems, my honeycomb."

"Well, your honeycomb needs a bee guy. Now. There's a swarm of them hovering over our bed."

"Relax, my lazy Susan. I can take care of this."

"You can?"

"I absolutely can. Keep the bedroom door shut. I'll call you right back."

Quinn called fifteen minutes later. I had opened the bedroom door three times, checking to see if they were still there.

"The bee guy will be there in an hour. I should get there about the same time he does. Don't forget to put Lurch in the second bedroom. You know how he hates strangers."

"I think I already know what my dog does and does not like, Quinn."

"There's nothing wrong with being reminded. It makes me feel loved and needed to make these observations."

A man with a rusty Chevy pickup showed up, which alarmed me at first. How was *this* guy going to get rid of the bees? He walked around the house twice, looking up the whole time, and then he stood on the front lawn, his hands crossed behind him, a few feet from the red-brick front face of my side of the twin house. He moved his head slowly clockwise, and then counterclockwise.

"I think we have just enough light," he said, positioning himself with his legs spread parallel to the width of his shoulders.

I nudged Quinn after five minutes. The man was just standing there, doing nothing. Quinn's arms were crossed over his chest and he put his finger in front of his lips, giving me an annoyed look. I started to watch the front of the house with the same focused intensity as Quinn and the bee guy. Eventually, a picture began to form: bees, floating about, not a swarm but definitely a building crowd scattered around the upper-left section of the front face of the house.

"The problem starts on the outside, leading to a problem on the inside. Come here and I'll show you where they are getting in," the bee guy said, not turning around to address me, just extending his right hand in a beckoning motion.

"Look a bit below that window up there," he said, a large arm pointing to a small hole in the mortar between two bricks. "See the hole, up there?"

"Yeah," I answered in a whisper.

"Watch that hole. You won't notice it right away, so just keep watching."

I finally saw it. One by one tired bees, slowed by the fatigue of summer's end, flew into the hole and flew out. It was barely noticeable unless you stood there staring.

"That's how they are getting in. The queen's in there," the bee guy said.

"She's about to be dethroned, eh?" I said with a chuckle, giddy that I was in on the secret.

Neither the bee guy nor Quinn saw anything to laugh about, and turned to look at me.

"I'll smoke them out," the bee guy said. "The rest will die. Some will go straight into your room, and they're likely to be angry. Before I smoke them out you may want to take a few things from your bedroom. If you keep the door shut, the bees that get in there will die in a day or so."

Quinn and I slept in the guest room for the next two nights. But I couldn't sleep. All I could think about was that the bees were slowly dying in our bedroom.

"Yes, you're the bee guy," I say to the man on Cardigan Avenue, holding my clipboard tightly to my chest.

"What can I do you for, dear?"

I hold up my laminated card.

"I have the form—not filled out, mind you—on my dining room table."

"You and a few thousand others in this county," I say.

My cell phone begins to ring, startling both of us. I secretly wonder if the bee guy is as unconnected to this world as I am used to being.

"You go on and answer that, and I'll be right back," he says.

I pick up the phone and look on the miniature screen. The incoming phone number flashes. A number I have dialed exactly thirty-two times. *But I didn't call you this time. You are not calling back. You are just calling.* I hold the phone, feeling it vibrate with each chirpy shrill. I do not know how to program it so that it doesn't have such a happy ring. I shove the phone back in my purse and wait for the bee guy, the shrill ending by the time he comes back outside.

"This is going to take a hell of a long time to do," he says, handing me the form he was sent.

"Oh, you got the Long Form," I say, trying to regain my composure.

My dad is calling me at work.

"One out of six people are sent the Long Form, which obviously asks many more questions than the Short Form."

"Will it get you in trouble if we do the short one?"

"I'll never tell," I say.

I get out my pen and begin.

"I need the names of all of the people who reside in this house, starting with preferably the homeowner," I said.

"I'm the homeowner. My name is Linus Snowwind."

"Thank you, Mr. Snowwind. I remember the name now."

"Call me Linus."

"Okay, Linus. Can you tell me the names of anybody else in the home, starting first with any people related to you?"

"My great-nephew, Hammond, also lives here."

"Is he just visiting temporarily or is he here for more than a year? I don't want to count him if he's going to be counted on the form his parents complete."

"He's here for the long haul, at least until he finishes high school."

"Can you tell me his last name and his age?"

"That's Hammond Covington. He's sixteen."

"Is that two m's in Hammond?"

"Yes, ma'am."

"Okay, anybody else?"

"Just the two of us. I've had him for a year now."

"Yeah?" I say nonchalantly. "That must be nice."

"I don't know if that's the word for it. I have him because nobody knows what else to do with him. So they gave him to me."

"Oh," I say.

"Everybody knows I fix problems."

Fourth house on Cardigan. Subtotal of thirteen people. Five people in house one. Three each in houses two and three. Now two in four.

"This a single-unit dwelling, correct?"

I am paid to confirm even the most obvious.

"Yes, it is. But sometimes it feels like a studio apartment. A teenager takes up a lot of space. Makes your house feel so much smaller. You know what I mean?"

I don't know why he is telling me everything, answering questions I haven't yet begun to ask but was planning to. I want to ask him if he is clairvoyant. I want my little sister here to look at his palm and read it.

"Yes, I do," I say. "But that feels good, too, the whole less-space feeling."

"Depends what kind of music that extra person is listening to. Black Sabbath isn't so good for my hearing—or my ceilings for that matter."

"Are you glad he's in your life?" I ask, wanting to know if Grace was happy about Quinn during the time she had him, the months leading up to his leaving, those few days before he died, if my father felt joy in his relationship with Stella, if he felt guilt and relief, too.

"Excuse me?" Linus asks.

"This person—this nephew of yours. Are you glad that he is in your life?"

"That's a loaded question, dear."

He stares at me for a while, contemplating my question.

"I am certainly not glad in many ways that he is in my life. He's a difficult boy with too many problems for his years, and too many problems that I'm too old for. But he's blood. And that makes him mine, in a way."

I nod at him. I will need to write this down when I get home. When I get a good answer to an unsanctioned question, I write it on the back of a blank Census form. I drink wine and smoke cigarettes when I do this. I keep this particular list in the top drawer in my kitchen, with all of my silverware. I am not eating a lot these days and I mostly open the drawer for the list.

"So have they ever come back?" he asks, as I begin to leave.

"Who?"

"The bees. Did they come back?"

A normal act: a father calling his daughter at work. I still haven't set up voice mail, much to Stella's chagrin, so he can't leave a message. I wonder, however, what on earth he would say. I love my father's phone number: 215-727-2345. I like when digits tumble like a gymnast—5969, the last four digits of my current phone number. The phone number Stella and I grew up with—484-262-6776—a three-ply palindrome that was one digit off from the local movie theater. People called daily asking for movie showing times. Through my teen years, I cataloged the movies and number of callers in a pink notebook I kept by the phone. When I was in high school, Stella would write parodies of movies in the notebook— *The Way We Weren't, Gandhi Schmandi, A Passage to Indiana, Ben Hurl.* I asked my mother why we didn't get our phone number changed. *There's no need to change something because of a minor inconvenience,* she said.

I turn my body east. My father lives in the Society Hill section of the city. I know his address. I've seen his house. I've been making detours during my lunch for years now—on anniversaries of deaths and births and celebrations—to walk past his small home. I never see him outside; I don't want to, and I'm convinced that is precisely why I haven't. I am standing on Cardigan Avenue, facing east while dialing his number. The phone rings only once, and I will myself not to hang up on him when I hear him say *Hello.*

"Hello," I say back.

"How are you?" he asks.

Stella and I are his children. He knows it's me before he knows that he knows.

"I don't know," I say.

And then it gets very, very quiet. Quinn once told me that people should live with that bubble of silence, not try to fill the moment for the sake of getting past an awkward pause. *Just wait. Just wait and see what may be possible,* he said.

"I'm glad to hear from you," he finally says.

"Okay."

And then that silence. You cannot begin anything—engaging in small talk or meaningful revelations—when you haven't spoken to somebody in seventeen years. You cannot just begin asking questions. There is no place to actually begin. So I find a beginning anyway, and it is a true beginning.

"My boyfriend died, and that's why I'm calling you."

"I'm sorry, Anjou. I'm very sorry."

"I have to go," I say.

And I hang up.

5

NEW MOONS

QUINN LEFT ME FOR A WOMAN named Grace, a professor at the university where he taught. A total different department—and school—altogether. She is in the College of Medicine in the Department of Pathology. She is pale skinned with wavy brown hair heavily streaked with gray and startlingly green eyes. Older than him—by five or six years. She looked a bit gaunt, hungry almost, the first time I met her, at a faculty happy hour at Green's Bar, a dive on 18th and Sansom. It was smoky, full of poorly nourished alcoholics and cranky barmaids and a scattering of tragically hip grad students, a bar that Quinn loved completely because he said it was just like the bar in Bethlehem in which his adopted grandfather had drunk himself to death. Quinn loved familiarity, even the most depressing kind. He hated all things new: homes, hotels, malls, restaurants. Anything built less than thirty years ago frustrated him. He was glad that his office was probably asbestos-filled.

Quinn loved my old house, my old postcards, and Lurch and Kip—both old. Quinn loved how stuck I was, and I loved how present he was. Quinn was friends with a doctor named Bernie in the Department of Psychiatry. They had been running partners for years, and the two of them brought together faculty in their respective departments for regular, and odd-houred, happy hours. *Strange bedfellows,* Quinn said. *Researchers and poets and doctors and anthropologists all getting soused together.*

What surprised me the most was not that he was having an affair but that I hadn't figured it out sooner. Quinn pursued women with the strategy of a night-enshrouded thief, moving with stealth and intense focus. I always figured it out because he did not choose the Jennifers or Marys or Lisas of the world. Quinn once told me that people with unusual names tend to seek out the most simple pleasures and struggle with the most mundane in their lives, himself included.

Mirjana was the first woman who made me understand how Lily must have felt. She was the bohemian owner of the flower shop on King Edward's Avenue. Every Friday, Quinn would buy me flowers from Mirjana's shop on his walk home from the Glyn Neath train station. He brought roses mixed with baby's breath or daisies or snapdragons. We socialized with Mirjana. I imagine he thought he was safeguarding himself from suspicion by introducing me to the woman he was sleeping with, inviting her over with her boyfriend, Sam, whom I knew from working together on the yearly 10-K race that the Glyn Neath Fire Department sponsored. It was all connected, cozy. Mirjana and Sam would come to the house that summer for gin-and-tonics on the porch. Kip would join us with tall tales of climbing Mt. Washington in Vermont or sailing in the South Pacific. Liz and Andy would come over and we'd grill, drinking and eating long into the night and too relaxed to care that our arms and legs were riddled with mosquito bites.

Mirjana was violently thin and a step away from beautiful. She had an uptilted nose, demanding brown eyes, faded freckles running a path from cheek to cheek, and a long mane of red hair that shot out in different directions, giving a wildness to her presence. Her breathy voice was so hypnotic, I believed if she asked a man to eat broken glass he'd hold out his palms as if receiving Holy Communion.

I knew, in a rushing explosion of my heart, when he began sleeping with her. He began coming home late on Wednesday nights from the class he was teaching that summer—*I'm off to the HOTEL,* he'd say, savoring the acronym of the course, History of the English Language. I'm sure he was secretly thrilled despite his guilt at the layers of this farewell. When he'd come home, he'd smell like moonflowers—a sticky citrus scent laced with a beach-combed breeze. Sweet and fresh and salty, and poisonous. I knew he was sleeping with Mirjana because of the moonflower. She had moonflower plants along the side of her porch that reached up through the wrought-iron railing. I imagined Quinn on her porch those evenings, not even ten blocks away, his head leaned back in a chair, laughing maybe, sighing, his head against the sprouting flowers.

I possess the olfactory nerves of a dog. I can smell the salmon that my next-door neighbor cooks, the burned air that follows the screeching brakes of the R8 train at the station, the Port-a-Potty that rested on the front sidewalk of my house during the four weeks that the township was widening our sidewalks.

"The windows are shut, Anjou. It's in your head," Quinn said.

"I can smell that Port-a-Potty. That disinfectant smell. Nothing but a futile attempt to mask the smell of shit, which, incidentally, I also smell."

"The window is closed," Quinn said.

"I can still smell it."

There was nothing else to give away the affair: no moods altering from intolerably detached one day to a suffocating affection the next. Just moonflowers. I imagine that Lily had had a clue to my presence, something equally small and distinct. On Wednesdays, while Quinn slept, curled on his side facing me, his arm around my waist, I would lean my face against his hair, smelling the night-blooming flowers, the release from their round webbed blossoms.

At summer's end, I ended the affair. On a languid Saturday in September, I walked into Mirjana's crowded and buzzing store. Mirjana spotted me at the back of the store, and welcomed me with a slinky hug.

"Let me guess, Quinn sent you out to buy your own bouquet this week."

She tossed her hip at mine.

"Not quite, but I was hoping you could help me."

"Sure," she said, stepping back a bit, sensing that something had shifted. During the affair, when I saw Mirjana, I acted normal. Disgusted and confused and scared—and yes, in love—I shared him. I honestly believed there was no other choice, that now that he had left Lily and lived with me, I had truly gotten what I wanted. And I knew that he didn't love her. Somehow this made it easier.

"I need carnations," I said.

"Sure thing," she said. "What kind of arrangement do you want?"

"Just white," I said.

"All white?"

"All white."

White carnations, the flower of death. White that faked out the black that we associate with death, the flowers we bring to the grieving, to pay homage to the end.

"A dozen."

Her face dropped and she walked to the freezer, tying the stems together with a ribbon, wrapping them in a pale green paper. She waved my money away when I drew out bills from my wallet.

"No charge," she said, shaking her head.

I didn't thank her.

"Anjou, I hate to pry, but has someone died?"

"Not someone. But hopefully something will."

I walked out of the store and threw the carnations in the nearest trash can. I never smelled moonflowers on Quinn again.

I am fiercely loyal, even to the wrong people. Even to my father. He is not dead to me. I never doubted that I would speak to him again. I knew I would. I was waiting. I have a freakish level of patience when it comes to getting answers or collecting data. Liz calls this trait of mine Anjou's Wall of Steel. Stella calls it denial. I prefer to call it patience. I once left twelve e-mails in my inbox, unread, for eight months when I had a falling out with my friend Joan, a friendship that died in a fiery crash over some perceived injustice on both of our parts, whether real or not, each of us pointing the finger at the other. I ignored her e-mails, ultimately deleting them, unread. When my boyfriend Jamie and I broke up after college, he mailed a box to me, which I took to Liz's apartment. We both lived in Lansdowne at the time, a neighborhood on the fringe of West Philly, and I put the box under her bed and told her not to open it.

"I've had sex with Andy over that box for almost two years," Liz finally said one day. "You gonna open it?"

"Maybe," I said with a shrug.

It would be another two years before I did; inside was the key chain I had bought him in Puerto Rico, a silver ring with two garnets that I must have left at his place, the instructions to the cordless phone I had purchased when we lived together during our senior year. And he had enclosed every letter and postcard I had sent to him during our four years together. His intention at the time, no doubt, was a dramatic and emotional proclamation that I was gone from his life. But the only emotion I felt when I saw the letters was joy. The history: It was mine. I did not miss Jamie. My heart did not ache for him. I did not feel sad or angry or regretful. I loved him in those years that we were together, but it was a love that would never change the landscape of who I was.

My father spent my childhood choosing when he would be in our lives; I'm his daughter. I learned everything I know from him. Stella has been and always will be the black sheep of our family. She sees the dynamics of our family as a continuum of choices and emotions and decisions and forgiveness and pardons. She sees all of us as partly responsible, partly guilty for what transpired. It is not that simple for me.

That winter after Mirjana, a woman named January created a new triangle in the household Quinn and I shared: a business card: *January Phillips, Real Estate Agent, Roach and Preston Realtors. Our homes are your homes.* And a neon-orange flyer: *Parents Without Partners invites you to a spaghetti dinner at the Chestnut Hill Presbyterian Church.*

Quinn had no children, but that was beside the point. I simply imagined how those two pieces of paper formed a sentence: Quinn, sitting on a plastic chair in the basement of the Chestnut Hill Presbytarian Church, talking about his youngest daughter, Olivia, who didn't exist. January had a daughter, too. I imagined that her name was Claire. That she was eight years old.

I found the flyer, folded like origami, and the business card in the front pocket of his Adidas gym jacket. I called Stella and told her about the business card and the Parents Without Partners flyer.

"Christ on a cross, Anjou, why should you be surprised?"

"No lectures today. Just listening. Please."

There was a pregnant pause, and Stella drew in her breath.

"Mom used to go to Parents Without Partners, remember?" she said, defeated but engaged.

"I remember that. She only went twice, though," I said.

Parents Without Partners was our mother's brief foray into dating, the year before she died. She went during one of the many periods when our father lived with the woman we didn't talk about. Although very much married, clinging to her commitment, still wearing the thick platinum band on her ring finger, our mother made one attempt to see something outside her world if she said *No* instead of *Yes*.

"She had a date, too," Stella said.

"No, she didn't. She just went to those two meetings."

"Two meetings, one date."

"Did she tell you this?"

"Jack told me," she said.

When a parent is dead, you want to know all the things you're convinced they would have told you, eventually. You want to know not just what they would have told you on your wedding day or graduation from college—you also want their minuscule and private-world moments.

"Mom told him herself," Stella said.

"I don't think I want to hear any more about this," I said.

"Yes, you do."

For a long time, Stella had been my only ally in a silent war I raged against my father, but one day—prompted by her marriage to

Bruce—she laid to rest the demons of our past and looked past the flaws and transgressions. Ever since then, the notable imperfections and screwups she created and experienced as a wife and then a mother freed her to an encompassing forgiveness of our father for his own mistakes. She called him on the phone. She handed her granddaughter to him. She visited him here and brought him to Newfoundland.

"Go ahead," I said, the desire to know building with each second.

"Apparently Mom met Mr. Callahan at the Parents Without Partners meeting and went on a date with him."

"You've got to be kidding me. Mr. Callahan?"

"Yup. Mr. Callahan."

"God, that's so creepy."

"She only went out with him once, and she never went back to another Parents Without Partners meeting."

"And Mom told Dad about this?"

"She told him right after Mr. Callahan's body was found."

Mr. Callahan was the librarian of the Tindell Memorial Library. He was widowed, forty-eight years old, with two children in college. During my sophmore year in high school, his body was found behind a gas station in Flourtown. He had been shot in the head, and beside him were three library books—*Sometimes a Great Notion* by Ken Kesey, *The Art of Mexican Cooking,* and a biography of Winston Churchill. They never found his killer.

"You have officially creeped me out, Stella."

"Ready for more?"

"There's more?"

"The police questioned her."

"Get the fuck out of town. Why?"

"The police were questioning everybody who had been in contact with Mr. Callahan during that year."

"She must have been so freaked out."

"No, she wasn't. At least Jack said she wasn't. Mom could keep a cool head. You know that."

"I wonder what she said to the police."

"Apparently they asked her why she stopped dating him. I guess they wanted to know if there was anything strange about him—or about Mom."

"What did she say?"

"She told the cops she wasn't *dating* him but had only gone on a date *with* him."

"Dear God," I whispered, thrown back to the memory of my mother's pointed analysis of the world around her, her ability to see things for exactly what they were, and accept them that way, too.

"It gets better. So Jack says she told the police she didn't go on another date with him because his eyes were too close together."

"What!"

"Yeah, I know. Crazy. She told the cops that men whose eyes were too close together tended to be intolerant and mean-spirited."

I burst out in a sound that was a cross between a yell and a laugh. I thought of our father's eyes, spaced so wide apart they were practically on the sides of his head, a sloping mountain of bone between each brow, a space Stella would tease him about, saying you could land a plane on his forehead.

"How is it possible that we didn't know this?" I asked, all humor gone.

"There's a lot we don't know, Anjou."

And I would never know about January, if she was his lover or not. What I believed in more was his life in mine: a life we shared, where we never talked in the morning because we both loved the silence—rare moments of Quinn just being Quinn without words—where he made love to me and I to him, where he read the same book after I was done just so we could talk about it. This was his idea, his desire to share words, and he always—always—let me choose the book. Even when I had chosen three books in a row that he hated, he kept letting me choose. The nights when I made him my mother's recipe of tuna-noodle casserole that stuck to your ribs, a casserole that he took leftovers of to work for three days, that he thanked me profusely for every time, with sincerity, with appreciation, with an undeniable sense of love that yes, was dichotomous, but love is love, and sometimes you'll take any that you can get. A life where he never talked about Lily after he left her, something that I had hated at first but then grew to appreciate. A life where he'd join Kip and me once a month for mass. The days when we fought over who would clean the bathroom or whose turn it was to take Lurch for a walk and decided in the end we would do it together. The days when he'd bring me watery tea and biscotti when I was leveled by a migraine. I would be huddled under the covers, crying for him to shut all the blinds; he'd rub my back and sing Simon and Garfunkel songs quietly. The phone calls with Stella, who didn't like him (and he knew this), where he'd insist on talking to her and in a genuine voice ask her how her horse-riding lessons were or what her daughter's latest developmental milestone was. The long rides to his parents' house, a swarm of people and hugs. His father loved to cook, filling our bellies with rib-sticking comfort dishes from his native Austria: Wiener schnitzel of veal with cranberries and parsley potatoes, beef broth with cheese dumplings, farmer's potato cakes with bacon and onion, curd apricot strudel. Quinn's arm around my shoulder for hours and my love of that weight, making impossibly quiet love on the floor before

climbing onto the tiny bunk bed in the bedroom he'd grown up in. I
slept against the wall and he'd be on the outer side, arm around me.

⌒ⁿ⌒

On the night Quinn announced he was leaving, he came home
from work, loosened his tie, and announced that we needed to talk.
It was after 10 o'clock, a common hour for him to arrive home from
teaching evening classes. He looked beautiful, even in that moment, in a rumpled suit with an exhausted look on his face. Looking like he needed something—or someone—was when Quinn
seemed most vulnerable.

"About what?" I asked, barely looking up from the thick novel
I was reading—*The Man of Property* by John Galsworthy, a family
drama set in high-society London in the early 1900s. Quinn would
be reading it next, of course, so I was already formulating my opening line for our one-on-one book club: The story is the same everywhere in every time period, cheating hearts and bleeding hearts
and lonely hearts and hungry hearts.

"I'm leaving," he said. The words clipped like scissors in the
air, metal-sharp-metal.

For an immeasurable three-dimensional period, I stared at the
sentence I was reading when he walked in: *Love is no hot-house
flower, but a wild plant, born of a wet night, born of an hour of sunshine.* If I understood that sentence, I would have to look up. This
was Quinn: he was leaving.

"Do you want to be more specific than that?" I asked, finally
looking up, and for the first time in three years it began: my breaths
(four), the number of times he scratched behind his right ear
(three), the number of back-and-forth glances from Lurch (six).

He said nothing, staring straight at me, visibly detached, gone
already.

"You said we needed to talk. Then you said *I'm leaving.* But you haven't really said that much at all."

I felt deliberate, relaxed almost, from the shock. But I wasn't surprised: I had always known it was coming but never quite believed, not completely, that it would. I got up and walked toward the kitchen. I was acutely aware of the way my feet carefully navigated the hardwood floors.

"Who is it?" I asked.

"Listen, Anjou, I didn't—"

"Who is it?" I repeated, not raising my voice.

There was a long pause. I was standing at the kitchen counter, staring at his back.

"It's Grace," he said. His ability to be honest without wavering when his step was headed in the next direction was remarkable.

"Grace?" I asked, convinced I had not met her, not remembering yet.

"She's in the College of Medicine."

Grace. Of course. Grace. Grace. I said her name in my head fifteen times. She was not gorgeous and she did not have a captivating name and all of this made it abundantly clear, with nary a word spoken, that he loved her.

I opened the cupboard where we kept our plates. I took all of them and put them on the counter.

"Yes. Grace. Of course. Grace."

"Listen—"

"Grace. Grace," I said, my turn to put her name out there, in my own tone and intention.

"Anjou, I'm so sorry about this," he said.

He did sound sorry, honestly sorry, a weighted and saddened sorry, a sorry that was real but fleeting. It wouldn't last. Quinn left people more sorry than himself.

"When are you leaving?" I asked.

I had said her name aloud five times and in my head twenty-two times.

"Tonight."

"Are you going to her house?"

Lurch began to whine, his heightened sensory system detecting my distress. Quinn stood up from the chair and began to walk toward the kitchen. I heard a door slam, a phantom door in an unused room upstairs. I blinked, sniffed the air, picked up a plate, and threw it at Quinn's head, aimed at his marvelous cheekbones, jutting chin, and bump-marred aquiline nose. But I missed—with relief, actually—the plate hurtling past his face close enough to scare him, close enough to make his sphincter wince, his eyes bug out in surprise, as the plate slammed atop a wooden chest behind him. Blue shrapnel flew everywhere in every direction, hitting Quinn's back, sending Lurch hobbling out of the room. I closed my eyes, and the moment felt like a prayer.

"What the hell—" Quinn choked.

He spread his arms, stretched wide like a savior on a cross.

"Jesus Christ, Anjou, let's not do this, okay?"

"I would like to know about Grace, you pathetic piece of shit," I screamed in a voice I did not know I had. I was halfway between myself and Stella.

Grace: eight times.

"I should leave right now," he said, starting to shake. I couldn't tell if he was mad or agitated. I just liked that he shook.

I sent another plate airborne, an intentionally bad shot meant strictly for show—the truth was that I couldn't hurt him.

"I want to know what song you sing to yourself when you think about Grace," I hollered, feeling hoarse already.

"What on earth are you talking about?" he asked, looking confused.

I threw another plate at him, because three is a good number. He stopped ducking, as if he knew he wouldn't get hit, as if he knew the crashing around him was part of what he needed to get through.

"I don't know what you're talking about," he said, his voice trembling. It is scary to walk out on a woman, to go choose another love.

"I just want you to answer my question," I said, still loud but breaking into something like a moan. "I need you to tell me about her. And then I need you to tell me what song you think of when you think of her. You have to tell me about Grace, and the song. I need to know these things."

"Why, Anjou?"

"Because details are what make a memory. You told me that. Remember?"

"No, I don't."

"You told me when were in Graz. Don't you remember? It was our first time in Austria together. It was a sunny July day, warm but not hot. We stood at the corner of Sporgasse and Hofgasse, those old cobblestone roads, and at that corner was the court bakery. The façade was sculpted in a pattern like a china cup, like a cake, really, like you could eat it. I told you that—that I wanted to take a bite—and you stood behind me and put your hands across my eyes and told me to save the view, to store it as a memory. Then we went to a beer garden and got drunk, and I was still thinking about that sculpted façade. I still see it, Quinn. I need to know about Grace because I need to form a very specific memory."

"Anjou, I'm so sorry. I cannot say anything right. I know this. But I don't know what you are talking about."

"I'm talking about remembering this moment. Because I can't kill you, which would inarguably leave quite a memory, I want a memory of this moment."

His voice was shaky, a rare break in his near impenetrable confidence.

"Christ, Anjou. I don't know—she's bright—"

"Grace. Her name is Grace. Don't call her she," I interrupted.

"Grace is a doctor. And has a garden in her backyard. And she—Grace—has a son, in college. And Grace is a widow," he stammered.

"You've told me nothing," I said, shaking my head at him.

"I don't know what you want me to tell you," Quinn said, his face falling. He wouldn't say much because it would hurt me too much. He did love me. He just couldn't love in a linear pattern.

"What's a nice thing that she does?" I ask.

"What?" Quinn said, his face twisted in confusion. This was not the argument he expected.

"I mean for you, what's a nice thing she does for you?"

He had an answer, an immediate one—I saw the blink of his eyes. He waited, so it wouldn't look like he was that in love with her.

"She tells me to drive safe," he finally said, sitting down again.

"When you drive home, you mean?"

"Yes."

"What's her house like?"

"Do we have to do this?"

"Yes, we do. Help me here."

"It's a twin, her house," Quinn said, shaking his head.

"Of course it is. Is it as nice as mine?"

"Anjou, I didn't mean for this to happen and it had nothing to do with her house."

Lurch had came back into the room and went over to sniff his feet.

"I need to ask you more questions."

"Okay," he said calmly.

"Don't patronize me."

"I'm not, Anjou."

"What did you expect?"

"I thought you'd keep throwing plates."

"Is that what Lily did?"

"No."

"What did she do?"

"She put on a sweater and left the house. She told me to be gone by the time she got back," he said.

"Were you gone when she got back?"

"No."

"Why not?"

"Because she was my wife, Anjou."

"Well, I don't want to throw plates. Everybody throws plates. Fuck the plates. I want you dead—some sort of assurance of you being dead—so that you can no longer be loved. I believe in God—you know that, Quinn, you know that, at least today I certainly do—and so I will actually pray for this, for you to be dead. But it might take God a little while to answer this prayer, so in the meantime I'd like something substantive. I want some answers."

Quinn stared at Lurch for a long time, his hand stroking my dog's neck, as if he knew everything that he would miss in this house.

"Anjou, I will answer any questions you have."

I stacked them in no time: *In what hallway or where on campus did you first see her? Did you ask Bernie about her or did you suddenly see her at Green's Bar as fate having put her there at your feet? Did you ask her what a pathologist sees when staring at all of those slides? Does her office smell like formaldehyde and are there biohazard stickers on her door and does she wear big plastic goggles all day and do they leave an imprint on the side of her cheek and do you touch that imprint? When did you know you loved her? Will you miss me? Will you regret your decision? Will you forget me? Do you ever want to stop all this and just stop, just with one? Did you love Grace and me—and even Lily—all at the same time, in varying degrees? How do you explain the complexity of your heart? Do you feel guilty because you don't feel guilty, because you know that you are not alone, that this capacity, this layered bloom-ing of love, can involve so many people? Do you think you'll be this young and beautiful forever? Has anybody ever hurt you? Are you afraid to die?*

I was still holding two plates, and I could not figure out how to ask. I knew that in a few days I'd be able to. I need time to work up to these things. I am not impulsive by nature.

"What song?" I finally said, floating almost.

"What do you mean?"

"The song you think of when you think of Grace. What song is it?"

"I don't have one," he said, shaking his head.

"You do. Think. This is an easy question."

"I can't think of one," he said. His elbows were on his knees, his head in his hands, fingers moving back and forth through his thick black curls.

He has a Jesus chest, his Austrian side, flat and hairless, that I won't touch again, I thought, shocked at the trivial things that come to our minds at the breaking points in our lives.

"Try," I said.

"I don't know why you want me to pick a song."

"You don't have to pick anything, Quinn. You have a song already, even if you don't know that you do. You would not leave me for a woman with a normal name if you didn't love her. So you had to get to a song in your head when you started to love her, and I want to know what it is. What song?"

Quinn shook his head slowly at me, looking worried, like there was something wrong with me, not him. Lurch was nudging his snout against Quinn's leg. Quinn squatted down and whispered something in my dog's ear.

"Try," I said.

"God, Anjou, I'm so tired," he said, putting his hands over his face with the back of his head against the couch, looking more exhausted than I had ever seen him.

I stared at him for a long time, the plates at my side, my hands cramping. *I'm so tired.*

"Side one, track 10, the Beatles' *White Album*," I finally said.

I stood for one long hour after Quinn left. Trance-like and suspended, I waited until my breathing finally slowed. When I am scared or sad or upset, I do not readily break down in tears. Instead, my insides collapse, and the world around me feels hyper and static-filled and too bright. Shaking and nervous—scared shitless—I made a list. A list! Things had to be done, taken care of. My lists are always numbered, although rarely chronological. Computers could never graph a lifetime of lists and the order in which they are accomplished. I was dizzy, not sure when I should start moving through my house and calling Stella or going over to Kip's—when and how do you start telling people things that you don't want to be real? I came up with one item. Stark revenge is difficult for me. The item: shopping. I had always turned up my nose at online shopping, preferring the act of perusing through a store, touching the clothing, smelling the soaps, picking up the down comforter. But it was 11 P.M. and I had Quinn's computer and his American Express card number, which he had given to me on a Post-It with expiration date and PIN so I could order our tickets to London for Thanksgiving.

I ordered him a year's subscription to nine pornographic magazines, keying in Grace's address—courtesy of online Yellow Pages—for delivery. I ordered fifteen Turduckens—a boned chicken stuffed into a boned duck stuffed into a boned turkey, spiced with Cajun flavoring, sent to Grace's house. I booked him a one-week nonrefundable stay for two at the Lake Edgewood Spa and Resort in Sedona. I gave them his cell-phone number so he could schedule the all-inclusive spa treatments—mango-grapefruit body scrubs, Swedish massages, and lemon facials. Then I booked Quinn two first-class round-trip nonrefundable tickets to Portugal. I tried to purchase two round-trip tickets to Moscow, but there was a problem with his credit card going through.

My phone rang at 1 o'clock in the morning.

"Hello, this is Lynette from American Express calling for Mr. Quinn Forster."

She sounded chipper. And Southern. Customer service representatives were always in Georgia. Or India.

"I'm his fiancée. Can I help you with something?"

"There's been some suspicious activity on his card this evening, and it's vitally important that we talk with him."

"He's asleep, and he took two Ambien," I said.

"I'm sorry, ma'am, but I don't know what the Ambien is, ma'am."

"Not *the* Ambien," I said. "Just Ambien. They're sleeping pills. He's out."

"These suspicious activities are vitally important to resolve, ma'am."

"What do you mean by vitally suspicious?"

"Vitally important."

"Well, they must be vitally suspicious to be vitally important."

I waited for her to catch up.

"Well, there was a notable increase in purchases in a short time frame—specifically, from 11 P.M. until 12:30 A.M. We'd like to confirm that these are intended purchases as opposed to purchases by someone other than the card holder."

"Are you talking about booking the Lake Edgewood Spa? And the tickets to Portugal?" I asked.

"Yes ma'am, well, yes, but there were others, ma'am."

"I know, ma'am," I said in a delicate mockery of her. "We share this credit card."

"Are you on the account, ma'am? I don't see anybody except for Mr. Forster listed on this account."

"I will be, soon. He is my fiancé. We share everything. I have his PIN number."

"Well, that doesn't necessarily mean anything."

"Maybe not to you, but it does to me. His PIN is 725. That stands for Raj. He was the little Indian boy on the cartoon *Johnny Quest*. He was Johnny's sidekick."

"Ma'am, unfortunately, knowing the PIN code is not enough information to confirm that there has been no security breach on the card."

"If you call me ma'am one more fucking time, I'm going to reach through the receiver and strangle you."

For the first time that night, I was feeling close to collapse.

"Clearly you are knowledgeable about the card holder, and I do not question that," she said, all friendliness gone from her voice and replaced with a cool stone edge. "And, yes, this phone number and associated address have been on his account for over a year. And yes, this is a very active account. But it is my responsibility to ensure that there has not been a breach in security of Mr. Forster's account."

"I know more, though. I know the answer to the secret question if you forget your PIN number."

Lynette was silent.

"What is Mr. Forster's mother's birthday?" I said in a mock game-show-host voice. "That's the question, isn't it?"

Lynette still said nothing. I imagined she was confused. I imagined she had blond hair that was winged back, something from the late 1970s, that she was in her early forties and had three children.

"The answer is March 14th," I say in a game-show-contestant voice.

The day before my father's birthday. My mother used to say, in an increasingly somber tone as we grew up, *Beware the Ides of March,* as she walked across the kitchen with a seven-layer chocolate cake that she had bought at the Amish stand in Reading Terminal Market. She walked balancing his cake with candles aglow, setting it in front of my smiling father.

"When's your birthday?" I asked.

"I'm not sure I understand, ma'am."

"I told you not to call me ma'am."

"I'm sorry. I'm not sure how to respond to you."

"Of course you don't. You are afforded a set of responses to a limited number of questions. This phone call is being recorded and so I know you aren't going to be mean. You also haven't reached a point at which you are able to fairly interrupt your manager because of this situation. You don't get paid very much money, you have problems I cannot begin to relate to, and your job is more stressful than most people will ever—ever—give you credit for. So now that you know that I have a certain level of sympathy for your life there in that horrible cubicle, please just indulge me and answer this one question. Your birthday. I'm just asking you when your fucking birthday is."

"November 19," she whispered.

I hung up the phone, relieved. It was the start of my understanding that challenges are not conquered by talking about them but instead by gathering information. Shocky and light, I drove to Circle K to buy cigarettes. I hadn't smoked in eleven years. A teenager, tall and skinny with acne and short hair, was behind the counter.

"Camel Lights," I said, my nose starting to run.

He was so young. His acne—red and screaming—would clear up. His lanky frame would fill out. He would love, go to college. He would marry. He doesn't know this now, I thought, but he will have babies.

"Hard pack or soft?"

"Hard pack. A carton."

He bent down and sifted through the stacks of cartons. He stood up, and it finally started. I was shaking my head, forgetting if I had brought my wallet, rummaging through my purse, and I couldn't stop everything coming up through my throat.

"Ma'am, are you okay?" the boy asked.

"Why does everybody keep calling me ma'am?" I said, pushing my hair out of my eyes, my cheeks wet and snot coming out of my nose, not even recognizing these sobs as mine, still searching for my wallet.

Three teenaged girls walked into the store, giggling and pushing at each other playfully. They got in line behind me, and their chatter stopped suddenly. They didn't ask me if I was okay, but their stillness was palpable. I was the only one moving in the store, shaking and crying.

"My boyfriend just left me," I sobbed, uncontrollably now.

I handed him two twenties. The girls behind me were still there, and I felt their eyes burning at my back.

"Just now. A few hours ago," I continued, wondering why the boy wasn't wearing a name tag, wiping my nose on my sleeve repeatedly.

The boy nervously sorted out my change.

"I'm sorry, ma'am," he said, handing me the change and not looking me in the eye.

"What is your name?" I asked. I wiped my face across my sleeve, sniffing in and coughing.

"Jonathan," he said.

The girls behind me whispered and shuffled.

"Do they call you Jack?" I asked, looking less alarmed. He needed to know how to deal with a woman crying.

"No, my mom hates that name."

"So do I." And I walked out of the store with the carton of cigarettes under my arm.

When I got home, I tore open the cigarettes, lit one, unplugged my answering machine, and picked up the phone. I had memorized those ten numbers. I dialed them and let it ring and ring. When he picked up the phone I just listened. He said *Hello*, and then again. And again.

At 3 A.M. I sat on a green plastic chair on my wooden deck at the back of the house. Kip, a night owl known for wandering the neighborhood at all hours, walked into my backyard.

"Heard your car," he said.

"Come on up," I said, my feet on the railing of my deck.

"You're up late."

"Technically, it's early," I said.

"Where's Quinn?"

"At Grace's," I said.

"Who?"

"Grace. He's at Grace's house."

Kip pulled up a chair next to me. He was wearing a Penn State sweatshirt, flannel pajama bottoms, and construction boots.

"Something on your mind?"

"Yup," I said.

"Wanna tell me about it?"

"I want to know why everybody keeps calling me ma'am tonight."

"Not sure what you mean, my dear."

"Every person I talked to tonight called me ma'am. When did I go from being miss to being ma'am?"

"You going to tell me what's going on?"

"Eventually," I said. "Eventually."

I reached in my pocket and took out a cigarette, my ninth one of the evening. I lit it and sucked the smoke in deep.

"Since when did you start smoking?" Kip asked, reaching to take it from my hand and squashing it under his boot.

"Since tonight."

I didn't care that he had wasted the cigarette. I still had 231 left.

6

EXTRAORDINARY LOVE, 1982

OUR MOTHER BEGAN TO DIE LATE IN THE NIGHT. I sat in a chair in her hospital room, Stella on my lap wide awake. Our Aunt Vicky sat on the other side of the room with a manic stare on her face. It was 1 A.M. A sixteen-year-old boy from a neighboring high school, stoned and drunk, had put our mother there—flat on her back, face and body swollen, organs unrepairable, tubes coming out of her arms and chest with the ongoing beeping of machines. The boy's Ford pickup truck had driven head-on into our 1980 Chevy Cavalier. The night before the accident, our father had been welcomed home for the eighteenth time in eleven years. At the moment she died, he was somewhere else: getting coffee, outside smoking a cigarette, somewhere. The machines started singing, three nurses and two doctors hustled in, and we were pushed out of the room. The three of us stared through the half-open door as a man twice as big as our mother leaned over her, placing instruments on her chest, making her body lurch upward in a majestic arch. At one point they knelt on the bed over her, pushing both hands, one on top of the other, onto her chest. Over and over—the machines screaming now, the doctors and nurses talking quickly, shouting, our mother's body pounded and pummeled. And then they stopped.

Our father was found outside, staring up at the sky. We all stood in the fluorescent-lit hallway, lined up in a row as the doctor explained about her lacerated liver and collapsed lungs and burst spleen and head trauma. These were just details about her body, though. I wanted to ask him questions about what our mother had felt, what she had been thinking, if she had come to consciousness at any one point and said something—a word, a thought, a question. Stella was holding Aunt Vicky's hand and, as the doctor talked, she began screaming, pulling Aunt Vicky down to the floor with her. I stared at my father, whose hands were over his face, his head shaking back and forth. From his mouth came a disturbing high-pitched sound, like a wounded animal. I didn't cry at first, not there in the hospital, not even at the funeral, where everybody gathered: all of our cousins, our neighbors, my mother's friends from her bridge club, my father's coworkers, who solemnly sat in the pews and whispered to each other. These people came up to me where I sat with Stella, who was shocked and red-eyed, and they murmured condolences to our father and touched my shoulder and looked at us with sympathetic eyes. All I could feel was a burning shame. The privacy of my family was on display, and it was impossible to respond in an appropriate way. It came to me, this gathering wave of grief, in Primo's Pizzeria, later that night after the funeral. Aunt Vicky had convinced our father that a large reception would be too much for us, too overwhelming and impersonal—we were not close with all of these people, as our mother had led a relatively isolated life. Aunt Vicky ordered us pizza, and I joined her on the short ride to pick it up.

"You really are your mother's kid, you know that?" Aunt Vicky said to me in the car.

I shrugged in confusion. I took her literally, and I didn't understand what she meant. I had never questioned my maternity.

"I mean that about your personality, the way you are. Sort of like that saying, *The fruit doesn't fall far from the tree.*"

"Oh," I said.

"That's a good thing, Anjou. Your mother was very sensitive, very loving, and she was pretty stoic about things. Didn't let people see her pain. You're a lot like her."

"I kept the notes, Aunt Vicky."

"What do you mean, sweetie pie?"

Aunt Vicky looked like hell, sallow and limp. She hadn't eaten in a week, and it showed on her already trim frame.

"I kept the notes Mom would leave me on the kitchen table, like to mop the floor or take the hamburger out of the fridge. I keep them in a candy box."

Aunt Vicky looked over at me.

"Mom did the same thing. Maybe I learned it from her," I said.

"She did?"

"Yeah. I snooped once, and I found them."

"Who were the notes from?"

"Dad, mostly."

Aunt Vicky said nothing for a while, and then she reached out with her right hand and softly tucked my long hair behind my ear.

"You know what your mother said to me once?"

"What?"

"She said, *Anjou is more me than me.*"

Aunt Vicky pulled into a parking space in front of Primo's. She handed me a twenty-dollar bill and I went inside and stood in line at the counter with teenagers and fathers with babies in their arms. I was immediately enveloped in warmth and doughy air and the noise of people and clanking pans. The Italian men behind the counter, young and greasy, were yelling at each other and slamming ovens open and shut. I was ready then, and this true fact—that my mother was dead—seemed so stunning. I didn't recognize anybody but Sandy McKernan, tucked into a booth toward the back of the restaurant. *She's such a slut,* I thought as the first tear fell and my throat choked and the weight of grief and loss exploded through me, a moan rising from the depths of memory. The crowd seemed to shift, the shouts and calls of Italian men, a hand of a stranger on my shoulder, Aunt Vicky finally coming in and picking me up from the floor.

That night our father packed his suitcase. He sat on the couch in the family room, where Stella and I stared at the television like shell-shocked soldiers on the battlefield. We were eating potato chips and drinking Pepsi.

"I'm sorry, girls," he said, his voice low and sad.

Stella stared at him, confused. I don't think she knew right then what this meant. She would have screamed if she did. I wouldn't look at him, focusing on the television and eating potato chip after potato chip. It seemed like he levitated a few inches off the ground, his body light, and Stella's neck seemed to follow an upward path.

Aunt Vicky was in the kitchen, organizing the casseroles in the freezer and putting tinfoil over the cakes, offerings from well-intentioned neighbors and friends. When she saw him walk by with that suitcase, she dropped a strawberry cheesecake on the kitchen floor. She followed him outside, fury spread across her young and beautiful face. She was outside with him for a while. Her voice was crackly and loud, but I didn't hear my father. Aunt Vicky canceled her lease on her apartment the next day and moved in with us. Our father sent checks that arrived every Tuesday. Like always.

Stella would tell me that he had grieved heavily, that he never really did get over our mother. Stella said that grief is a personal experience, that we can't blame him forever for his failures. Listening is hard for me.

Those months after my mother's death, I was overcome with anxiety. Not because our father was gone but because of a compelling need to tell my mother that I loved her even though she kept taking him back—something I had never said directly—that I knew she had done what she had to do for reasons that I never needed to know. I had never found the nerve to ask my mother about this love. I tried to figure out what had kept her from ending her marriage. I eventually believed—simply enough—that it was love and commitment. My mother ignored liberation on America's terms. She had an unopened open marriage, riding between two divides. There was no real abuse or neglect. This marriage did not fall on either side of the diagnostic pendulum—it was truly neither pathological nor normal. It was somewhere in between, something I would grow to learn was not that uncommon, manifested in different ways, but still not uncommon. But even when I grew to realize that the choices they made were made together, I still held my father more accountable. Our mother was softer—weaker, really—and always more hopeful. Our father, quite simply, knew better.

I wanted her to know that I was aware of her pain, the price of impossible love—I rarely saw this pain or understood how it may have been manifested because she always took him back without complaint. When you finally understand your parents' pain, it is scary how deeply you feel it. It is an extraordinary inheritance, unbearable at times, oddly comforting at others.

I never wanted to be anything extraordinary. Especially not that year, not two short months after my mother died. My high school guidance counselor, Mr. Lehman, tried to convince me otherwise. Like all good guidance counselors, it was his job to make sure you were aiming to *be* someone.

"Anjou, your SAT scores on the math portion are phenomenal. And your other tests show that you have a real inclination in the visual arts. Do you have a particular college or major in mind?"

Mr. Lehman knew my mother had died recently; he knew my father was somewhere other than where he should be. Stella was the only one who spoke of this, pelting Aunt Vicky with questions, challenging her, demanding information on where she could find him. She yelled about it, yelled at me for leaving the room when the topic came up, for walking out of the house when Aunt Vicky tried to soothe her. She made phone calls to his office, yelled at our father's secretary, and, still, nothing. It was as if he was living in Guam instead of twenty miles away in downtown Philadelphia. Stella refused to funnel her pain and curiosity through other avenues and shouts and distractions. With our mother gone, she no longer felt the need to be respectful or considerate of other people's feelings. She tried once to go to our father's office. Public transportation didn't run through Gulph Mills, but Stella was undeterred. She was picked up by the township police trying to hitchhike into the city. Stella didn't speak to me or Aunt Vicky for four days.

After that incident, Stella resigned, gave up. More accurately, she moved on. I made no attempts to contact our father and call him on his abandonment—mainly because I didn't want to upset

Aunt Vicky. Our world seemed very tenuous, and had made Stella louder than ever. Aunt Vicky was a thirty-year-old single woman—edgy and sexy and brazen—who dated men who rode motorcycles and owned homes in Miami or boats in North Carolina, men who never, never got married. She had suddenly inherited an eleven-year old and a sixteen-year old and was doing an admirable, if shaky, job of holding it together for us. I did not want to send the new order of the house into a tailspin. The truth was, we could have become addicted to cocaine and committed grand theft auto and shown up pregnant and it wouldn't have mattered—Aunt Vicky wouldn't have budged from our lives. So Stella found new avenues to yell at the world, whether it was from the sideline of a field hockey game or the front of an eight-man boat as coxswain hollering at her rowers down the Schuylkill River. I rarely cried, except in odd places: on the bleachers at the Homecoming football game with Liz and her boyfriend Trent trying to comfort me, on the third floor at John Wanamakers buying new bras, in the dusty back row of the American history section of the Tindell Memorial Library, where I checked out and rechecked out *The Rise and Fall of the Third Reich.* And when I cried it was hard and fast and violent; it rattled me, a rush toward relief that never seemed to come. I kept collecting notes, waiting for somebody to give me a box of candy so I could store them somewhere. Notes from Stella or Aunt Vicky: *Liz called twice, Pick up your sister at 8 from the Mall, Pizza tonight for dinner.* Aunt Vicky, in silent solidarity, bought me candy from all over the country, having friends ship me Frango Mints from Minneapolis and See's Candy from California and hunks of dark chocolate from Ecuador that arrived in flat rectangular wooden boxes.

"Do you have any ideas what you want to major in?" Mr. Lehman asked.

"I'm not sure," I said flatly.

"You have entirely too much potential to be so ambivalent, Anjou."

I was sixteen years old and exhausted by a proxy version of being orphaned. I had no ambition or desire to pursue an extraordinary career. I longed only to wrap my hands around extraordinary love. So I sighed and told Mr. Lehman I could probably be an accountant.

"Accounting," Mr. Lehman responded, his pointy dry elbows on the desk and his hairy-knuckled fingers clasped in a prayer hold.

"Yes," he continued. I can see accounting, I can see it. Very interesting."

Not really, I thought. There was nothing very interesting about it to me. And the truth was, Mr. Lehman was right: I was a visual person. I could see Stella's screams in light and color. I could capture my mother's strained expression the first night after our father would not come home from work. I could recast my father's smile, relieved and joyful—abundant—on the first night of a homecoming and then stilted and insincere a few months later. But I didn't do anything about it. Every painter I had read about—Vincent van Gogh and Frida Kahlo and Pablo Picasso—had led a life that was marked with pain and wounds that could only be treated with brushstrokes. I saw things, but I didn't want to.

"Let's talk about a few colleges you can apply to," Mr. Lehman said, looking relieved. He took a tissue and wiped the brow of his angular face.

"Any state school, I suppose. Something like that," I offered.

"Anjou, this is where I worry about you. You can do better than the *something like that's* of the world."

Something like this was lodged in my throat: *Mr. Lehman, did you know that my mother died exactly sixty-four days ago? Did you know it took seventeen hours from the moment the truck hit our mother's car until her last breath? So it really doesn't matter where I go to college—Penn State or Harvard or fucking Oxford University.*

That deep river of words was caught behind a dam, raging and pushing. So I said what he wanted to hear: "Okay, Mr. Lehman, I'll check into some private schools. I'll have my Aunt Vicky help me out."

"Great," he said, rising from his chair and extending a sweaty palm to shake, trying to convince me that he knew what I should become.

7

St. Clears Avenue

715 St. Clears Avenue

Davıd Lawrence Spergel, a middle-aged man who stands straight as a ruler, has been on his porch talking to me for nearly twenty minutes. It is April 12. It is unusually cold today. He is not wearing a coat and he doesn't seem to care. I am wearing a pink down jacket and grief; together these keep me warm. Mr. Spergel is a single man, in a single-family dwelling—a three-bedroom white stone house, shaped like a box with a slanting slate roof and dormers in the front. He has no curtains on his windows and his door is painted colonial blue. He lives alone, no pets and no house plants. He answers all eleven questions on the Census Short Form with more detail than I need. He tells me his occupation—freelance graphic designer—which is information I do not need. He talks to me for a very long time about the hermit crabs he is breeding and how, in the summer, he will paint their shells with patterns as intricate as Ukrainian Easter eggs and sell them to souvenir shops at the Jersey Shore.

"Which shore?" I ask.

"Wildwood and Ocean City. Sometimes I go to Stone Harbor, but they don't have a boardwalk. I get the best business on the boardwalks," he said.

I am a lousy enumerator. I have become entirely too comfortable asking my own questions. Old neighborhoods like Glyn Neath have an impenetrable aura around them; they maintain certain types of values—nothing morally pretentious but things that are easily stripped in the fast-paced world of technology and city-quick lifestyles. People in very old neighborhoods talk to everybody, they converse, they consider questions and listen to answers, they are kind but also calmly rude and inappropriate—all very acceptable—but they are always responsive.

I am a lousy enumerator because I will listen to people who want to talk. Despite my meticulously completed Census forms, my supervisor, Thadius, will stress the importance of quantity along with quality. I actually want to please Thadius because he let me enumerate in Glyn Neath, which is against the rules. I want to hear from my neighbors who are strangers but not quite. This seems reasonable.

"What shore do you go to?" he asks when he notes my interest in his hermit crabs. I am more interested in the Shore than his crabs, but I do not tell him this.

"Long Beach Island."

"Lovely," he says.

"I was just there a few weeks ago."

He is the fourteenth person I've accounted for today. Soon it will become dark.

"Ah," he says, nodding, "you're one of those."

"I'm not sure I understand."

"An off-season type."

"Yes. Well, it's an off season for me."

"How do you mean?"

"It's just off," I say with a shrug.

"I'm keeping you, aren't I?" he says, a sheepish look spreading across his pale thin face. He has a cleanly shaven head, and I wonder if he is impervious to the cold—he is not even shaking.

"No. Not really," I say, putting his completed form in the government-issued military-green envelope. He has signed the form, a squat signature that is modest and firm.

"So that's all the questions then?"

I turn to him and look him straight in the eye, with the gaze of a professional, of a regimented federal employee, emotionless, stark, polite. Not every resident gets an extra question, but here it feels right.

"Is it possible to be in love with more than one person at the same time?"

Mr. Spergel looks at me for a long time. This seems to be the way with my neighbors. For the most part they do not get violent or vitriolic. They ponder. I now see a slight chatter of his teeth. It is a cold April and I recall an Easter when Stella and I hunted for painted eggs in the sparse backyard of our house; we were wearing galoshes and red winter coats. Our parents were huddled by the side of the house, my father rubbing my mother's arm, the two of them whispering about things I'll never know about. This question, about love, is actually a question I have for Grace.

"I'm guessing that the answer to this question is of no interest to the United States Census?"

"None at all," I say, nodding my head evenly.

Tears start to come down my cheek, a warmth in this gray, still dusk. He is not prepared for this. But he must be a strong man, I decide. Because he stands firm. He is short, but his back straightens.

"Yes. You can," he answers. "It happens all the time. All the time."

I don't ask him anything else because I don't want to influence. He is with me now, Mr. Spergel. A man who has the security of a home.

"There's a catch, though. There's a catch if you love two people at the same time. You have to keep it to yourself. Nothing's going to stop it from happening—I think it happens to most of us at least once in our lives. But it should stay a secret. Oh, I'm not saying you should lie or cheat or anything. Just keep it to yourself. Otherwise it's unfair. To everybody."

Unfair. That was really the most important thing he said that I would write down later.

Mr. Spergel is now shivering. I shake his hand and thank him, and I walk down his porch stairs. He isn't going inside yet, I can still see him out of the corner of my eye, but his arms are wrapped all the way around himself now.

⌐⌐

730 St. Clears Avenue

The twin homes on the south side of St. Clears Avenue are bigger than the postage-stamp homes on my block. They have great big square facades for the bottom story, and the top two stories are shaped like half of an octagon—a stop sign severed through the middle. A brotherhood of geometric trees. Rebecca Duzen is a nurse or a doctor or an x-ray tech or something surgical and anti-septic. She is wearing hospital-green scrubs and purple plastic clogs. She ushers me into her front hall after I introduce myself. Great big tufts of dog hair float up as the door shuts, and the sound of music and foot-thuds can be heard above. At the end of the hall, a television breaks the darkness of the unlit room. Rebecca Duzen lives in this home with her husband, Patrick, their twin daughters, Rachel and Renee, and her elderly mother, Miriam. Rebecca Duzen is helpful. She answers my questions clearly, spelling out the names of her husband and children and mother, providing me with everybody's ages as I complete the form. She has a strong voice, so I can hear her despite the television, which is blaring.

"My mother is half deaf and half blind and she refuses to wear glasses or a hearing aide. She says the world is a lot softer when you can barely hear or see. The crazy thing is, she winds up squinting at everything and turning up the television loud enough to burst your eardrums—now, that doesn't strike me as too soft of a world, eh?"

I hand her a pen and turn the clipboard so she can sign the completed form.

"Do you think there's such thing as a softer world?" I ask.

"What do you mean?" she asks, scratching her name across the form and handing the clipboard back to me.

"Do you think there's such thing as a softer world?"

She stares at me for a moment, and she has just realized that I want to take this benign, rudimentary interview somewhere else. She looks tired, and I realize I have misjudged her. I realize that she is a person who sees enough reality every day in whatever office or hospital she works in. She sees people who have arrived by ambu-lance or arrived to hear some awful diagnosis or futile attempt at treatment. She has seen people die. She has done her part, really, and it is asinine—simply despicable—for me to ask anything more of her. I make a mental note to leave the doctors and nurses alone. She looks close to being mad at me.

Her hands are positioned on her hips. I know I should leave, that she will not tell me anything I don't already know. I am not ashamed of my invasiveness—it is an invasive world, and I'm trying to join in, at least here in my neighborhood.

⌒*⌒*

734 St. Clears Avenue

I love the night-cold of April, how it touches but does not penetrate like that of February or March. You can smell the infancy of spring in the chill layer of darkness. In about a month I will be in the warm clear waters of the Italian sea, floating in a grotto. I want to tell my father I'm going there. I want to know if the world still rhymes in his eyes. I want to know if he coats his days with easy words and phrases that match.

A woman in gray yoga pants and a zip-up sweatshirt—both of them fitted and flattering—answers the door. I start asking her questions and she complies, spelling names and listing ages. Confirming that nobody lives there four days a week but three days somewhere else. We can't double up our numbers inadvertently. Her name is Ryan O'Toole.

"Do you like poetry?" I ask finally, without a lead-in.

Poetry. It is not a big question to most people. But a small percentage of the population—suicidal academics, the truly enlightened, the truly patient, the truly perceptive, Quinn, my father—would see the gravity of this question.

"Excuse me?" she asks. "What did you say?"

A child is crying in the background.

"Poetry, do you like it?" I say, hugging the clipboard to my chest.

I am annoyed with her. Because I have asked what should be, for her, a very simple question. I want a suburban mother's point of view. I am annoyed because she is probably not going to afford me an answer, which makes my venom all the worse because I think she has a perfect life. I know this is not possible, but I am biased and prejudiced about educated middle-class suburbs, which, despite its small section of blue-collar residents and its left-of-center, nonsprawled, noncorporate, unconsolidated, and unfranchised way, Glyn Neath is still guilty of being. I have been working on this for a while, to get over it; Stella tells me it's not that I'm jealous of these women, just that I am close-minded about people I cannot relate to. Stella told me to buy a house in the city, but Stella knows that I need quiet places to run, trees that will change colors, leaves that I must rake, houses that creak and collect cobwebs, and drainpipes that get rusty and clogged with wet leaves.

Ryan O'Toole's demeanor has revealed nothing to me about whether she has any pains or insults or discrepancies. I'm sure she does. We all do. But she is the woman I hate when I hate the mothers in this town, the mothers who don't have to work and who are raising kids in such a way that their children will grow up confident—with self-esteem!—with a balanced view of the world, without racial or socioeconomic prejudices. It is not their fault that I hate them, that I love my town but am disgusted with the superficial homogeneity (all the while knowing that indeed there is a murky heterogeneous complexity of pain and kindness and compassion underneath). But yes, this is the woman I hate when I tell Liz I am an illegal alien in my own town, that, at thirty-five, I am beginning, just beginning, to see wrinkles and sprouts of gray in my hair and that I am lost in disbelief, that I am waiting for somebody in this town, an official, to evict me, to tell me to leave. That I have woken up, finally, and realized that Quinn is dead and that I need to start talking to my father again because the numbers in my life naturally gravitate toward balance. This waking-up does not fit in this town that I love. So I'll make it fit. I am not one of these wives or mothers or widows or divorcées. I am not an old person (which would make me respected and revered in this town). I am not a visitor, a renter in the Victorian-converted-into-apartments who lives here for convenience (twelve minutes to the city on the R8), a middle-aged woman living with her elderly parents in a nine-bedroom stone house on Tremadog Avenue, a pastor's wife who lives across the street from First Presbyterian Church. I am not a lesbian or a gay man or a medical student at the University of Pennsylvania. I am not a retired electrician who lives in a row house on Yorkshire Avenue, part of a small patch of streets warmed by blue-collar residents whose homes have been in the family since Glyn Neath was a working-class town.

I cannot see where I fit in, in this town that is so diverse in all ways except for color. I cannot decide what block I really belong on. (Although I am not special. There is nothing special to this situation. When I am depressed or self-pitying, Stella always yells at me—forcefully—that I am not special. She loves me more than anybody ever has because not only is she right, but she's brave enough to give me the straight story. Stella tells me that not being special opens up all of your possibilities and makes all of your faults and mishaps seem bearable. In my home, this town where I am not special, I am comforted by Kip, by his house right next to mine, his seat beside me on Sundays at church, the way my dog loves him. I am certain that God put me here in a house next to him, for me to drink Scotch with him and socialize my dog properly, for him to love Quinn with me, to help me understand that none of this is very special.)

This woman I am pathetic for hating is annoyed with me. Clearly she has a life to live and probably talks to her father if he's alive and probably doesn't think much about whether or not she's special—why should she? she's not—but no doubt she thinks that Census enumerators should not be asking her if she likes poetry.

"Do you like poetry?" I ask one more time.

I am certain now, by the look on her face, that this is an important question to be answered, particularly by her.

"No. Not at all," she spits and she slams the door in my face.

"But you don't know what you're missing," I say, starting to cry there on her porch.

~

804 St. Clears Avenue

Gary Thomas and his partner, Anthony Duncan, live in a stop-sign twin. They meet a stereotype of mine, for better or for worse: They are immediately engaging and demonstrative, and invite me in without hesitation. I am shuffled over a glossy-wood floor into a massive kitchen, where everything is white. It is dark outside now, and the rows of windows are like mirrors.

"Do you meet a lot of weirdos doing this?" Gary asks with a tensed forehead and a concerned expression.

Gary is very tall, and he is muscular and imposing. Anthony is also tall, but he is thin and fleshy, with shiny brown hair pulled back in a short ponytail.

"Not any bad weirdos," I say.

I am aware that I am a weirdo, not special, but a weirdo.

"Well, a weirdo is a weirdo. You can never be too careful these days," Gary says.

"Glyn Neath is safe."

"Too safe," Anthony says.

"Exactly. I doubt that I have much to worry about."

"That's true. But the really tame types are the ones you need to watch out for. They are the ones who are dying to explode," Gary says.

He has begun pouring wine and hands me a glass.

"No, thank you," I say. "Really, this will only take a few minutes."

He continues to hold the glass in front of me.

"It's against the rules," I say, putting my clipboard on the table, pen poised.

"The feds may not let us get married, but at least they know we count," Anthony says sarcastically, and we all laugh.

Gary is thirty-eight and Anthony is forty-one. Gary is an attorney and Anthony designs flatware. I do not need to know this, but they tell me anyway. People who are courteous to Census enumerators will provide more information than required. We're all dying to be specific, detailed, important—special, really.

"That's it? Where are the personal questions about my income? What about my ethnicity? I may look white but for all you know I'm not a Caucasian," Anthony says after they answer the benign and brief list of questions.

"She doesn't need to ask you that question. It's against the law not to be white in this town," Gary says, and we all break into a laugh. I am halfway through the glass of wine I didn't want.

"Well, what about asking me how many hours a week I work and how many I spend commuting or cooking or wallpapering my bathroom or going to the bathroom, mind you? I want to answer *those* questions," Anthony says.

"How do you forgive somebody who has wronged you in unforgivable ways, but for reasons that you technically can't blame them for?" I say suddenly, pen still in my hands, straight-faced and official.

They are in freeze-frame, looking at me. I get up from the table and pick up the merlot we have been drinking. I top off each of our glasses and sit back down. They are still staring at me, and I realize that I have begun to cry.

"Honey, are you okay?" Anthony finally says. I have swallowed anything that would resemble a sob.

I nod up and down at him, letting him know that yes, truly, I am, without a doubt, simply not okay.

"Do you want to tell us what happened?" Gary asks.

"I'm the one who gets to ask the questions here," I say, sniffing in hard.

The two of them laugh tentatively and I offer a small, weak smile.

"Then you, my dear, shall be answered," Anthony says.

"May I smoke?" I ask.

Gary runs to fetch a cup of water for my ashes, opening the window on my left. This will be my second cigarette of the day. I went running this morning—averaging a nine-minute forty-second mile, which I sustained for fifty-six minutes and fifty-seven seconds—and on days that I run I do not allow myself more than five cigarettes. Yesterday I did not run; I smoked thirty-one cigarettes.

"Well, at least you finally got a sensitive question," I say to Anthony, deadpan.

He breaks into a wide grin. He is very handsome, and I am acutely aware that he is completely unaware of this fact. He asks for a cigarette, looking over guiltily at Gary, saying, *I promise, just this one.*

"Basically, you have to wait until you are damn well ready to forgive a person. Because forgiveness has nothing to do with the other person, the person who wronged you. They don't need your forgiveness—you do. So you'll forgive them, blameless or not, when you are ready," Gary says.

I feel snot coming down my nose, and Anthony hands me a tissue. I thank him, and drink the wine in large gulps. I finally light my cigarette.

"The word *unforgivable*—you used that in your question—is an oxymoron," Anthony says in a long slow breath. "Even the most heinous and hurtful actions—even unforgivable ones—are forgivable. No matter the circumstances."

"Anthony believes in God," Gary says to me across the table in a conspiratorial whisper.

I nod and smile in communion. I stay with Gary and Anthony for another hour. We don't talk about Quinn or why I asked an unsanctioned question. Instead we talk like the neighbors we are: We drink wine and talk about the neighborhood. We talk about the movie theater on King Edward's Avenue, how they are renovating from its preserved 1940s decor to have stadium seating and modern facilities. We talk about our homes, the discoveries that happen when you own a house so old—there are roofs to consider and hardwood planks to be replaced and porches that decompose and only one bathroom most times—just one—so there's always the question of where to add on the second bathroom. We talk about the things we invariably find in an attic or crawl space, something that a previous owner left behind—a rotted suitcase, a box of moldy winter coats, a stack of old board games like Twister and Risk and Monopoly. We talk about collecting all of these rare finds, putting them in a showcase in town, opening up our neighborhood to the words the trees have whispered and the pictures the walls have seen.

I have begun to think of my father in terms of streets. I first called him on my own street, Conway Avenue. When I got my cell phone, I began calling during walks through the neighborhood. Twice I called him from King Edward's Avenue. Three times from Sompton Avenue. On my first day of enumerating I called him while standing on Kent Avenue. I remember calling him on Pembroke, right before I stood at the doorstep of a man with a wishbone scar. And now I think of St. Clears: My father is going to visit me today, a week in which I am still accountable for the tallies of St. Clears Avenue. My father is coming to my house because I invited him here. It is Sunday, April 16, and it has been raining since I woke up.

I am hoping that if we are face to face I will figure out something to say. So I have fine-tuned a list of ten questions. It became very difficult to choose which ten—this is just a place to start—but I think I have chosen the most important. I wrote the list on a piece of unlined paper from a notepad from my former job. It says *A. L. Lovett* in fat capital letters. My middle name is Long, my mother's maiden name.

When I decided to meet with my father, I knew it would have to be at my house. Stella tells me that potentially emotional meetings should be held in public, because you are less likely to act out or make a scene. This approach won't work for me, and I explain this to Stella, who tries to convince me that my psychiatrist, David, is right, that I should take antidepressants—if only temporarily. So I remind her—and this humbles her, it does—of the animal-howl cries that came out of her for months after our mother died, her failure to eat properly for a year, her nocturnal walks through the cemetery on Heidler Road. The cemetery was Old World, with thirty, forty graves at the most that had sand-colored modest headstones dating back to the early 1900s, when our town was nothing but farmland. The cemetery was a half-mile walk from the tract-housing development we lived in and, late at night, when Stella was only in the seventh grade, she would walk there on autumn evenings and make etchings of names on notebook paper with pencils and tuck them away in the bottom drawer—her "junk drawer"—of her dresser. *I want to know who else is dead,* she said to me, cavalier and refreshed, when I caught her sneaking back into the house one night. She was clutching a piece of paper that read *Ezekiel Williams, 1910 to 1931, Our son who is now with the Son.* I explain to Stella—who agrees—that it is not far from my public strolls through brightly lit, heavily populated public places where tears or sobs or guttural moans mark my desire to know who else is living.

A few hours before my father arrives, I take Lurch next door to Kip's. Lurch is testy at best with strangers, and Kip has agreed to keep him for the afternoon. I hand Kip a plate of brownies as he takes Lurch from me, the three of us crowded into the foyer.

"These are for you."

"You didn't have to make me brownies."

"I didn't make them just for you."

"Ah, for your dad?" Kip says, and the three of us make our way into Kip's cluttered and warm kitchen.

Lurch is thrilled to be here, knowing he will be fed forbidden table food and taken for a long walk through the woodsy patch of property on the cusp of Glyn Neath. Kip is undeterred by rain.

"It's not like I wanted to make him brownies. I'm not trying to make him happy or anything. It's just what I'm supposed to do, right, make something to eat? Right? That's what you do for guests, right?"

"It's going to be fine," he says, rubbing my shoulder.

"I don't even know why I'm doing this."

"You don't need to know why. Just open the door, pour him a cup of coffee, relax."

"Why did I make him brownies? He's going to think everything's okay. He's going to misread this whole visit."

"Don't overthink the brownies, Anjou."

Kip kisses me on the cheek and sends me back into the rain. I go upstairs to the guest bedroom and take a small wooden cross from the drawer of my nightstand. The cross is dark brown, with a shellacked decoupage print of Jesus. I bought the cross at an open-air market in Athens with Liz. I lie flat on my back, clutching the cross. I do this when I am worried: lie on my back clutching a cheap souvenir and praying silently. Eyes open, no sound, and I can see the tree tops budding with new leaves.

I learned to pray from our father. It was the only time I knew him to be quiet and unassuming—when he was in church, when he was being a Catholic. It fascinated me, just sitting next to him without him talking or explaining or being so loving or so much larger than life. When we went to the 8:30 mass, Stella and I insisted on sitting in a front pew, captivated during the music portion of the service, when a quartet of nuns played guitars up front with an eye-closed body-shaking emotion that I would later understand to be passion.

I can't pray in St. Theresa's. When I bought my house in Glyn Neath, I decided that if I was going to pay a mortgage once a month, I should start going to church once a month, too. In my mind, it was all about investments. I shopped around for a while. The Baptists were too friendly, the Methodists sang too much, the Unitarians believed in everything short of alien spacecrafts landing on Earth. The Lutherans and Presbyterians were too staid. But the Catholics left me alone, which was what I liked most—they were courteous, unobtrusive, methodical, and well attended. When Kip and I became close, I started going every week. I always took Communion despite the rules (I refused to go into the confession box), paid strict attention to the homily, resented the hypocrisy of the doctrine, but carefully acknowledged my own hypocrisy. I was soothed. I liked the ritual. I liked trying to make my belief in God a permanent thing. I liked volunteering for steering committees and selling cookies at the church bazaar and writing articles for the church's newsletter. Most of all, I liked the people in the church—all of them, the sanctimonious, the humble, the righteous, the prayerful, the hypocritical, the hopeful, the earnest, and the apathetic. I felt part of a bigger world walking to church on Sundays with Kip, going to Mc-Clanaghan's Diner afterward for banana pancakes. Quinn would always join us the first Sunday of the month. He'd sleep through the sermon, smile widely at the old ladies and charm them to no end, and then bring a flask of Bailey's Irish Cream into Mc-Clanaghan's and spike our coffee. I loved him for supporting my fumbling toward faith.

But praying was far too personal to do at church. So I'd come into my guest room, lie on my back, clutch a cross, and begin a delicate conversation that seemed unaffected, uncomplicated. Quinn walked in on me once. *What are you doing, masturbating?* he asked, laughing warmly, completely unaware how unfunny it was to me. The prayer this day my father is coming is a simple one:

Please. Please. Please. I am not done praying this word, but I hear a car, a hubcap scraping against the curb out front. I know it is him and I don't want to hear a doorbell ring, the formality of having to answer the door and say *Come in.* I run downstairs and open the door and stand there.

My father is not carrying an umbrella, and he is wearing gray slacks and black shoes, a bright yellow raincoat—so bright it looks ridiculous. He looks old: older than his sixty-five years. His hair is still a curly mass of twisted locks, but is now gray and dull. His forehead is riddled with lines, stepping stones of a worried expression fixed upon the fair slope of his brow down his nose and across his mouth. His chin is smooth—still. My father rarely needed to shave, his body practically hairless. Although he has always been lean, he looks gaunt, as if he's swimming in his jacket and clothes. I am not Stella, who is quick to anger and equally quick to forgive. I am not Stella, who is succinct and competent at choices and decisions. I don't know what I want to do with this man, who looks sad, who is making me sad, who is my father and my ghost and my phantom blood, but I am certain that we need to try to cut the barbed-wire fence we have of linked pain, sharp and unyielding.

"Come in," I say.

"I'm wet," he says.

"It's okay," I say, stepping back into the hallway. It is hard for me to look him in the eyes. The list of questions for him is folded into a four-square and deep in the back pocket of my blue jeans. I even titled the list: *Things I Need to Know.*

"I don't want to get your house wet."

"It's okay. My dog always comes in wet and muddy."

He steps into the foyer, staring at me, a puddle quickly forming from the trickle off his raincoat.

"You look beautiful," he says without display or grandeur, and he offers me a weak smile.

"I made brownies," I reply, the only possible thing I could say that would make any sense.

"I like brownies," he replies.

"Good."

"What I meant to say was *Thank you*," and he pauses. "I'm sorry."

"Don't be sorry."

"I meant to thank you."

I reach out my hand to take his wet coat, but he misunderstands my gesture. He takes my hand in a hesitant grip. I'd rather touch his hand than talk.

"I'm sorry," he whispers, dropping my hand.

I walk into the kitchen and he follows me, his coat still on, leaving a trail of water.

"How do you like your coffee?" I ask, and I know my voice is shaking. (I also know the answer to this question. Three sugars, no cream.)

"Three sugars," he says. "No cream."

A lengthy and uncomfortable silence ensues: I pour coffee and put the plate of brownies between us and we are sitting at the table and he is in this wet yellow jacket that, because of the lighting of my kitchen, is difficult to look at. He is thin and wet and probably cold. He is not supposed to look sad. And he certainly isn't supposed to be quiet. Stella did not tell me this would happen. I am annoyed that Stella has not helped me with this. And I am more annoyed with my father, for catching me off guard, for failing to be the person I remember—lyrical and charming, bursting and textured, talkative and filling every silence and space.

"You said you had a dog?" he says finally.

"I do. His name is Lurch, but he's next door at my friend's house. He's a bit nervous around strangers."

"I see."

"He's a border collie."

"They're protective dogs, they shepherd people in."

"They do, but Lurch is temperamental. He doesn't like many people. Men in particular."

"Did he like Quinn?" my father asks, for reasons that baffle me and, quickly I see, that baffle him, too.

"I don't want to talk about Quinn."

"I'm sorry," he says, sincerely regretful.

"It's okay. I just don't want to talk about him."

"I'm sorry," he says again, eyes widening in desperation.

"Please stop saying you're sorry," I say, too harshly, and I regret it instantly.

He is a stranger. Treat him like you are supposed to treat strangers. Nicely.

My father's eyes fill, right there in my kitchen. Embarrassed and surprised at himself, he stares down at the table top.

"Dad," I say hesitantly, for my heart has sunk because of this stranger.

I wanted to call him Jack.

"I don't know how to do this," he says, still not looking up at me.

"What did you do when you last saw Stella?"

It is a question that is not on the list in my pocket. I am aware of a weight in the room, a barometric drop—it must have come inside with him, with the rain.

"We played with the baby," he says.

"You went to Newfoundland this winter, right?"

"I spent a week there. I really like Bruce. He's very nice and protective."

"Yes, he is."

"Do you like Bruce?"

"I love him," I say. "He's good for Stella. She always needs a bit of reining in, and he does that."

"That sister of yours has a good head on her shoulders."

"That she does."

"Merry is a beautiful baby."

"She is."

That is all we come up with. I wait for him to speak, to tell me things, to answer the questions I cannot pull out of my pocket. I wait for him to go first. We sit, saying nothing, for what seems like hours and we don't eat my brownies and he barely drinks his coffee and, as we listen to the rain, the heavy and burdensome silence becomes just a little bit bearable.

Finally he stands up. He is still wearing his jacket, but it has dried. He looks rumpled and tired.

"I should leave," he says.

He has been in my house for eighteen minutes. That is a very, very long time to be in a room with somebody and not saying very much. I have started to adjust to seeing him, the depth of his age, the lines in his face, the slowness of his movements.

"Okay," I say, looking up at him.

"Can we try again?"

"Yes."

"Good," he says, his eyes glassy and wet.

I hear his car pull out of my driveway. I stand up, biting my thumbnail, and I eat a brownie. I take a sip of his coffee. It is cold and sweet. I hate coffee that is sweet, but I take several more sips. I eat another brownie, slowly this time. They taste amazing.

~~*~~

822 St. Clears Avenue

Today I started calling Grace. It is Monday, April 17. Monday is always a good day to start something new. I've called her twice so far. I still have the list of questions for her that I brought to Quinn's service. I have a question that isn't on the list—*Why didn't you come to Quinn's service?*—but I have already promised myself that I will not ask her anything not on the list. I called at 6:15 this morning, and I got her voice mail. Her voice is more chipper than it seemed that one time I met her. I was so fixed by her voice that I almost called back right there and then to hear it again. The second time I called, at 9:30, she answered. She sounded rushed. *Hello,* she said. *Hello, Hello.* Then a long pause, then she hung up.

I almost call her again, on the porch of 822 St. Clears Avenue, before I ring the bell, but it is early evening now and dark, and I can't find any redial button on the face of this cell phone and I have not yet memorized her phone number or the process of finding a phone number for an outgoing call in the phone's memory. I ring the doorbell, and a tall, thin woman with hair the color of a chocolate truffle, monochromatic and thick, answers. Her name is Wendy Reynolds and she is wearing a Blondie concert tee-shirt, a faded denim miniskirt, black fishnet stockings, and clunky Dr. Martens shoes that have a cat face at the top of each toe, pink and bright. In the background, I can hear a man retching. Wendy thinks it's too cold outside to even ask me why I am at her door and she promptly shuffles me into her foyer, saying *Come in, come in, come in.* This

April has been harsh, as if winter refuses to let spring take control. Two bushy black cats rub up against my legs, and the retching sound starts again.

"Dear God, I don't think he's ever going to stop puking," she says, shaking her head.

She looks off through the kitchen but she stays next to me, picking up one of the cats.

"Is everything okay?" I ask, feeling sheepish about being in the middle of this private moment—the violence of vomiting would always make Stella cry and I would rub her back to calm her.

"It's fine, it's fine," she says, waving her hand back and forth.

"Maybe I should come back at another time. I can schedule a call-back—"

"I don't even know why you're here," she says, holding the cat like it was a baby.

"The Census. I'm an enumerator. My name is Anjou, and nobody from your household completed the form that was mailed to you."

"No surprise there," she quips, stroking the cat's head, the second one walking in circles around her feet, mewing loudly.

"I should probably schedule a time to come back."

"No, no, let's do this now. Jeff and I are never around and, really, he's fine. Really, he is. He's a bit dramatic, always wanted to be in theater, you know the type," she says, inspecting my laminated ID card.

"Helluva picture," she continues. "Makes a passport photo look like a glamour shot, eh?"

I am white and hungover in the photograph. The retching gets very loud suddenly and my eyes widen.

"Seriously, don't worry. My husband ate a star fruit. That's what we think it was, food poisoning from the star fruit. Have you ever had one?"

"No," I say.

"They're from Indonesia. Or Belize. I can't quite remember. Hold on," she says, putting a hand up at me and turning around to holler, *Where were those star fruit from? Was it Honduras?*

"Oh, anyway, we bought them at the Food Source. They sounded like they would be good and the thing looked pretty, but it must have been infected by some parasite. He's been puking all day."

"I'm sorry to hear this," I say.

"I knew something would happen with this fruit. I get premonitions about things like this. My mother says I'm too middle-class for premonitions but I *knew* this fruit was trouble when we were at the check-out line. The cashier couldn't figure out the pricing. Nine times out of ten if you buy anything more exotic than an orange or an apple there, the cashier won't know what the pricing is. So, of course, the star fruit is entirely too much of a fruit challenge for the cashier and she gets annoyed with us because she doesn't know what the hell this star fruit is, let alone what it costs, all of this causing a major kerfuffle in her kingdom of grocery order. You would think that they would have some basic fruit training in that place, especially with the cost of their produce. I don't know, maybe my standards are too high."

"Maybe you should see if you can get your money back," I offer.

"That isn't too bad of an idea, actually. I may just have to do that. If I wind up having to take him to the hospital, you can be guaranteed I'm going to do that."

With the sound of Jeff retching in the background, I ask Wendy who lives there, anybody else besides her and Jeff, their ages, the type of dwelling it is. She answers the eleventh item and I scratch at my wrists—they have been rashy and itchy for weeks now. When I think, I itch.

"How much would you do for love?" I ask her, handing her the Short Form for her signature, a long relaxing breath releasing from me.

She doesn't take my clipboard but instead puts her hands on her hips, scrunches up her face, and then puts a hand on my forehead.

"You feeling okay?" she asks with skeptical concern, annoyed almost.

"Yes. No. Yes."

"That's two answers, one twice," she says, her hands back on her hips.

Wendy is a person who loves being bothered but doesn't want you to know this. She will take her husband to the hospital later. She will bitch the entire time, in an edgy but humorous way, telling her husband how lucky he is. She will tell me how they married young, how she knew right away that she would love him until she was dead—the only part of the marriage vow she subscribed to in whole. Love to death. She will tell me this the day before I leave for Capri. She and I will talk again, because I asked about love.

Jeff retches again in the background.

"Stay here," she commands with a pointed finger.

She is gone for a few moments, and her two cats slink over and wind around my legs, mewing up at me. I don't like cats, but I smile at them, thinking this is the nice thing to do.

"Okay, now I've been thinking about your question while I was cleaning up rather offensive vomit," she says while walking back through the kitchen and into the hallway, where I am still standing.

"I believe your exact question was *How much would you do for love?* Correct? That was it?"

"Yes," I say.

I am mesmerized by her frenetic activity, the way her hands keep moving, a cat picked up here and put down there. She keeps looking back toward the kitchen, waiting to hear the sounds of her sick husband. Her foot is tapping, too.

"You're serious, aren't you?"

"I am," I say.

"'Cause it's a little weird—no, a lot weird—for the Census chick to ask me how much I would do for love? *That* is just a bit weird, and probably illegal."

"Probably," I say.

I don't smile, because I don't want her to think this is a joke to me.

"All right then," she says with a shake of her head, "how much would I do for love? Well, not much actually. I wouldn't die for it, wouldn't kill for it, not likely to give up my cats for it either. Jeff takes allergy pills because of the cats. He's been taking a pill every morning since our fourth date. Now, see, he'd do anything for love. If he had two cats that made me sneeze and break out in hives, he'd get rid of the cats. There is, I confess, great disparity in our relationship. But I know for a fact that I'm doing a whole lot of things for love and I'm not even aware of it. 'Cause Jeff is no Milquetoast, and it's highly unlikely he'd stay with me if I wasn't doing something. So I may not be able to do much for love, but for one person I'm doing enough."

"Thank you," I say.

"You're welcome."

I want to shake her hand, but it seems inappropriate, so I offer a weak smile and shrug my shoulders. I turn to leave.

"You know, you're a strange bird?"

"Not really," I say.

"Oh, no, really, you are. Trust me. But I like that in a person. We should get together sometime and drink beers. Or go to a concert. Or make curtains, you know?"

"I'd like that," I say, surprised at myself.

Stella frequently reminds me that a middle-aged guy who lives next door and a childhood friend who lives in Hong Kong should not be the extent of my social life. When I first met Quinn, she accused me of just being too lazy to make friends, that Quinn was a quick fix to my need to increase my social network.

"Great. Now, in keeping with my theme of not doing much for anybody, I'll let you get in touch with me. You know where I live, and we're in the phone book."

"Okay," I say.

"But make it soon," she says. "I have a shitty short-term memory, and I'll forget who you are in a few weeks."

"I will," I say.

(And I do—I will call her and we will eat brunch one Sunday morning at McClanaghan's Diner before I leave for Capri. She will tell me that her husband would have joined us but he wanted her to make sure I wasn't boring first. She will tell me she hates chocolate when I order chocolate-chip pancakes. She will insist on paying and she will order a side of bacon to take home to Jeff. *He loves all breakfast meats*, she will say. Kip will not be hurt when I tell him I'm meeting a woman after church for brunch, that I'd invite him but that I don't know her that well. Kip will not be even the least bit wounded and will tell me that he'll take Lurch for a walk. He'll tell me to enjoy brunch. And I will. And three days afterward I will receive a card in the mail from Wendy. It will be "written" by her two cats, Holly and Jolly, inviting me to a small dinner party the following Saturday. I will call her on the phone immediately, to RSVP, to follow through on a social opportunity. Eventually, I will tell her about Quinn because she will become more than a stranger-neighbor, because she told me what she would do for love.)

The retching begins again.

"Christ on a Popsicle stick," she says, shaking her head. "I think that husband of mine is puking up an intestine. Looks like the Reynoldses shall be making a road trip to Lankenau Hospital."

"I hope he feels better," I say, walking out the door, wondering what it will be like to call her.

"Oh, he will. He's just barfing extra loud to get some sympathy out of me."

I step out into the cool air; the sun has just set, but a trace of light coats the atmosphere. Everything is eerie this time of day; you can see big structures and imposing trees, but everything else disappears into the gray. I turn around and she is slowly shutting the door. She looks much softer from here, her pale skin and thin legs. I do not know this woman but I know for certain that she loves her husband with such depth and intensity that she doesn't need to talk about it or analyze it or quantify it or ever prove it.

8

IN THE WATER WITH YOU

TWELVE HOURS AFTER QUINN LEFT, Stella's plane touched down at Philadelphia International Airport. I hadn't cried since buying cigarettes at the Circle K, but the airport was a wide berth of brightly lit public space, an offering really. I arrived a full hour before Stella's plane landed and there, in the last seat of the last row at Gate C19, where the gamut of emotions is expressed with little regard for social norms (tears and laughter and silences are expected), I looked at my watch, 9:05, and I began to mourn. It was a glorious belonging, and it went on for fifty-four minutes. I was red-eyed and puffy-faced and exhausted, hiccuping like a drunk, watching Stella's plane taxi to the gate.

She came through the crowd of travel-weary passengers and we wrapped ourselves around each other with a fierceness close to anger. I took in her smell—grapefruit shampoo, stale plane air. I associate Stella with scents, a way to find her. She is sandalwood. She is ocean breeze and baked potatoes and laundered towels and muddy boots. She is dust behind the couch and peach soap and peppermint.

"You look like shit," she said, ending our embrace and eyeing me up and down, repeatedly kissing my cheeks, stroking my back and squeezing my hand.

We drove directly to Long Beach Island—LBI, our mother always called it—where we were staying for three days. LBI is four miles off the coast of New Jersey, connected to the mainland by the Manahawkin Bridge. Its shorelines are flat, with a cream-colored sandscape, littered with a rainbow of sea nature: horseshoe-crab shells, tangles of seaweed, broken clamshells whose insides are hues of gold and purple and pink, an occasional bone-white sand dollar. Gray-and-white gulls gather on jagged black jetties to fish in the breaking waves and shallow water. The island is eighteen miles long and exceedingly thin—the space between the ocean and bay seems frighteningly narrow—with small hamlets that have comforting names such as Loveladies, Beach Haven, Harvey Cedars, Barnegat Light, Brighton Beach. The north end of the island is luxurious, full of newly constructed houses with angular outcroppings, multilevel decks, and porthole windows, modern replicas of old sailing ships. The south end of the island is more modest. Smaller, older homes are settled close together, an instantaneous notion of a neighborhood with whitewashed cottages, weathered beach bungalows, formulaic boxes-on-stilts, all painted from a palette of sky-blue and yellow and salmon and seashell gray. Stella and I grew up going to the Jersey Shore every summer with our parents, all of August every year. Our father would stay home to work in the city during the week and then come down on the weekends to join us. We always stayed in the south end, in a yellow saltbox-style house in Spray Beach.

It was 42 degrees, a biting February day. Stella rolled the windows halfway down, cranked up the heat. Route 72—the back road to LBI—is a hypnotizing two-lane broken-line highway. Ruler-straight and flat, the horizon stretches on forever, as if you will eventually drive right into the ocean, which you quite literally will if you want to. On either side are dense thickets of skinny white pines that grow out like matchsticks with feathery needles on top. I had booked us a room at Wida's Hotel & Seafood Restaurant in Brant Beach. During our childhood summers, Stella obsessed about staying at Wida's, an old-fashioned resort, a big white hotel with green shutters and an Old World charm.

"Why can't we stay there, Mom? We should *experience* a hotel," Stella had said, stretching out the window of our car as we drove down Long Beach Boulevard.

My mother didn't need to slow down when we passed Wida's. She adhered strictly to the island's 25-mph speed limit, which was enforced with an equality of fervor I would later relate to in Glyn Neath.

"Why do you want to stay there so badly?" our mother asked, smiling at my sister in the rearview mirror.

"Because we're at the seashore. And we should eat seafood at the seashore and stay in a seashore resort."

"I see," my mother said.

"Nice pun, Mom," I said.

"Can you just imagine staying there?" Stella went on, hanging out the window, looking at Wida's as if it was a golden palace.

"Maybe we can stay there one day, sweetheart," my mother said sincerely. "Maybe we can go on Monday."

"I don't want to go during the week. It's not the same. I want to go on the weekend. I want to stay over on a *Saturday* night. When it's really a seashore resort. When everybody is there. When it's *full*."

"Honey, it's August. Wida's is always full in August."

"No, it has to be a weekend. I bet that's when there's dancing in the restaurant. And I want the surf-and-turf special. That's always on Saturday night. You've seen the signs. And we can eat salmon at the restaurant, or crabs, and then we can wash our hair like an official hen party," she said dreamily.

Stella was fascinated by gatherings, private and public. She loved events and parties and celebrations. Anniversaries and commencements and awards and accolades. She loved fanfare and traditions—church on Sunday, Wednesday-night bowling, a large cheese pizza from Primo's every Thursday night. She wanted to celebrate Hanukkah even though we were Catholic. Irrepressible, she convinced our mother to buy a plastic menorah and wrap small gifts—Play-Doh and jacks—for the first night of Hanukkah. She taped a piece of black construction paper on the front bay window of the house in Spray Beach every August 16, to honor the death of Elvis. We never did stay at Wida's. I imagined there'd be a cozy crowdedness, the three of us—the girls—in an ocean-front room, sleeping in the same bed and getting ready in the morning, watching our mother apply her makeup and trying it ourselves. We never stayed at Wida's because of our father, who never missed coming down for the weekends during our August at the Shore. Even if our father was living with Maggie at the time, he still came to the Shore. He'd burst in late on a Friday night from wherever he had been—our house, hers, playing squash with Uncle Tim, who wasn't really our uncle. Stella and I would be on the floor reading or playing cards or backgammon, the television on in the background. He'd stand in the middle of the living room, still holding his suitcase, and pretend he was on a surfboard riding a wave. *Try not to wipe out, Jack,* our mother would holler from the bedroom. She couldn't see what he was doing, but she knew. Our father was a creature of habit.

I had called Stella at 4 A.M. the night Quinn left. By then I had made $8,000 worth of charges on Quinn's credit card, broken down at the Circle K, smoked twenty-one cigarettes, and drunk half a bottle of whiskey on my back porch with Kip.

"Christ almighty, I'm so sorry. I'm so very sorry," she had said, her voice still laced with sleep.

"You're supposed to say *I told you so.* You've been waiting three years for the opportunity."

"I'll be there tomorrow," she said.

"I don't want to stay here. I don't want to be here. I want to go to the Shore," I said.

"Honey, what are you talking about? You want to go to the Shore?"

"Yes, the Shore. The Jersey Shore."

"Are you sure?"

"Nice pun," I said, the memory flooding me of our mother, our summers, our father, the safety of being there on days during the week that blended together as one. Everything could be a mess in our lives, but looking out at the unlimited horizon, the water and its shift of colors by light, by angle, reminded me that there was something that was constant, reliable through the seasons.

∾⁊ℓ∽

It was early evening and February had already forced the sky to begin its night cover. Stella and I had slept late that day, taken a long walk on the beach, eaten lunch at Scojo's in Surf City, and then driven down to Barnegat to see the lighthouse. We bought cheap shell-covered jewelry boxes lined with chintzy red velvet, and then we drove up and down the island looking at the kaleidoscope of architecture and color. There were very few year-rounders, but they carried a brave and tempered demeanor. They were respectful of the wrath and joy of their ocean. I went for a run along Ocean Boulevard while Stella napped, and then together we sat outside on the deck of our room smoking cigarettes. Stella was always a social smoker, never needing to quit because a few cigarettes a year was all she ever really wanted. She sat on a plastic chair, painting her toenails while I watched the gray-purple waves, laughing gulls overhead.

"Why are you painting your toenails?" I asked.

We were dressed in wool sweaters and jeans and hot-pink fleece scarves that Stella had bought for us at Ron Jon's Surf Shop in Ship Bottom.

"Because we always painted our toes at the Shore," she said, motioning for me to remove my footwear, too.

"It was summer when we did that," I said.

"A minor technicality."

She handed me the pink nail polish and then leaned back and put her feet up on the railing to let her toes dry in the cold salty air.

"I think I know what I'm going to do," I said to Stella.

"What's that, kid?"

"I'm going to go away."

"If you haven't noticed, you are away. Right now, in fact."

"I mean really go away. Overseas."

"Do you have a specific place in mind?" she asked, examining her toes critically.

"Capri."

I put my sneakers on the deck and reached for a cigarette. Stella stared at me while I tried to light it, the flame blown out with every click of the lighter. I gave up and sat back in my chair, wiggling my toes and trying to summon up the courage to be barefoot.

"Capri," she said slowly, evenly.

"Capri," I repeated.

"I see."

"Just me," I continued, egging her on.

"To swim in the sea?"

"Oui."

Capri, off the western coast of Italy, toward the southern portion of the leg of the boot. On the upper section of the island, in Anacapri, is a blue grotto, a cave-like opening off the craggy-rock side of the island. During the day men in small boats row you into the grotto so you can see how the sun reflects off the walls to make the water a magical blue, glassy-aquamarine and supernatural. After the sun lowers, when the men in the boats are gone, handfuls of tourists go to the small docking area where you jump into the Bay of Naples and swim about fifty feet into the grotto, just in time to catch the dusk light and see the water around you, a shade of blue you never thought your eyes could see.

"I met your mother on the moon, married her on a star, and then you see, we went to Capri, to eat gelato and swim in the grotto," Stella said with a gentle cadence, a sweep of syllables and pauses, a sad look on her face.

I rubbed my arms. We both hated the confinement of winter jackets but loved to be outside when temperatures plummeted. As kids we'd sneak outside without a jacket—bundled in hats and scarves and gloves—and breathe in the silence. And then we'd break into a run, screaming *Nobody else knows this world,* over and over, running down the streets with plumes of steam coming from our mouths.

Stella took the cigarette from my hand, put it in her mouth, and brought the lighter up to cupped hands. It lit immediately, and she handed it to me. We passed the cigarette back and forth for a while in silence.

"You better not start smoking again. You'll have to quit. It'll shave years from your life," she said.

"Longevity is overrated."

"How long are you planning to be gone?"

"Two weeks, maybe three. Probably four," I said, feeling like I had run away in just those words.

"What about work?"

"A minor technicality," I said, giving her a sideways look.

"So you think it's a good idea to take off for Italian waters right now?"

She frequently asked me questions that, based on delivery and tone, had nothing to do with wanting a concrete answer; the question served solely as a vehicle to get her opinion across.

"No. It's a lousy idea. But I've made quite a few lousy decisions these past few years, so why break the streak?"

"Fine," she said. "I think it's a marvelous idea. So marvelous that I'll go with you."

"That's a major technicality. You have a family last time I checked. You can't abandon them for a month."

"Honey, you have me more worried than usual. Quinn left two days ago. Two days. You have a lot of shit—pure shit, Anjou—coming your way. Don't run from this."

"I'm going," I said, imagining Quinn in his car, idle at a long traffic light, waiting to go somewhere, to get to his next place that he already knew about.

"I need an island, Stella."

"You're on one right this minute. Take two weeks off of work. I'll stay another week. Why do you have to fly halfway across the world to find your island?"

"Because it has to be Capri."

"Why?" Stella burst out. "You won't even talk to Jack. You haven't spoken to him in over seventeen years. Why in God's name do you want anything to do with a fairy-tale poem of his?"

"Because that's the only time I ever believed him. When he lied about their honeymoon."

"You believed that they went to Capri?"

"No. I believed that he loved Mom. When he would say that poem, I believed he dropped from the sky to love her. It seemed possible. Remember after Mom died, remember what Aunt Vicky told us? How they got married by the Justice of the Peace in Norristown and they drove directly here to LBI, to Surf City. How they went crabbing and walked on the beach and played shuffleboard at the vacant Senior Center in Beach Haven. Remember?"

"Yup."

"Well, I still don't quite believe that. I always thought Capri was their parallel universe. It's the only poem that made Mom look, well, so at ease. And it's the only poem of Dad's that I believed."

Stella's eyes were glassy and she stared at the water.

"She actually thought she was going to go," she finally said.

"What do you mean?"

"Mom, she really thought she was going. Every year she'd buy the new Frommer's Guide to Italy."

"How do you know that?"

"I found them in the attic. I was eight years old. I was snooping for Christmas gifts and found them in a big cardboard box. There were years and years of them."

"Why didn't you tell me?" I asked, surprised at how much we learn about someone who has died long after they were alive. There is a constant discovery, a new and haphazard map of unturned stones and secret caves, a journey that begins only when lives had ended.

"I don't know, Anjou. I only put it all together now, with you talking about wanting to go to Capri. There was about ten years' worth of Italys."

Our mother was an armchair tourist. She would have loved that I'd been to Italy and Greece and France and Wales. That Stella had lived in Norway for her senior year of college and then spent six months after college in Newfoundland, where she met Bruce. That I'd gone to Austria with Quinn to eat strudel and to Germany to drink beer and to France to float down the River Seine. She would have hated that I had become an accountant. She always said, *Make art or make babies. The rest the men can handle.*

"She'd love that you live in Newfoundland," I said.

"No doubt," Stella said, nodding her head at the ocean.

The wind blew the back of her hair forward in shooting wisps around her face. I licked my lips, the faint taste of salt.

"You're going to need to let go of this one day," she said.

"I know he loved me," I said.

"He still does," Stella replied.

"Who are we talking about?" I asked, forgetting where our father began and Quinn ended.

On February 17, while I was at Wida's with Stella, three days after Quinn left me, he was struck by a car and killed. He died instantly, or as close to instantly as one can measure. He was dead when the ambulance arrived. He was in the city, and he was standing at a place where four streets converge in a cluster of traffic lights and crosswalks. It's a zigzag formation—16th Street, Benjamin Franklin Parkway, Arch Street—16th Street going north, the other two streets each with two lanes running east and west. The convergence of these streets is a star, pointing in five directions. This complex topography is overwhelming, mindboggling, to a first-time visitor. But people who live or work in the city understand the nuances of this intersection, what limits you can push when navigating it.

Quinn died because he was struck by a car, but really he died from words. He died because he was buried in the pages of a book—Marcel Proust's *Swann's Way*, I would later find out. I would ask Grace about the book when I went to her house.

Based on the flow of traffic for these streets, when a certain light is red, you can walk across the south side of Arch Street and hover there near the two dividing yellow lines; eastbound traffic is stopped on the south side of that street as the westbound traffic zooms by you on its north side. You can literally stand there in the middle of the street with traffic going in almost every direction around you. You can do this safely, but only if you are careful. You have to pay attention to the movement around you. You cannot step over the yellow lines headed north, or fast-moving traffic will seal your fate. In the chronic rush of modern times, it makes no sense for people—these workers trying to get to work!—to simply wait at the corner of Arch and 16th to cross both sides. If the south side of Arch is passable, then it should be passed.

And so there Quinn stood, inches behind the yellow lines, in the middle of it all, with ten people or twenty or more or less (you didn't know how many, you were in a pack, you just sensed them there, comfortably, all around you with the noise). And because he sensed the crowd—just as he always did—he kept reading. See, this was the problem, this unbreakable habit: to read. Anywhere. At any time. He would read sitting, standing still, in motion. Even when walking across a street.

He was among the crowd at the yellow line, but very alone I imagine, in the middle of one of Proust's sentences that went on for pages. He started to move forward. The light had not changed, and his crowd had not begun to bring him forward into a fold of safe crossing. But he moved forward anyway, deep in an unending sentence. I wondered about that moment, while he was walking and reading: What was Proust saying when Quinn's life ended? What did he hear as he stood on the yellow dividing line, distracted and reading and in love? Did he hear the swoosh of cars in every direction, the wind sweeping against his calves, the clunk-and-slam of trucks lumbering over manholes and the horns and the people around him talking on cell phones or to friends and office mates? A common sound. A typical sound. A rush-hour sound at the star of streets.

It was only three steps across the yellow line—I imagine it as three steps—that Quinn heard the voice. Not mine. Not Grace's. Not a woman's voice. Not a man's voice. Nothing celestial or mystical. He heard the solitary voice of a crowd, a crescendo of pitches and decibels—cries, even—a collective voice telling him nothing in particular—it was just a jumble of words that were one—something close to *Stop* or *Wait* or *No* or *Stop* or *Stop* or *Stop*. His head came up from the book to see where all of those words were coming from, finally ignoring the ones he was busy with (Proust! Of course!), and that was it. I like to imagine he felt nothing, that the car hit—words everywhere in the air from behind him and flying out of his hands—and his body flew, and the cars on the side of the street you shouldn't walk on tried to stop but he was already three steps into the westbound lane and even though the people yelled and even though they tried to brake everything was moving too fast so all of those words they yelled and the words he read were useless, just useless, and then he was hit. It was all useless, a waste. He was hit and then he was thrown and then he flew and then he landed on the car (which one?) and on the ground, his head first, all of it over in that instant.

He had started reading the Proust book one week before he left me.

"How is it so far?" I asked.

"I'm forty-four pages in. But I've read it twice already."

"I heard that Proust is hard to read."

Marcel Proust, a French novelist, had been in the periphery of my consciousness ever since college. I had fuzzy recollections of people saying *Swann's Way* was impossible to read. I never heard one person say one good thing about the book, that it was enjoyable, that it evoked great emotion. Proust sounded like something to read for the sake of having said you'd read it. I could never have predicted that not soon after that brief conversation I wouldn't be able to get Proust out of my mind, that I would never read a single word of his book but that I would want a copy, simply to hold in my hands.

Quinn took the book with him in the blue Delta Airlines duffel bag he packed the night he left. He was engrossed in it three days later when crossing Arch Street to go to a meeting at the Friends Society Meeting House on 16th and Cherry Streets, his life carrying on as it always had, but with a different woman, with no transition or slow movement to the next step. Everything else had stayed the same, even the book he was reading.

I thought a lot about how the book had landed. Grace looked confused when I asked her where she thought the book had ended up. (The sidewalk? The street? Under a tire?) I remember the mundane details that first time Quinn asked me about my half-moon scar. A man with a flaky scalp sat in front of me, and a woman in a burgundy suit with too much perfume sat in front of Quinn. I needed this mundane detail of Quinn's last moments. I needed to know about the book and, really, I can't imagine why anybody wouldn't need to know this. Did the book land on its spine, open up like outstretched arms, pages going back and forth from the swoosh of traffic on the other side of the street, from the rush of people toward Quinn? (He was twisted then, right arm and left leg bent in directions in which they should simply not be bent. No blood. Only his insides leaking and ending all of the promise. Eyes closed. Hands in fists. Grace told me. I made her tell me. A witness had told somebody who had told somebody who had told Quinn's friend Bernie who had told Grace. We all had the right to know.) The book was probably smudged and scratched, with gravel in the creases, a forgotten piece of nothing just feet away from a dead man, a beautiful man, inconsistent and half-bred and deeply loved and hated—as we all are.

Quinn couldn't let go of words. It was his job. It was his research. It was what he taught and how he spun the world around him. He capitalized on the tiered levels of vocabulary, on the power of inflection that made his words bigger than they were. He read everywhere, his appetite ceaseless. In the kitchen, the bedroom, the bathroom, the car. On the train, and at the platform waiting for the train. He brought a book with him for any appointment—the doctor, the dentist, the optometrist—snubbing the magazine selection in the waiting room. He kept a book in the backseat of his car, to grab for standing in line at the bank or waiting for a prescription to be filled in the pharmacy. He read while sitting at traffic lights, and he had several dents in the rear bumper of his Honda to prove the stupidity of this action. Once I found him standing on the sidewalk in front of my house. It was 6:30 on a June evening and he stood there, his briefcase at his feet, his tie loosened and his suit rumpled from an early burst of high temperatures and heavy humidity. He was standing there as his fellow commuters walked to their cars and homes from the train station just a block away. He was standing there, reading.

"What are you doing?" I asked him with a laugh.

He put his worn leather bag down, not looking up from the magazine that held his attention.

"Quinn," I called out.

He stretched his free arm out, his palm upturned, as if waiting for my hand, reassuring me of his love despite his unquestionable signal of *Hold on. Wait. Wait.* I watched him for a while, his ability to focus like that. To start something and hold on and finish it even if it was something small, there on the sidewalk in front of his lover's house. He finally looked up, a smile spread across his face.

"What was it?" I asked.

"A story," he said, looking relaxed. "Story," he repeated, tasting the word. "A girl should be named that, don't you think? A baby. A baby girl named Story."

I smiled at him. We hadn't talked about children. Not until that moment. He was the first man to unleash what was a very real desire to have a baby.

"Yes, Anjou, my tree, my fruit, my sweet, sweet love. Just think of it. A pear and a story."

"You're crazy," I said, because it scared me to think he might be half serious. (I wanted to have a Story—a girl, a baby with a name of words, a beginning, a middle, no end—with him.)

"You know you should be D'Anjou? Do you know that? That's what the pear is really called. D'Anjou pears."

"My father thought that a child's name should never have an apostrophe."

"Your father is a smart man," he said, the commuters walking by him.

"Some would argue that," I said.

Quinn always read during the ten-minute walk from 30th Street Station to his office on campus. I imagine that day he must have been a bit disoriented, coming out of Suburban Station instead of 30th Street, having taken the train in farther because of his meeting at the Friends Society Meeting House. There at 16th Street, he probably stood outside the brassy art-deco doors of the station and looked up for several minutes. It was Quinn who taught me to always look up in a city, to take in the breadth of a metropolis by looking up, having your scope of vision halfway up a building or structure, cupped by the sky. I bet he looked up that day, stared at the frame: the spraying fountain of Love Park across the street, behind it the imposing City Hall with the statue of William Penn on top, behind that the Philadelphia Savings Fund Society skyscraper, built in 1932, a majestic steel sky-shooting frame with the blocky letters PSFS emblazoned across its top—seeing all of the history new and old in a frame. Then he would begin his leisurely walk— as all walks were for him, rain or shine—from Suburban Station heading north, toward that constellation of streets. I made Grace tell me who had made the phone call to her: Was it Bernie and did he try to talk to her like a psychiatrist, did he handle her well, her emotional state, or was he just a friend to her?

It was a glitch in Quinn's routine, heading north not south, but he still read because glitches were to be filled with the ordinary and mundane. And so he read along the path he took that day. He learned early in his career how to memorize the cracks and rises on the sidewalks and streets of the city, how to navigate the flow of people with his face down in a book. But sometimes he missed; he'd forget the contour or curve of a sidewalk, the height of a step and the slope of a curb, and he'd trip. He'd get up, brush himself off, move forward. His scratched knees and nicked elbows were a badge of honor for his commitment to words.

Enough falls and you'd think he'd stop reading while in motion. But he didn't. I didn't mind. I sympathized with Quinn's plight. Because I tripped a lot, too, and for reasons that had nothing to do with klutziness and certainly nothing to do with reading. I tripped because I had mean thoughts, and sometimes these thoughts—so mean and harsh that I didn't know what to do with them—got caught up together, entangled, and they required so much focus that I wouldn't pay attention to where I was going, and I wouldn't remember where I was headed, and I wouldn't listen to what the person next to me was saying, and I'd trip. I had abrasions on my palms and scrapes on my elbows. I gathered street dust on my knees. I tripped a lot during third and fourth grades, the year after my mother died, the year Stella got married, and during the three years I was with Quinn. And in the dawn hours, walking to get contact solution from my car, there in the parking lot of Wida's Hotel & Seafood Restaurant where it was dark and the only sound was crashing waves, I thought about Quinn and I fell.

ↄℳ৴

Time is funny: how what is happening to you in one brief moment can be so trivial, while at that same moment another person's life changes forever, and then changes yours forever. The whole time you're oblivious, the thickness of that moment unrealized, until the perspectives converge. You remember where you were when somebody dies. There's a running list of encapsulated moments stored in a box in our brain. You can open the lid and out pours what creates the skeleton of our knowledge of grief.

While Quinn read and walked and paused and read and moved forward and died on a Monday morning at a crossroads in downtown Philadelphia, I was about a mile up the road from Wida's Hotel & Seafood Restaurant. I was at an antique store, the first customer of the morning. While Quinn was at the intersection, I was in Ship Bottom buying vintage postcards at A Moment in Time Antiques. It was 10:08 A.M.

I stood in the back of the antique store rifling through two shoeboxes of old postcards as Quinn died. I bought eleven of them, a dollar each. Each was a site in Europe. My favorite was a black-and-white photograph of the Pantheon in Rome. It was mailed June 14, 1936, to Mrs. Hannah Caraway in Brooklyn from a woman named Alathea. In tight black script she wrote, *Hannah, Today we went to the Pantheon, the Coliseum, and Vatican City. I thought about how Jesus died when he was 33 years old. Think about what he did in 33 years. I have done nothing in my life. I fast approach 63 and I wonder if I'll do anything, if I'll know anything. I am growing melancholy. Rome is beautiful. You must come see it.*

ↄℳ৴

"You want to go to Capri so you can swim in a cave?" Liz asked.

Stella was in the shower, still unconvinced that a month in Italy would have any healing qualities. Quinn was dead at that moment, but neither of us knew it yet.

"It's a grotto, not a cave. A blue grotto," I said.

It was 4:39 A.M. in Hong Kong, 3:39 P.M. at the Jersey Shore. Liz and her husband, Andy, had been living in Hong Kong for almost four months. The company Andy worked for, a communications conglomerate, had placed him on a three-year assignment there. Liz, a seasoned traveler, quickly adapted to life halfway across the world. I teased her when she left that Hong Kong would rip the loner right out of her. Liz also adapted quickly to my inconsiderate and very consistent lack of respect for the time difference. I am a selfish friend, but Liz is a chronic insomniac. In the two days since Quinn had left, she had spoken to me at the most ungodly hours. She offered to come home, but she had spoken with Stella several times and been reassured that flying home wasn't necessary.

"Grotto, cave, it's all the same, Anjou. Just be careful. You know you'll need to be careful."

"We never really knew if that was what it was," I said.

"It was."

"We don't know."

"What else could it have been?" she said. "I don't mean to be superstitious, but a cave? It can change everything, you know that."

I know, I thought. *I hope.*

As teenagers, Liz and her brother always spent the month of July on the island of Santorini with their grandparents. When I met Quinn, I tried to convince Liz that I attracted people who were somehow from the Greek islands. Liz and her brother were immersed in the chaotic and rich and sun-drenched life of their extended family of aunts and uncles and cousins. Liz's grand-parents had been born and raised and would most certainly die in their island town, Imerovigli, which sits atop the Caldera, Santorini's crater. Perched on stone, lava, and ash, Imerovigli indoctrinated Liz from an early age: She evoked the subtle pressing sentiment of the Old World, was at home in the sea, and quietly brimmed with a salt-of-the-earth temperament.

I would cling to Liz the night before she boarded an Air Olympia jet, holding back the bursting dam in my heart, needing her too much. She was my K factor, my X and Y axes. The summer before our senior year in high school, months after my mother died, Liz handed me a ticket to Athens the night before she flew to Santorini. I shook my head, confused.

"What's this? What? I mean—"

"You're coming with me this year," she said nonchalantly, trying to act contained.

"What are you talking about?"

"We cleared it with Aunt Vicky weeks ago. I wanted to surprise you," she said, laughing and tossing clothes in the air.

I felt like crying, but she wouldn't let me. *This is not something to cry about. It's joy, Anjou. Joy.* She slammed into my open arms and together we crashed, laughing and screaming, holding on. Free.

That magical month in Greece, Liz and I were joined at the hip with her cousin Dina, who was far more daring than Liz or I ever would be. It was Dina who swam farthest out into the ocean, farther than even the arrogant boy cousins. *The boy cousins are pussies,* she'd say after swimming back in, cackling and shaking her wet hair at a pack of them lying on the beach. It was Dina who convinced Liz and me to hitch a ride to Kamari Beach—Dina could drive, but she liked to see if she could get a tourist to pick her up. At Kamari she would walk across the beach's black and red and green pebbles slowly, as if they were cool blankets instead of the hot coals they felt like. And it was Dina who on our first night there told us that she had given her virginity to a university student from Australia weeks before we arrived. She talked endlessly about the university student, what it felt like to have a man between your legs, how there was no pain at all: *Oh, there never is if you are ready for him.* The more Dina talked about the university student, the more Liz doubted the story. Liz, who was shy with boys, had only kissed one boy at that point—Ned Rosenthal, a short Jewish boy, a boy whose kiss she described clinically as *interesting.* She said his tongue was velvety but hesitant. And it was Dina who convinced all of her cousins—Dimitri and Nikolas and Christakis—to join the girls to go cave swimming. That day Dina had been in high gear, manic, prattling on endlessly about her deflowering. Liz pressed her with questions, hoping to find a crack in the story.

"Where in Australia is he from?" Liz asked as she stood in the tub shaving her bikini line. I was sitting on the toilet seat, and Dina stood in the bathroom doorway, her shoulder leaning on the frame, arms crossed, confident.

"The north."

"Yeah, but where in the north?" Liz asked, shaking her foamy razor under the spray of spigot water.

"Brisbane," Dina said, looking bored, a radically different demeanor than when she herself would broach the subject.

"What did it feel like?"

"Why so many questions? I told you."

"What did it feel like?" Liz repeated, now focusing on her left calf.

"Perfect."

"Well, how did the whole condom thing work?"

"Oh, fine. Good. See, I'm not pregnant," she said with a toothy grin and a laugh, her wild black hair flying in every direction.

But Liz wanted to know who put it on, not whether or not it functioned.

The boy cousins knew of a cave near Kamari Beach, in a secluded section cut off from tourists and foot traffic. They brought some of their friends, a deep-throated crowd that split off like an atom, clusters of shirtless boy-men moving into cars and jeeps. At the impending dusk, Liz would later tell me that while she jumped into the waters of Kamari with the boy cousins and Dina and me, the early evening spoke to her: an insidious uneven wordless whisper, the water reaching up to take her warm and inviting—alive. The laughter and whooping calls echoed as we made our way to the cave, an arched outcrop of stone just a short swim away. One of the friends of the boy cousins, an olive-skinned boy named Kormos, stayed behind with Liz and me as the pack formed a line toward the cave. I knew his name was Kormos because I had asked Liz who he was. He had been smiling at her all day, and they'd nod at each other. He spoke little English, and Liz was too shy to talk to him in her choppy Greek.

We swam around in the cave, splashing each other and yelling, our languages becoming one as our voices bounced back and forth. It was noisy to be in the cave and in the falling light reflections off Dina's small diamond earrings bounced on the water. Liz told me later that it was when she saw the reflecting earrings that she felt something brush past her thighs—something different, but not necessarily foreign; it belonged there. The brush was a long thick pass across her legs, reliable and cold and solid. Liz froze and quickly turned to look at Dina and just as Dina looked at Liz, Dina felt it, too. Dina's eyes locked on Liz's, six feet from each other but somehow attached. Then the boys, all of them—was it six boys or seven or eight or nine?—looked over, saw that we had stopped shrieking (I didn't feel it, it didn't touch me, but I knew). Then the boys knew. They saw the look on Liz's and Dina's faces and everybody knew what the truth was: that our history had suddenly shifted, that all of life is packaged in moments and seconds and the uncontrollable.

The truth about the Aegean Sea and sharks is still a controversy. Some will say that there are no sharks in Greek waters, not anymore. Some say they are regularly in those waters, particularly sandtigers. Some agree that sharks come to the shores of the Cyclades Islands, but they are very rare, very few and far between. The ambiguity floats in the glass-clear water, what is fable or denial or reality is up to the swimmer.

The hush settled. Our arms and legs were still moving. It was Dina who started whispering first, a stream of frantic Greek bubbling out of her. And then like a crescendo, the furtive and frenetic syllables and vowels poured out in fluid fearful tones. I started to tabulate the boys, which were cousins, which were friends. *We should know how many are here.* I kept losing count because of Dina, her whisper, the fear in her words I did not understand. Liz was next to me, now on her back floating, staring at the ceiling of the cave. The cousins continued to whisper, looking like they were coming to an agreement. Liz was still close to me, and I held out my hand for hers, waiting. Then the olive-skinned boy, Kormos, looked at her with a fake sense of calm, but a very real desire to calm her—she could read it, she later told me. He whispered her name so she would look at him. He said to her slowly, enunciating his Greek so that she could understand, "We need to swim out. Slow. It's okay. Slow."

Liz shook her head *No* at him.

"What did he say?" I asked, shivering.

Liz did not know how to get past how her history had just switched and how a boy who did not speak English was going to lead her. The sun was setting, somewhere Liz's parents were thousands of miles away probably still playing bridge in the early-morning hours at their kitchen table with the Marquardts, somewhere Liz's grandparents were drinking Mythos beer with her Uncle Dominick—and there we were, with Dina who may or may not have had sex, her boy cousins, a shark or two or maybe none, and a boy named Kormos who would lead the way.

We all locked hands, all of us floating like a paper chain of people that young children make, softly kicking our way out of the cave and steadily back to shore. We piled into the cars in a frenzy and drove back to her grandparents', where, after thinking long and hard about what had touched her, Dina got glassy-eyed and silent and shivered uncontrollably. A flurry of cries and yells came from the family. *The hospital,* Liz said. *Dina's in shock.* We all piled into cars in confusion and in need—to not be alone. And it wasn't until an hour later, there in the emergency room with her grandmother, who chain-smoked cigarettes and kept yelling at her husband, that I noticed that Liz wasn't there. Neither was Kormos.

The next day, when we were lying on towels on the hot sand taking deep drags on Peter Stuyvesant cigarettes, Liz told me how she and Kormos, both in a state, had watched as the rest of us drove off in jeeps and a rusty Mercedes and on mopeds. Liz took Kormos by the hand and led him to the room we shared with Dina, and there, on Dina's bed, she touched his mouth and then tasted it. She softly bit his tongue. She took off her clothes and kissed his elbows and touched his thighs. So many firsts—sharks, one or two or none, and bodies—all of them shared with the olive-skinned boy who had led her out of the cave.

"I want to float in a cave," I said.

"But you'll be alone."

"It'll be okay."

"But you'll be alone."

9

KNIGHTON AVENUE

245 Knighton Avenue

THE PROBLEM IS THIS: A woman named Jessica St. James called my supervisor, Thadius. Jessica St. James lives at 445 Briton Ferry Lane. She has a single-family dwelling, a white Cape Cod with red shutters, neat grass, and dirty windows. According to Thadius, I asked her a question about emptiness. I remember this and, specifically, I asked her what she thought defined emptiness. She was short and sprightly, with copper-red hair in a crazy mess of curls. She had smooth lovely hands, and although she looked a little surprised at first, she answered my question as if I were a schoolteacher asking her to recite the ABCs. She looked nervous but eager to please, and she gave me an answer, tentatively—*It's when there's nothing left, when everything is gone. I think. I mean I know, but that sounds like an official definition to me.* Her answer was useless, and I made very little of it. But I underestimated her. Two days later, when I came to the office to hand in my daily counts, Thadius asked me to come into his office. I had been in the field for twelve days and Glyn Neath was becoming smaller and smaller.

"Anjou, we need to have a word," he said.

Thadius' demeanor is instructive and managerial, but cracks do appear. There are times when a softness billows out from the drill-sergeant shield. I enjoy this the most, when he is funny, even when he doesn't intend to be, in his earnestness to account for every single person in my town. I respect this immensely.

"My office," he said, and he pointed down the hall, signaling for me to walk first.

Horatio Mendelworth, I thought. A sweaty and eye-squinted man, too old for his young age in dress and demeanor and smell, a man who stared at my breasts and repeatedly asked me if I liked being an enumerator. Horatio's flesh was like that of a chicken, yellow, wet-looking. *What is your most painful childhood memory?* I had asked him.

"Anjou, I've received a complaint from a resident with whom you conducted an interview."

"What kind of complaint?" I asked with feigned innocence, thinking *Horatio, Horatio.*

"Apparently you asked a strange question," he said.

He started twirling his ballpoint pen with his fingers but didn't shift his gaze from mine.

"I don't recall asking a strange question," I said, telling myself that this was not a lie, because there is nothing strange about trying to get to the bottom of things.

"Well, apparently you did. Jessica St. James said you asked a question about emptiness."

"Emptiness? I don't understand."

"Nor did Jessica St. James. She did not understand why the United States government wants to know what she thinks about emptiness."

"Thadius, I ask people every day how many people live in their house. She must have misunderstood something."

"I'm not sure what you are trying to say."

"Well, when you have one person in a house, that could be interpreted as empty. Ten people in a house could be interpreted as full. Maybe she misread what I was asking her."

"I don't think so."

"Well, what did she say I specifically asked?" I huffed, trying to mask a slow shake that had begun in my legs.

"She didn't exactly say, although that's really not the point. She said you asked a strange question about emptiness. And, well, there are no strange questions on the Census Short Form."

"I don't remember this St. James person."

I like Thadius—and it dawned on me that Kip would love him—and I felt guilty lying to him.

"It's Jessica St. James," he said.

"I'm not sure what you want me to do, Thadius. I've been handing my forms in on time."

"Yes, I know. And they are always complete. Always neat. You follow up on your call-backs. You know the importance of closure."

"Then I'm not sure what you want me to say."

His shoulders caved a bit. I knew what he was thinking: *Not enough evidence. Performance otherwise flawless. Do nothing unless another complaint comes in.*

"I'm going to give you the benefit of the doubt. But I'm going to remind you again that the Census process—even with only the Short Form—is a sensitive process. Be careful of how you ask questions."

And here I am at 245 Knighton Avenue and I know I should take Thadius seriously, his warning. But a teenaged boy opens the door, and I know it is useless—I will need to talk to him. He is tall and lanky, with a stance that mixes swagger and stumble, living somewhere between boyhood and manhood with peachy hair sprouting from his chin.

"Is your mom or dad around?"

The boy walks away from the door, leaving it open, yelling *Dad*, stretching the word into many syllables. In that bellow, I can tell that he hates his father. This is my last house for the evening, and I am wearing a wool sweater with horizontal stripes of every imaginable orange. Quinn bought it for me when he went to Scotland with his former college roommates. I am able to wear a few cherished items that he gave me, that I held on to after he died: a ring made from a centuries-old Greek coin that he bought while in Corfu with his father; a choker necklace—pink leather with a tiny silver heart charm—that he bought at Harrods when we were in London, just so I could have a gift from Harrods. I hate Quinn for leaving me, and even more for dying. But it is impossible to hate our past, what we were, what we had, even the wrongness of our love. How can anybody hate all of that time? How else will we keep our hearts from going cold?

The boy's father comes to the door. He is middle-aged with a graying handlebar mustache and a beer belly that hangs over dirty blue jeans; a leather tool belt hangs low below his stomach. He has short and callused hands with stubby fingers, everything in his appearance is such contrast to the coltish nature of his son.

"Can I help you?" he asks.

"My name is Anjou Lovett and I'm from the United States Census. Do you have a few minutes to answer some questions?"

"Is this the law or something?"

"Technically you can refuse to answer the questions, but this will make it difficult for your local and state governments to make decisions about allocating resources effectively, fairly, and to the advantage of all citizens. It also potentially prevents your local and state governments from receiving monies that are reasonable based on population."

I raise my head and look at him. He is staring at me, bug-eyed and surprised. My spiel is formula at this point, although in Glyn Neath very few people resist the Census process and I rarely need to say it.

"Go ahead," he says.

One adult male—Brian Palmer, a plumber by trade, a fact he volunteers after telling me he is working on his own pipes for a change. *My son decided that he'd pour a bowl of lentil soup down the sink, even though the disposal is broken. So now instead of fixing just the disposal, I'm also unclogging the sink. He thought lentils were soft, that they'd go down just fine.* He has a wife and she is forty-three. Her name is Paula. They have three children: a seventeen-year-old daughter named Laurie and twin boys who are fifteen—Joshua, the lentil-soup culprit, and Jason. He suddenly remembers one more person—a seventy-seven-year-old woman named Beatrice. Paula's mother. *Almost forgot her, which is not necessarily a bad thing,* he says with a chuckle. They live in a gray stone house with a mother-in-law suite built over the garage. This apartment unit (that's what it is, according to the Census) needs special notation on the Short Form.

He is helpful and kind, signs the form, and goes inside. But it's the boy I want to talk to. He won't tell his mom or dad. Conspiracies are respected, hoarded almost, among the young. He is on the driveway shooting hoops at a net near the garage, and the only light for him is the glow from the mother-in-law suite.

I walk over, still clutching my clipboard. He stops dribbling and looks at me queerly.

"Did you need me to get you my dad again?"

"Actually I wanted to talk to you. I was wondering if I could ask you a question."

"Me?"

"Yes."

"Who are you?"

"My name is Anjou. I work for the United States Census."

"What's the Census?"

"You don't know?" I ask with a genuine smile.

"Why else would I ask you?" he says with a bit of edge.

"Oh, well, every four years, the government counts how many people are in the United States. They do other things, too, like asking questions about people's ages and what kind of homes they live in and where they work and how much money they make and what their ethnicity is."

"Did you ask my father how much money he makes?" he asks with a chuckle.

"No."

"Okay," he says nonchalantly, an honest indifference that makes possibility endless.

"What is it that you love most about your father?"

People never stop surprising me. The woman least likely to call Thadius calls Thadius. The woman most likely to call was the woman on Chestnut Street who called me a fucking lunatic and slammed her door shut when I asked her which loved one's death would she least be upset by. I wanted to tell her that people in Glyn Neath do not use the F-word in public, but I simply burst into tears on the sidewalk while walking to the next house.

He starts dribbling his ball again, recognizing the ease with which we should converse with the strangers of our neighborhood. He dribbles for a few moments, looking like he doesn't have a care in the world.

"He shows up," he says, throwing a shot that swooshed through the net.

"What do you mean?"

I have already been caught by Thadius. I am leaving for Capri in one month. My mortgage is paid this month and will be paid next month and the month thereafter, and Kip will take care of Lurch while I am gone. Stella loves me. My father is repositioned in my landscape, but not nailed down. I will talk with Grace—I will—and I will ask her where the book is that Quinn was reading when he died. There is less and less to lose here in my life; I see all the things that are already permanent. The freedom this affords me is breathtaking.

"I mean he shows up. To my basketball games. To my older sister's recitals, whatever they call it. Shit like that."

He is dribbling the ball, ignoring me almost.

"You are a wise person, you know that?"

"No, I'm not," he says, and he holds the ball and looks at me. "He's a prick. Trust me. But he shows up."

I walk away and take out my cell phone. The phone rings seven times before she picks up. This is the eleventh time I have called her this week. I still haven't said anything to her when I call. Quinn and Grace's friend Bernie, the psychiatrist, has been calling me and leaving messages on my voice mail at home—I have thrown out my answering machine and upgraded. His voice is a poker-faced vocal outreach, asking me to call him, telling me we should get together and talk, that he's been thinking a lot about Quinn lately. That is how I know Grace knows that it is me calling. She must be making a breakthrough, because Grace answers without a *Hello.*

"Anjou," she says.

⌒*⌒*

310 Knighton Avenue

Thadius would be mad at me. I am standing in front of the home of Gus and Angela Gunther, and I know them. I have sworn to Thadius that I do not know anybody in the section of Glyn Neath I am assigned to. I had forgotten about the Gunthers, mainly because I have not seen them in a long time.

They have a house so big you can't truly tell how many floors there are—there are upper decks and spires and a wraparound porch with ivy crawling up the beams. The home is painted a deep gray-blue with windows everywhere. Gus is a chiropractor, and Angela is a licensed massage therapist. They run their offices out of the third floor of their home, a staircase in the back leading to a separate entrance. For the first three months after Quinn moved in with me, I frequented the Guntherses' practice twice a week. Quinn always called them the back cracker and the body rubber.

"Anjou Lovett. Well, look at you," Gus says when he answers the door.

"You still recognize me," I say. I am thinner than I used to be, and my hair has been cut pixie-short with a black dye job. This was a superficial catharsis the week after Quinn died.

"I never forget a client. Never. It's freakish because I can barely remember my wife's birthday."

Gus himself is freakishly thin. Tall and angular with an emaciated look that comes from a fat-free raw-foods diet, exercise, no drinking, no smoking, and too many vitamins. His face resembles a grinning skeleton with skin stretched across it topped with downy reddish hair and a painfully protruding Adam's apple. Quinn used to say that Gus made good health look scary, that people should not be too skinny, especially women. *Who wants to go to bed with a bicycle?* he'd say when I complained about my thick waist and hearty inner thighs.

"Did you need to make an appointment? You could have just come in from the back. You know where it is," he says.

"Actually, I'm here about the Census," I say, flashing my enumerator ID. "You didn't fill out the forms that were mailed to you, so they send me here to get the information."

"I thought you were an accountant?" he asks with a confused look.

"I was."

"Okay. Well. Let's see. How about you come on inside," he says with a concern that he's futilely trying to mask.

"I was just making some tea. You look like you could use some—maybe a ginseng with freshly cut ginger root," he says, leaning in, cupping my chin with his hand, and inspecting my face. "My, my, you look, well—let me think how to phrase this—you look beleaguered."

I shrug my shoulders and walk into their living room. It is filled with modern Swedish furniture, all squares and rectangles, carefully arranged. Feng shui. *Old house, modern furniture. Balance,* Gus once said.

"I can see Veraguth's fold on your forehead," he says, sitting us on the couch and moving his thumb softly across the spot between my eyes.

"You can see what?" I ask.

"Veraguth's fold—it's a crease at the top of your nose, right between your eyebrows. It can indicate a couple of things—a major depressive episode or just a mild depressive affect. Sit down. I'll pour us tea."

Gus prepares me a glass of tea that tastes like tree bark. I feign pleasure, drink some, smile. We start going through the questions.

"We've added a third person to the household. She's three months old. Isabella."

"Congratulations," I say genuinely. I am relieved that, despite this surreal season of losing Quinn, I am able to understand that other people are being loved even when I am not. I feel less selfish than I know I am.

"Speaking of life changes, when are you and Finn going to take a stroll down the aisle of love?"

"It's Quinn."

"Yes, Quinn. Yes, he came here once. For a massage. He said he'd take a rubdown but not a crackdown. He was funny. So how is he?"

"He died. Over a month ago," I say, finalizing the data on the form, not even looking up at Gus because, really, I have little to say.

"What?" Gus asks.

I look at Gus sympathetically. I know that in my few words, Gus sees his world as sealed—he knows it is marvelous and fragile. That's the look on his face: he has received a sudden gift, and then the pity—and, more so, the relief——when somebody we know, even superficially, somebody young for all intents and purposes, dies.

"I'm so sorry, Anjou. I don't know what to say. What happened?"

"There was an accident."

"I'm so sorry. I didn't know. I had no idea. Are you okay? What kind of accident?" he asks, talking quickly, filling the void.

Be silent, I think. *You will feel better if you just be silent.*

"How is it possible that I didn't hear this? Nobody told me. I don't understand. Angela and I were at her parents' all last month—that's probably why. I must have missed when CoCo talked about him over the air."

Glyn Neath holds tight to ritual. A seventy-seven-year-old native of Glyn Neath, Miriam "CoCo" Oliver, reads the obituaries on the local radio station, AM 1080. CoCo is wealthy, eccentric, tightfisted, and loud. She has been reading the obits for over three decades. She curses like a sailor, smokes Pall Mall unfiltereds, and wears wigs with variety like neckties. She is short and thin, with leathery skin so yellow that I would tell Quinn she must certainly have jaundice. She comes on at 7 A.M., talks about herself, her bridge club, her dog Drift Wood, and then, without a single shift of her husky voice, launches into the obituaries, peppering each with her personal commentary. Quinn and I listened to CoCo in the mornings. Her approach was far from somber, less than dignified. CoCo kept life in that old sourpuss Death: *Well, my friends, I'm sorry to announce the passing of the always lovely, never late, and irrepressibly honest Ms. Eileen Caroline Jenkins of Aberdeen Station. She was quiet as a church mouse but damn didn't she make one mean ambrosia?* After Quinn died, I didn't turn on the radio for three weeks. I couldn't listen to his achievements and his alma mater and the absurdity of him being forty-one and dead.

"Why don't I go get Angela? She should be finishing up a session by now," Gus says, eyes wide and earnest.

"That's thoughtful of you, but I don't really want to talk about it."

I know it is unfair to ask a question of a man who loves his wife implicitly and is awash in fatigue and enamored by his newborn, every gurgle and shitty diaper and her clutches at Angela's breast. I look at Gus, a man who looks like he hasn't slept in days.

"Gus," I say, bittersweet and regretful already, "have you ever thought about leaving your wife?"

My father hasn't called me. It has been four days since he came to my house.

"It's out of respect," Stella tells me.

"Respect?"

"He doesn't want to make you uncomfortable. He's being unassuming, Anjou. You need to make the moves for now if you think you want a relationship with him. He's too respectful, and he thinks that he doesn't deserve anything from us."

"Maybe he doesn't," I offer.

"That's really up to you to decide."

When I was twenty-eight years old, I stopped hating my father. I didn't forgive him. I just stopped hating him.

"Don't you think ten years is long enough?" Stella had asked me after she invited our father back into her life.

She and Bruce had just married. They were still living in Philadelphia. Neither of us had spoken to our father in ten years, but the day after she and Bruce came back from their honeymoon in Quebec City, she called our father and announced that she was coming to visit. She showed up at his doorstep, holding tightly to Bruce's hand, presenting her new husband to him, and presenting herself as well. I look back now and realize that Stella, always confident and full of bravado, was petrified. She wasn't scared of our dad but of her husband, the permanence of her decision. She was twenty-three and the assertiveness and level-headedness and old-soulness of her could not prepare her for the gravity of her decision to get married. She was admittedly blinded by the belief that the two of them would make it and, furthermore, make it the right way.

She was also too bright for her own expectations and, when she got home after her honeymoon, she realized how she had set herself up to fail. Not wanting to fail, she went straight to our father, because he was the only one left. He could teach her a few things. Aunt Vicky was always available, always. She lived in Tucson with her second husband. But Stella needed her father for this one.

"I'm not full of posthoneymoon idealistic zeal right now, Stella," I had said, instantly regretting my bitter comment.

"I'm not telling you to reconcile with him. That's up to you when you want to, if you want to. I'm just telling you to stop hating him, if only for yourself. It uses up a lot of energy."

"I have plenty of reserves stored up."

"Anjou, you're wasting your time—"

For the first time ever, I hung up on my sister. For two days I wouldn't answer her phone calls and on the third day she showed up at my house at 6 A.M. and pounded on my door. Dazed and sleep-silenced and confused, she barreled through the door and cried hysterically for thirty minutes, telling me that I couldn't do that—that I must answer her calls, that I must always talk to her—no matter what. So I stopped hating my father that morning with Stella in my living room bawling. I stopped hating him—not for me, not for him, but for Stella.

"Stella, I don't know what I want," I say.

I am standing on Knighton Avenue in front of the Guntherses' house. Gus responded to my question with a calm nod, then went and got Angela, and they talked to me in a bubble of words and warmth about marriage and choices and learning to live with the feelings we don't—and do—act on.

"I feel bad for him," I say. "He looked sad. That messed every- thing up, you know, when he came here. He wasn't supposed to look so sad. I wanted to ask him questions, but I felt sorry for him."

"He's not always like that," she says knowingly. "This is hard for him, Anjou. Please don't think because he doesn't call that he doesn't want to hear from you."

So I call my father that day. We talk for less than five minutes, and I direct the conversation by asking him various questions about the book he is currently reading. (*Dispatches, by Michael Herr. Probably the single best book written about Vietnam, he says.*) I keep asking about the book, as I am fascinated by Vietnam—its war, its history from long ago, its people, and its landscape. I tried for years to convince Liz to go there with me. *The food there is going to totally upset my stomach. I don't want to spend three weeks drinking Coke and chewing Tums,* Liz said.

The next day I call him, and this time we talk for ten minutes. I time it on my stove clock. I tell him as much as I can about Lurch. I will myself to talk. He listens patiently as I detail the shots Lurch receives every year, the brand of dog food I use, the places Kip and I walk him, his hatred of golden retrievers and love for cats. And the next day I call again, momentum built. I am still working Knighton Avenue, and I think that I should meet with my father again before I reach Portmeirion Lane.

"Maybe we could have dinner," I say with nervous relief. I am committed in this season to get things done. "Tomorrow night?"

"I'll come to you. You don't have to drive into the city."

We decide on Pizza Hut. My father tells me that it is his new favorite place, that it has comfortable booths, that he likes their breadsticks. "There's a Pizza Hut on Route 18 across from the Germantown Savings Bank."

"I can pick you up," he says.

"You don't have to do that."

I do not want to be in the car with him and watch him drive. If he continues not being the way I knew him—eyes barely on the road and taking curves with a deft sense of the movement of objects across surfaces—I will be upset. I can't bear to think that he will drive with clenched hands, leaning forward.

"I want to," he continues.

"Why?" I ask, feeling the rush of annoyance in my breath.

"I want to meet your dog."

Lurch is my heart song, a refuge. He has been a barometer of my judgment for a long time: He loved Kip immediately, greeted Stella with feigned indifference, much like a cat, but instead of slinking away, you could see Lurch in the corner of the room looking up at her periodically to stare, quickly turning his head the minute she noticed. His respect for Stella—and careful love—is a tempered emotion doled out with a cool and even ease of heart. Lurch barks incessantly if he even smells my neighbor Warren, who lives across the street, so much as walking out his door. Warren is an immaculately dressed man with dark hair, bright blue eyes, and a heavy New York accent. He is an investment banker, amiable and polite; he drives a BMW and lives with a woman who is not his wife but she does not work. There is nothing about Warren that appears threatening or underhanded. But Lurch knows otherwise; he can detect an alarming character trait not visible to the rest of us. Lurch hated Quinn, for a very, very long time, but then he grew to love Quinn with an exhausted sort of defeat, a deep and resentful love that was passionate and confusing and left me jealous of its complexity.

"I told you that Lurch can be kind of cranky."

"That's okay, Anjou," he says, a reassuring tone that I have not yet heard.

"All right. You can pick me up," I say. "How about 8:30?"

"I'll see you at 8:30."

"Okay, then."

"What shall I bring?"

"You don't need to bring anything, Dad. Pizza Hut serves beer and wine."

It feels strange to call my father Dad. I really want to call him Jack, which seems more impersonal. But I don't because of something Stella told me when I asked her why she calls him Jack: *He is a different man than he used to be. He's not the dad I knew as Dad. Not that this is a good thing—or a bad thing—it simply is*, she tells me.

"I'd still like to bring something, Anjou," he says.

"Why?" I ask, frustrated at his insistence.

"Because you made me brownies."

When my father arrives at my house, Lurch is slightly agitated. He is not aggressive, but there is a quiver in the skin along his back. He barked when the doorbell rang, but after a firm *At ease* command, and a sense that there is no danger, Lurch retreated to the end of the hallway and sat with his haunches just inside the kitchen door.

My father surprises me, making no gestures toward Lurch, not even looking him the eye, but instead walking up to me and saying, "Your dog is handsome. Rather distinguished, actually."

I look over at Lurch, who is staring at my father, his head tilted in a question.

"He's old," I say.

"But distinguished."

"Yeah, I guess you could say so." I smile at Lurch.

"Being distinguished is something we all hope for with age," my father says.

In this very moment, I wish that Quinn were alive so I could introduce him to my father. Because I like that my father knows how to walk into the room with a cranky border collie who's missing half of his left ear and not look him in the eye. Because I am thankful for this one gesture my father has made. Because he does not look sad, and this lifts a burden from me. Because, in a sweep, Quinn would have gotten my father seated comfortably on the couch in the living room. He'd be touching my father in small ways, taking his coat off, a hand on the shoulder, things like that. Quinn would point at me and say, *Dearest Pear, why don't you mix your father a drink?* I wouldn't have to do much. Quinn would handle this for me; he knew how to work a room, make every person feel at ease, important. I don't know how to put anybody at ease and I'm not sure where to begin redefining this loyalty that through the course of my years has gone from hatred to indifference to curiosity.

"It doesn't appear that he's going to bark at you," I say.

"Or bite, I hope."

"If he was going to bite, he'd have done so by now."

My father and I smile at each other.

"Maybe next time he'll let me pet him," my father says.

He has still not looked my dog in the eye. My father can be very smart.

"Maybe," I say.

"I brought you something," he says.

"You didn't have to do that."

"I wanted to. Here," he says, handing me a rumpled brown paper bag, the kind you pack lunches in for school or work.

It is a copy of Vera Brittain's *Testament of Youth*, an autobiography by a woman who was a nurse in the First World War.

I don't tell my father that I've read it several times. That it was assigned my sophomore year of college in a European history class I took. That I keep a copy under my bed. Because if I tell him it may make him feel bad but, worse yet, it may make me talk about what it was like reading that during college, about a war in Europe and the war inside my heart all mixed together. I decide that I will read it again, that maybe I'll get something different out of it.

"Thank you. That was very thoughtful," I say.

I touch my father's arm then because I am certain that this is something Quinn would do—or would make me do. I put on my coat and as we walk to the door I see that Lurch has moved from the end of the hallway. He is now in the doorframe from the hall into the living room, staring at us.

"See ya, old man," I say, and his tail sways back and forth on the smooth worn floor.

My father drives much the same way he did while I was growing up, fast and confident, understanding the touch of the wheels on the road. But he is quiet and looks straight ahead, alert and attentive, his eyes on the traffic and the cars around him instead of on me. In the restaurant we order breadsticks and a large pepperoni pizza. I order a glass of wine and listen to my father talk about the differences between Coke and Pepsi. The quiet nervousness that my father displayed when he was at my house two weeks ago has been lifted. He is far from exuberant, but he is talking.

I have the list of questions for him in my purse, still folded (but they have been read and reread, twice almost amended, and then refolded). What I want are his memories. I have to ask him in the form of a question, but really I just want to say to him directly: *I want your memories.* Quinn spoke like this—cutting past language and form and structure, saying something too broad and intensely specific at the same time. *I want your memories.* If Quinn had said that to me I could have talked for hours.

"I'm going to Capri," I say, because this seems like the closest I can get to his memories.

"I heard about this," he says, handing me a plate with a piece of pizza on it.

"Stella told you?"

"Yes, she did."

Stella is connecting all of us and this is a relief, for her to take some of the burden.

"How long are you going for?"

"A month."

"Why did you choose Capri?"

"I was hoping you could tell me."

631 Knighton Avenue

Some houses are deceiving. They look big but are small, or vice versa. This house appears dwarfed by the blockish and thick-stoned homes on either side, homes with three or four stories and rows of windows and shutters, homes that have floors closed off during the winter. This house is narrow, faded yellow paint job on the wood, two stories, with a long slate roof. But if you walk to the side of the house, you see that the narrow structure stretches back farther than you can imagine. An elderly man—wobbly and thin—answers the heavy door, and he is buffered by a thin screen door. I can smell him through this screen, a mixture of lemons and cigarette smoke and urine.

"Good afternoon, my name is Anjou Lovett, and I work for the United States Census. A completed form was not—"

"Look at you," he says with a wide grin.

I smile back, knowing I'll get a completed Short Form out of this interview but nothing more. I have sized up this man: he is a fruit loop, a crackpot, a man who will talk about nothing for a long, long time. In a little over a month I will be floating in the grotto. It is April 24, and the coolness from spring's start is finally gone.

"Julia. Julia. Julia," the man says, shaking his head as if he's been wondering where I've been.

"I'm sorry, sir, my name isn't—"

"Your mother is making lemon cake," he says.

He tries to open the screen door, but it is locked.

"Thomas, who are you talking to?" a woman asks, coming up behind him.

"Julia is here," he says to her, grinning widely.

"I'm, I'm, uh—"

"Spit it out, dear," the woman says, holding the man's hand.

"I think your husband has mistaken me for someone else. My name is Anjou, and I am here for the Census," I say, flashing my laminated badge.

"She's here, Gertie. Julia's here."

"I'm so sorry," she says, still holding her husband's hand upright and rubbing it between her two hands.

"Let her in, Gertie. Please move over and let her in."

"Perhaps I should come back another time? We can schedule a call-back," I offer.

I can't look at her husband now.

"Come in," the man yells at me, then looks over at his wife. "Gertie, move over and let her in."

"If you come back this time tomorrow, my husband will be at the Senior Center."

"Four o'clock then?" I say, and I am feeling ashamed.

"Perfect," she says with a warm grin.

"I know who you are," he says, his voice rising as I turn to go down the footpath.

He continues calling to me through the screen door as the first sob comes. Old people make me think of my father. And my father makes me think of Quinn. I am outside and a man is yelling at me. I love to be outside. I am starting to cry and it is dark and I am alone but surrounded by my neighborhood, my grief diluted by the air, and I still have a question, one that I wanted to ask the moment I noticed that their house only looked small but really stretched on.

⌒ff⌒

It was a secret. The Blue Grotto poem. It was a hope fulfilled, a promise made good. Where my mother wanted to honeymoon. My father told me as we sat in the Pizza Hut booth. The summer before our mother died, her dream of swimming in the grotto was realized, an escape to the marriage they both wanted and from the marriage they lived. When they went, Stella and I were at Camp Tweedale in the Poconos. Stella was bunking with five other eleven-year-old girls, corraling them for scheduled and unscheduled events with the mastery and command of any adult counselor. I was a junior counselor, having spent the first three weeks of June at Camp Tweedale every year since Stella was five years old. That year was our first year together; Camp Tweedale for three weeks in June and the Shore for the month of August had been a reliable summer rhythm. That year, our father was living with Maggie at the time we left for Camp Tweedale. I had recently acquired my driver's license and tried to convince our mother to let me do the driving when Aunt Vicky took us up there.

"You're too young to drive the turnpike. Besides, Stella wants to take the bus up there with all the other kids, so both of you can ride it."

"There's no way I'm going to take the bus, Mom. I'm a counselor now."

"A junior counselor."

"A counselor is a counselor, and counselors don't ride to Camp Tweedale in a yellow school bus."

Our mother hated long drives. She liked her world to have readily marked perimeters, landmarks that were not of a commercial nature: the poplar tree at the top of the hill on South Mansion Road, the broken-down and never-to-be-removed black Gremlin at the end of Sutton Mill Road, the giant rooster statue at the entrance of Nor-View Farms.

Stella would have none of it, insisting on going in the yellow bus.

"Do not deprive me of an authentic camping experience," Stella said, hands on her hips.

"I suppose I can't say No to such an articulate argument," my mother responded, laughing at Stella.

"I'm going on the bus," she demanded.

"Yes, it appears you are," my mother said, suppressing more giggles.

So Aunt Vicky drove me to Camp Tweedale. I asked her questions about her dates, her job, about sex. She gave me detailed and informative—albeit tempered—answers. She was spirited and wild—*a real kook,* our father would say with a warm and loving tone—but she knew when to be an adult. And for this I will always be grateful, for after our mother died she was our version of Newfoundland, our island of rock and fortitude, atop which life and greenery could flourish.

And it was Aunt Vicky who would mail letters to us every three days during those weeks at Tweedale when our parents were in Capri, a time of year when the island has the best weather and the fewest tourists. Camp Tweedale had a strict policy: no telephone calls home unless there was a medical emergency. It was before the world was connected technologically, and a child quickly adjusted to the sounds of the wood, the symphony of crickets and the creaking of tree branches overhead while hiking, the delicate pitter-patter of inchworms dropping onto the leaf-covered trails. We were allowed to receive letters and we were required to write to our moms and dads twice a week. Our Aunt Vicky's handwriting was identical to our mother's, and she had masked her tone to match that of our mother. Our mother's letters were practical and pointed—but at the end would be three or four sentences of a bittersweet love-burst, an escaped desperation in her desire for us to know that we were her glorious escapade, her only true goal. Our father added poems in the form of postscripts, futilely attempting to find words that rhymed with *mosquitoes* and *s'mores*. My father had written these postscripts on twenty sheets of writing paper so that Stella and I wouldn't suspect anything.

"You weren't even living with us at the time Stella and I left for camp. What made you two decide to go to Capri?"

"She needed me."

"Well, didn't she always need you?" I asked, a bit incredulous.

"Yes, yes, she did. But sometimes she needed me more."

"Why? What happened?"

"She called me up at work one day and said *Jack, we need to do something about this mess. Can we go swim in the Grotto first?*"

"So you took her to Capri?"

"Yes, because she asked me to. She said she wanted to make a good memory before stepping over the line."

"What line?"

"The line of her perimeter. You know your mother, she kept a small world. Geographically, emotionally. She wanted to get a divorce."

"She hadn't wanted that before?"

"No. Not at all. She didn't want to do it alone."

"But she did sort of do it alone."

"It's what she wanted, Anjou."

"You make it sound like it's her fault."

"I'm not saying that, not at all. But it's the deal we made. It's how we worked things out."

"People don't do that, Dad. They don't love two people at the same time."

"They do, Anjou. They do. I am sorry for what we—especially I—did to you and your sister."

"So obviously Mom didn't ask for a divorce."

"No, she decided that wasn't what she wanted after all. She wanted different things after that," my father said, and he looked out the window at the cars in the parking lot.

"I hope I see more clearly than she did when I swim there, Dad. I really do."

"Me, too," he said, and his eyes were teary and I just didn't know what I should ask, or if I would get answers when I dove into the Tyrrhenian Sea.

When Stella and I got home from Camp Tweedale that year, our father was living at home again. Our parents were both very tan, and Stella asked our mother if she had been sunbathing.

"Your father and I went to the Shore for the weekend," she said nonchalantly.

"The water was quite blue, wasn't it, my dear?" our father said to our mother while he swung Stella upside down by her legs, making her shriek with joy and beg him to put her down. She wanted to show him things from her time at Tweedale—a tiny birdhouse made from twigs she had collected, a butterfly wing she had unearthed from under a small patch of leaves next to her cabin.

"The Jersey Shore isn't blue, Dad. It's green. Puke green," I said.

I was actually less hostile than I sounded and I was angry only because I was actually glad to see him there. There was less swallowing required when I wasn't glad to see him, less of a front I would put on for my mother's sake. Our parents were not beating us or depriving us or in any real way neglecting us; they were making decisions, and Stella and I did our best to live with them. I was glad my father was there for one solitary reason—the express purpose of not telling him or anybody, except Liz, that I had given my virginity to a fellow counselor, a boy named Ishan, a half-Indian, half-Caucasian seventeen-year-old who lived in Germania, tucked in the hills on the border of New York. I thought he was snobby during the first week but soon discovered he was shy, and more than anything I wanted to know how a half-Indian boy had wound up in Potter County, in an area of the state my father always called God's country. Ishan never answered my question, but he helped me with others, and I was smug with my own secret.

"No, my dear, my pet, my pear. It is not green, not any green there. If there's one thing that is true, in June the water is most certainly blue," he said, walking over to our mother, who wasn't smiling but whose face was rested, at ease. Our father put his hand on her hip and with his other hand turned her face, a soft kiss to her cheek.

"Your rhyme is lousy," I said, seeing a fleeting moment of my father looking wounded.

"Anjou, apologize to your father," my mother said.

I stared at both of them for a long time, until my gaze made my mother uncomfortable. Then I left the room.

My parents stayed in Anacapri and every morning they spent hours exploring: Villa Jovis, a fortress on the northern section of the island that is reached by a long walk up narrow streets; Augustus's Gardens, which lead to a view of I Faraglioni, enormous gray jagged sea rocks—like vertical islands—jutting up through the water to implausible heights. When the sun started to set, they climbed down a metal staircase they reached from a small swim club built into the side of the cliff face. They stood on a small grated platform at the bottom of the cliff, where the ripple of the sea lapped at their feet. On most days there were a handful of tourists swimming with them. But on their last day there, it was empty. In the cave my mother swam nude.

"What was it like?"

"You'll soon see for yourself," my father said.

"I know, but what was it like for the two of you?"

Our pizza was now cold, the cheese and grease congealed and hardened. My father had taken only one bite of his. I had not touched mine.

"Your mother wanted a memory that was nobody else's but ours."

"I always liked your poem, about the Grotto and gelato."

"I liked that, too."

"Your rhymes annoyed me, all the time. I never believed what you were saying."

"I didn't either, Anjou."

"But I believed you when you talked about the Grotto."

My father put his hands on the table and nodded at me. We didn't talk for a few minutes. Four minutes. I watched the face of his digital watch.

"Does Stella know about you and Mom going to the Grotto?" I asked.

"No."

"Did you tell anybody else?"

"Of course not," he quickly answered.

"Not even Maggie?"

"No, Anjou. Not even Maggie."

"She's dead. Isn't she?"

"Four years ago," he said and I could see him try to stay stone-faced. He looked scared, though.

"Stella told me."

I stood up and went to the salad bar, picking up a wet warm plate, and I began to pile broccoli and shredded carrots and chick-peas and red cabbage on my plate. I was not going to eat the salad, but I could not sit in the red-seated booth with the two women my father had loved dead. I held a memory of my mother, so in love with my father, their time in clear waters where everything else did not matter, where my mother would not use a grotto to start the end of their marriage—a grotto she wanted to start their begin-ning—but instead for it to be a safe spot in the near-end of their marriage. I kept piling the plate up—cucumber slices and cherry tomatoes—and I was stirring up the bucket of buttermilk ranch dressing as the tears begin to fall down my face. So I stayed there for a few minutes crying, until I had swallowed enough of all of these histories to be private enough to go back there, back to the puffy booth where my father sat waiting.

It is 1 A.M., and I am just back from a run. Since Quinn died I mostly run late at night, when only the insomniacs and the drunks in front of their televisions are awake. Glyn Neath goes to sleep early, so the roads and trees and smells are all mine. It is safe to run here, no streetlights but still safe, and sometimes I pass an old man walking his dog or teenagers who have probably snuck out of their houses. We nod at each other. Kip tracks my movements. He comes over late at night when I am back from running, sharing a nightcap with me, retelling old stories I've heard for years. The stories change—the people, the moonlight, the quality of air, the ocean's stir—with each telling. Sometimes when I get home from a night run, he is already there with Lurch, the two of them stretched out on the couch watching television. Sometimes Quinn and I would find him in the morning asleep on the couch with Lurch; Kip would insist on making the coffee, telling Quinn he made it too weak. Kip has a sixth sense, never intruding on Quinn and me during private or difficult moments, smelling a fight or a need for passion, politely departing before Quinn and I even knew that we would come to blows or skin to skin.

"So you've been asking some strange questions around town," Kip says, pouring scotch into two tumblers.

"What are you talking about?" I say, dropping my keys on the coffee table and kissing him and Lurch.

"You knew I'd catch wind of this," he says, handing me a glass.

"It's all under control," I say.

I am still breathing hard and sweating, but I take a large gulp of the scotch.

"Asking Meredith Slavosky if during her honeymoon she was plagued by thoughts of having made a mistake tells me you've got nothing under control, kid."

"When did you hear about this?"

"Two nights ago. Surprised it wasn't sooner."

"And you're just bringing it up now?"

"Wanted to see if there was much more to it, asked around a bit."

"Did you hear this firsthand from Meredith or did someone else tell you? Truths become fiction around here, you know that."

"Heard it firsthand. I gave her my bar stool at Reilly's. She told me the whole story."

"Shit," I say softly, shaking my head, wondering if she'd call Thadius.

"She thought it was funny. She did an imitation of you, Anjou. Standing there holding a clipboard."

"As long as she didn't call Thadius."

"If not her, God knows somebody else has."

"Somebody called Thadius about me last week."

"Who?"

"It doesn't matter, Kip," I say exhaustedly.

"What street?"

"Briton Ferry," I say, giving up because he'd find out anyway.

"Let me guess . . . Lon Nussmeier?"

"Try again," I say.

"Jessica St. James?"

"Bingo."

"She's a skittish lady. Holds her own well, but the minute you turn your back, watch out."

"So I learned."

"I don't know what the hell you are up to, and I'm not going to lecture you while you're going through all of this with Quinn and your dad, but—"

"This has nothing to do with my father."

"Okay. Okay. But listen, you need to be careful. This may be Glyn Neath, where eccentric behavior is socially acceptable, but asking personal and philosophical questions on people's doorsteps is pushing the envelope a bit."

"I own property here, they can't exactly evict me."

"They can arrest you."

"Please, Kip. Spare me."

It seems unlikely—even to me, two weeks after I began enumerating—that Glyn Neath's residents are not up in arms about my behavior or reporting me in a string of calls to Thadius. Those who are noncompliant in answering my extra question seem tolerant on the most part, angry or annoyed, perhaps, but tolerant. Only Jessica St. James has called Thadius. I think Glyn Neath—its very body, its Welsh beginnings, its homes, its gargantuan old trees hanging like a canopy over the streets—has whispered in the ears of its townspeople to be still, to let me listen. And even those few people who get angry understand that I still get it right. I make it clear that they matter, that they are accounted for, and I think they appreciate this. I want to explain all of this to Kip, but I am too tired and he is too concerned.

When Kip leaves, after more scotches than necessary, I call my father. It is 3 A.M., and I wake him up.

"Dad, it's me," I say.

"Hello?"

"It's me. It's Anjou."

My father coughs and the sound rattles me. He doesn't smoke anymore, but it sounds as if he does. He has already had one heart attack. He had bypass surgery. Triple or quadruple. He changed his habits.

"Anjou, is everything okay? I, I, I didn't know you were going to call."

"Am I allowed to ask you any question I want?"

"What do you mean?"

"Am I allowed to ask you any question I want?"

"Yes. Of course you can. Anjou, hold on for a moment. I need to find my glasses so I can turn on the light."

"No, Dad. I don't want to talk anymore. Not tonight. I'm sorry I woke you up," I say sincerely.

"Don't be sorry, Anjou."

"But I am."

"Anjou, listen—"

"I've got to go, Dad," I say, and I hang up the phone and I fall into a drunken sleep.

Stella calls me fifteen minutes later. It is 4:15 A.M. in Newfoundland, an hour later than East Coast time because that island of rock pushes farther east into the Atlantic Ocean.

"Why the hell are you calling me so early? What happened?"

"You tell me," she says curtly.

"I don't know what you're talking about."

"Why are you calling Jack at 3 o'clock in the morning, worrying him like that?"

"Did he call you?"

"Yes. He was upset, Anjou. Said you called and asked him if you could ask him anything you want. What's this all about?"

Stella is the most consistent person I know. Once I let my father into my life again, I realized the depth to which Stella had already done so. She is—as she is with everyone she loves—fiercely protective.

"First of all, Stella, I apologized to him. I said I was sorry. Second of all, if he was that worried, he could have called me back."

"He did, you idiot. You just didn't hear the phone. Anjou, what the hell is going on? If you want to ask him a question, just ask him a fucking question. But don't call him up at 3 A.M. drunk and asking him if you can ask him anything."

"Fine, Stella. Got your point. I don't really want to talk right now, okay? I need to go back to sleep. I'm working tomorrow—or today—whichever it is."

"That's the other thing I want to talk to you about."

"What do you mean?"

"I spoke to Kip."

"When did you talk to Kip?"

"Yesterday."

"I'm going to kill that son of a bitch."

"I'm not going to let you sink, Anjou."

"I'm not sinking."

"Yes, Anjou, you are. I have not wanted to push you too much because this is your grief. I know this. I would never try to tell you how to mourn Quinn. Never. I wanted you to ride this out in whatever way you needed to. But I'm seriously worried."

"You should be," I say, hanging up her, because I love my sister, but I cannot change her ways and she cannot change mine.

I count my breaths and watch the clock for over three hours. I start counting Lurch's breaths as he sleeps next to me. Finally it feels safe. Everything is ready. I have held it all in and it's excruciating, keeping this bursting grief locked in my heart and throat, locked here in my house. I have to get outside, I have to go get something to eat, I have to get to the French Bakery. I am in my pajamas—a tee-shirt that Quinn and I got from running in a 10-K over the holidays, the Jingle Bell Run, Conshohocken, it said. Quinn was always a much faster runner, but he stuck with me during the race that year, talking the entire time, sometimes running backward next to me just to keep warm because my pace was so slow. He sang "Jingle Bells" to me until I screamed at him, and then he let me cross the finish line first. The bakery will be just open— maybe not quite yet—and I will walk in wearing pajamas, because this has to come out of me, and the kind French couple and the young girl behind the counter will let me in.

411 Knighton Avenue

"What did it feel like when Mom died?" I say into my father's answering machine. This is the first question on the list. My father bought the answering machine after I stopped hanging up on him. And I finally set up voice mail on my cell phone. I am on the corner of Knighton and Sompton Avenues. It is April 25.

I ring the doorbell of 411 Knighton Avenue. A middle-aged woman with curly brown hair, dark red lipstick, blue jeans, and a baggy tee-shirt emblazoned with large lettering that says *Branson, Missouri,* answers it.

"Good afternoon, my name is Anjou Lovett and I'm from the United States Census."

She grins widely at me, nodding her head up and down, pulling at my jacket to bring me inside.

"Yes, Ms. Lovett, tell me, how can I help you today?"

"A Census form was sent to your house for completion but it was never received. I need to ask you a few questions—"

"Ask away," she says. "I'm all ears."

"Do we know each other?" I ask, feeling nervous at the way she is staring at me.

"No, no, we never met," she says with spark.

People are not gleeful in Glyn Neath. They are nosy and kind and cranky and selective and quirky and odd and compassionate and impassioned. This is a town that embodies intimacy and all of its foibles. It has ghosts and cobwebbed corners. It is a place to marry and have babies and walk dogs and die in your own living room with friends and family around you in a comforting haze. But it is not a fun place to be, certainly not gleeful. And gleeful people like her are the serial killers of the world, Quinn would say.

And this is why Helen Calloway of 411 Knighton Avenue makes me nervous. She is so excited to see me that I know she has nothing to offer me.

"Thank you for your time, Mrs. Calloway. If you could just sign here," I say after asking the perfunctory questions.

"That's it?" she asks, a look of disappointment on her face. "You don't have any other questions?"

"Um, no," I say.

"But surely you have some more questions."

"No, I don't," I say, and my cell phone begins to ring.

"You had more questions for Emily Smith."

I look at my phone. It is my father's number.

"I'm sorry, excuse me?" I ask, suddenly worried that the bravery I had felt asking my father that question was not backed up by readiness to get an answer.

"Emily Smith. You had more questions for her," she says like a petulant child.

Emily Smith, 560 Sompton Avenue. I asked her if she'd ever prayed for somebody she hates.

"Now, what kind of question is that?" Emily Smith had said, crossing her arms and asking me to repeat myself.

"Did you ever pray for somebody you hate?" I repeated.

"Now, that'd be ridiculous to pray for somebody you hate, although I'm willing to bet that's exactly who you should be praying for. That's the craziest Census question I ever heard. That's not even a Census question, is it? It's not. Should I be calling your boss about this kind of question?"

"I'd prefer you wouldn't."

"What do I get out of it?" she said, arms crossed in a most unprayerful way.

"I have some gum in my purse," I said, deadpan.

"What flavor?"

"Teaberry."

Emily Smith opened her hand, popped the gum into her mouth, and told me about a friend she hated who had then gotten sick whom she still hated who died whom she still hated. And so on.

"I should get an extra question, too," Helen says. "I don't think this is fair, Ms. Lovett. Can I call you Anjou?"

"Yes."

"Anjou, I would like a question."

My phone has stopped ringing and I wonder what my father said. If he asked me to call him. If he broke: tears or shouts or spits of frustration and my failure to reengage with him in a manner that is more efficient, more linear, more straightforward. Maybe he just answered the question, there on my voice mail.

"Are your parents still alive?" I ask Helen.

"That's too easy. I want a question like some other people are getting. I want a question about prayer or pain."

"I'm getting to that," I say. "Are your parents still alive?"

Helen stands up straight. I am not wise or important or profound, but she recognizes the importance of paying attention to people who come to collect data.

"No, my parents are not alive. Both of them died years ago."

"Did you get along well with your parents?"

"Well, when I was younger I did, but after I had children it was my father who I was actually closest to."

"What about your mother?"

"Well, my mother and I sort of drifted," she says.

She's starting to look uncomfortable. This happens: We dig. The bones are ugly. I'm going to give her that extra question. Forensic accounting and Census enumerating have taught me how transparent people are: Helen Calloway probably very nearly hated her mother in her later years. She is probably guilt-ridden because of this. She probably doesn't really want to talk about this because then she'll have to think about it and, if she thinks about it, the fear will set in. The fear of knowing she could have handled it differently, she could have tolerated her mother's annoying habits and forgiven her questionable ethics and infuriatingly bad decisions. And a bigger fear of Helen's: that her own children will one day choose to drift from her, that they have inherited a legacy of how to forge forward in this world.

I am standing on Knighton Avenue. Helen was very upset with me and, after listening to my father's message—*Please call me, Anjou*—I stand on the sidewalk in front of Helen's house crying. A man walking his dog on the other side of the street calls out, asking if I'm okay. I nod my head *Yes,* and he keeps walking, looking back at me several times. I call Stella, who is in her car.

"Is the baby in the car?"

"Yes, why?"

"Then slow down," I say.

"I'm not speeding."

"So what, you're on the phone while driving. Slow down."

"Fine. I'm driving slowly. What's going on?"

"I left Dad a strange message. Well, it's not really strange because he said I could ask him anything I want. But maybe it's strange."

"What did you say in the message?" Stella asks, her voice preparing to stay calm.

"I asked him what it felt like when Mom died."

"I think I need to make another visit out there, Anjou."

"No, you don't," I say.

"That's probably an upsetting question for Jack," she says with tired resignation. She starts to cry.

"You will not discover who he is now, why he and our mother—remember that, Anjou, he *and* our mother—made the decisions they made, if you just ply him with these types of questions. We don't reenter people's lives with calculable explanations."

"Why not?"

"Because we don't," she says, crying in great chunks of heaves. Stella wants my life to be smoother than I will let it be.

"Think about Quinn, Anjou. He was your life and he had your heart and you knew everything he did wrong and you loved him anyway. You chose to love him, regardless. It was complicated. It was difficult to explain. You know as well as I do that you will not get any answers from Quinn and that you will forgive him anyway."

"Quinn is dead—of course I'm not going to get any answers."

"If he wasn't dead, you still wouldn't get any. And you'd have to figure out how to forgive him, and yourself."

"I would have gotten answers. Lily did. He told me."

"Lily was his wife."

"So what?"

"She was his wife. She would naturally get answers. When you are married one day, you will understand."

"Please, Stella, don't give me this sanctimonious bullshit that I wouldn't get any answers because I wasn't part of the Married Club. Do you really think you've got greater insight into Mom and Dad's marriage because you are married?"

"Yes," she said calmly.

I hear Merry start to cry in the background.

"Anjou, Dad's past is not ours."

"Yes, it is. What are you talking about?"

"Dad will never remember it the same way you and I do. He will never see it the same way we do. Even if he's sorry. Even if he apologizes every day for the rest of his life, his past is not ours."

"Then I want to know his."

"You'd better be sure you do."

"I've got to go, Stella. I'm going to call Dad."

"Okay," she says, sniffing through a cry that has calmed.

She will never let me sink, but I think she's starting to have faith that I will navigate this gap season.

"It's me," I say when my father picks up the phone.

"I'm glad you called."

"You said I could ask you anything. That's why I left that message. It's a question I have."

I wish more than anything I could be like Stella and talk directly to him instead of his answering machine, instead of clinging to a numbered list. I wish I could repeat the question—*What did it feel like when Mom died?*—now that he is on the phone. But I am not Stella. And I am not a wimp. I am not chicken shit. I just don't see the world in a forceful direct way: I don't communicate in the up-front and black-and-white manner with people I love. It is why I loved Quinn, because his life was revealed in twists of words, lending his viewpoint to interpretation. I could read the language of his life, the way words were more than they seemed.

"You can. You can ask me anything."

"But then I'll just keep asking you more questions. And Stella just told me that I won't get the answers I want or need if I go at you like that," I say, starting to cry.

There are birds in the bushes beside me. They are chirping, a fluttering playful sound. I don't know what kind of birds they are. Quinn would know. He knew the details of my neighborhood, of the architecture of the homes, of the timetables on which the trains ran. He knew the name of the dry cleaner's granddaughter—Chung He—and he would remind me to say *Hello, Chung-He* to her whenever I was in there because if you see a nine-year-old girl in a store like that all the time, it means she has to be there. *Show her something,* Quinn said. He noticed that kind of stuff. He would know the name of the birds in the bushes that make this chortling sound while I cry on the phone with my father.

"You can ask me anything you want," my father says again.

"It's not going to fix anything. Will it?"

"No," he says.

"I'm going to go home. I need to go home because I'm outside crying."

"Do you want me to come get you?"

"No."

"Are you sure?"

"No," I say.

My father sits just listening to me sob over the phone for a very long time.

~

416 Knighton Avenue

I almost said something to Grace when I called her today. She's much braver than my father was when I first started calling. She's been saying my name and offering up questions—*Do you want to talk, Anjou? Do you want to meet for coffee? Are you okay?* She's actually making this more difficult. Today she said something new—it's amazing, she does not get frustrated with me, at all—she said, *We can figure this out, Anjou.* That actually scared me. I wondered if she is telepathic. Grace never calls me back; she knows she doesn't have to.

I stood for a long time in front of 416 Knighton Avenue before ringing the doorbell. This is Dana Jayson's house. A run-of-the-mill boxy twin, painted pale blue, white shutters. The roof looks like it could use some work. The porch is nice. She has painted it white and stenciled daisies and ivy patterns across the railing. She lives here with her fiancé, Kirk, and their three dogs—standard poodles. They are ginger-colored and skittish and circle Dana's legs. The house is a mess. Dana seems unfazed by this fact and invites me in anyway. She is my age; I can tell by the just-blossoming crow's feet at her eyes, by her hands, by the way one hand rests contentedly at the small of the back. I am not getting very far with this question about dead mothers. Helen Calloway shook when I asked her, and then she slammed the door on me. She was so eager to get a personal question, and it was what I gave to her. I'm certainly not willing to let people screen the questions. I'm the enumerator. But she will figure out in about an hour that she actually wants to answer the question and she will probably think about how she can find me. People in Glyn Neath are industrious, and by tomorrow she will be on the phone with Thadius. Helen may be the person who will get me fired.

Dana Jayson is beautiful—she has long thin arms and pale skin and a long oval face and her hair is limp—but she is beautiful. So many people are. It has nothing to do with thinness or curves in the right places or the kind of clothes they wear or the clarity of their eye. The happy and contented people I meet on this job glow. They answer questions willingly, even the personal ones; when you are that content with your life, it is very, very hard to be offended by strangers who politely ask you probing or philosophical questions. When you are that content, questions about your love for your mother or the complexities of commitment—they do not leave you shocked and defensive.

Dana is bent at the knees, soothing her nervous dogs, and she spends the few minutes I need to answer questions about the house and the structure and who lives there besides the owner— and their ages

"Do the dogs count?" she asks with a lopsided grin.

"Dogs always count in my world."

"Oh, so I can get them added to that Census form?" she asks with a laugh.

"Probably," I say without laughing.

Helen may get me fired, and so I add the three dogs as Dana's children.

"How old are the dogs?" I ask.

Dana starts laughing.

"I was just kidding."

"I'm not."

"Holy shit, you are serious. I wouldn't think an enumerator would lie on the form. I thought that was our job—to do all the lying."

"How old are the dogs?"

"They're all five years old. They're from the same litter," she says, grinning at me.

I make notes, remarking on their witty names—Nina, Pinta, and Santa Maria. I have enrolled Dana. She now is connected with me on a small universal level—loving dogs.

"What gender?"

"Nina and Santa Maria are female, and Pinta's a boy."

I sign my name on the completed Census Short Form and hand it to her to sign. She has a neat, stretching signature.

"What's the most hurtful thing you've done to another person?"

She looks up at me.

"Excuse me?"

"What's the most hurtful thing you've done to another person?"

She looks angry, but I am ready for this. It's only the initial response. I am hoping she'll move past it. I am relying on the looseness of her long arms and the confidence of her signature as signs that her internal barometer will adjust to this invasive pressure. I stare at her, and my eyes are pleading. Time is closing in. Stella may show up on my doorstep clutching her baby and pulling me by my shirtsleeves out of my house, into a car, and onto a plane to Newfoundland, where she will sit next to me the whole ride and explain exactly how I am going to get over Quinn and exactly how I will make sense of my choice to love him and how, no, really, truly, I have not become our mother. I have little time before Kip straps me to my sofa and is angry with me. He has never once raised his voice but it's coming soon, it will come out of frustration and a sense that only action—physical action—will ensure that the path to self-destruction is halted. I have little time until my father starts giving me answers to the questions I have yet to ask—he is starting to remember the type of daughter I am. He is an old man and now is the time of his discontent, of his pain, and he wants me in his life. There is not a lot of time until I am at the Grotto swimming in clear cave water and I am holding on to hope that Dana is nothing like Helen, that she will settle in and just answer the question.

"What is up with you?" she spits at me, and her dogs, just like my Lurch, sense that the atmosphere has shifted toward a layer of the world far beyond the mundane niceties and neighborly ways.

"This is dangerous. What you are doing is dangerous," she barks.

"I know."

She still looks angry. The gravity of the pain we cause others should not be handled in a cavalier manner. Her phone starts to ring, but she doesn't notice.

"I can't believe you," she says, looking like she's gathering her thoughts in some way, figuring out whether to kick me out her door or slug me or simply answer me.

She slides down and sits down on the floor of her hallway, and she wraps her arms around her legs, knees up to her chin. The dogs surround her, lying down with their flanks pressed up against her in hopes of comforting her. I sit down across from her, as if this is natural.

"My fiancé isn't home. He'd kick you—he'd literally kick you. He'd call the cops."

I want to tell her I'm sorry, but I'm not. She has begun to cry already, this stranger, the warm distance of a person across from you, a hand stretch away.

Kip tells me there's no such thing as coincidence. *The whole notion is bullshit,* he says. He believes that God has hands, literally, to shape the events of our lives. We've argued this concept many times, usually after several stiff drinks late in the night. Although Kip is haphazardly frank and outspoken, his voice never rises when debating a topic that has anything to do with God. He is so certain of his beliefs that it coats him with a tolerance for the differing beliefs of others. He nods at me when I am arguing a counterpoint; he listens carefully, waiting until I have made my frenzied and emotional plea, buzzed and sloppy and self-righteous. Like Kip, I believe that there is no such thing as coincidence, but it has nothing to do with God. I think that when you want something to happen, you can will it. You can make coincidence, even if you don't realize you are doing it. You can set the stage and plant the seeds and turn yourself in the direction toward coincidence—a converging of factors and choices that aren't noticeable from any one angle. I learned this from my mother. I saw Maggie once—just once—before my mother died. It was a supposed coincidence, but I would realize later—when I saw Lily for the first time—that it was an act of will on my mother's part.

My mother and I were at Reading Terminal Market in downtown Philadelphia on a Friday afternoon. I didn't even know it was Maggie at the time. I was seven years old. My mother and I had come to Reading Terminal to buy fillets of grouper and lemon meringue pie. The farmers' market was lined with booths and stalls—butchers, fishmongers, loose-tea vendors, a chocolatier, vegetable stands, Italian specialty-meats vendors, greasy counters selling cheese steaks, three delis and two diners on either end of the football-stadium-sized hotbed of activity. The entire left-side market—a counter running a city block long—was owned and operated by Amish farmers. Their wives and daughters—wearing no makeup and white linen hats that tied under their chins—sold eggs, homemade potato chips, cheddar spreads, Dutch macaroni salad, potato bread, and an endless variety of pies.

We saw Maggie at Navine's Produce. Stella was home with Aunt Vicky, who was off on Fridays; she was a nurse at Jefferson Hospital and worked the 7-to-7 shift Monday through Thursday. I had accompanied my mother into the city for a doctor's appointment on Walnut Street; her migraines were bad then, lasting for days when they hit, and she saw a neurologist every few months. We rode the R8 into Market East Station. My mother was scared to drive in the city, and the train was an exciting novelty for me. In the bustling frenzy of 9-to-5ers on a late lunch hour and elderly women with canes, my mother was holding my hand in the vegetable section of Navine's looking for asparagus when we came upon her.

"Her," my mother said, her voice pitching up, as if she was thinking *Well, there she is,* as if she had been waiting all along.

My mother squeezed my hand too hard, and I could feel the strange sticky sweat of a heart-race coming off her palm. Frozen in place among the scent of pineapples, I stared at my mom, waiting for her grip to loosen, transfixed by her strange expression—my mother looked like she was spirited away. I caught one glimpse of Maggie before my mother pulled me, walking out of Navine's holding a cluster of asparagus stalks that she hadn't paid for. Maggie was tall, wearing a black wool coat with a pink fluffy scarf. She was pale-skinned and smiling to herself, sniffing grapefruits. My mother dragged me to the Amish stand and, there in the crowd crushed up against the counters, she began to cry. She was oblivious to the people staring at her, clutching my hand and wiping her nose on her sleeve, sobbing her request for potato bread and lemon meringue pie to a ruddy-cheeked Amish girl. I was too scared to say anything, but her cavalier display of pain sheltered me from feeling anything close to shame. The train ride home was silent. I knew something important just happened, and I comforted myself by savoring the sugary sweetness of the chocolate whoopee pie that she had bought for me.

When we got home, my mother put the lemon meringue pie and the paper-wrapped grouper on the table and sat down in a kitchen chair. Aunt Vicky came downstairs holding Stella. My mother took Stella from Aunt Vicky, kissed her forehead, chin, and both cheeks, and put her on the floor. But Stella wanted more, and she began to cry, arms reaching skyward in vain attempts to get my mother to pick her up. My mother had long ago stopped crying, but her face was awash in relief and a sense of accomplishment.

"I finally saw her," she said to Aunt Vicky, shrugging her shoulders.

And later I would realize that somehow, in some way I'll never know about—maybe in her subconscious—my mother had known all along that Maggie went to Reading Terminal, that eventually she would run into her, that she would finally see for herself what my father wanted so badly.

Twenty-five years later, I forced the hand of coincidence, if only subconsciously, so I could see Lily. It was simple: I switched doctors. I had kept all of my doctors where I had lived before moving to Glyn Neath, but several weeks into my affair with Quinn I switched to ones that were closer: my dentist and family practitioner and gynecologist, all in a five-mile radius. I never ran into Lily and Quinn while shopping in downtown Cynwyd or out to eat at the restaurants and bars along Route 18. I both dreaded and lived for the day when I could see her. I asked Quinn to let me know when they would be somewhere—a restaurant, the movies— so I could see her from afar.

"Anjou, I do believe you are sick," he said.

"I can't help it. I just want to see what she looks like."

I was unaware of the gravity of these haphazard choices, of the ways that small decisions wreak havoc on lives.

"It's not a competition."

"I know that," I said defensively. "I'm just curious."

"Cats die for that cause."

"I just want to see her."

"Worlds should not collide unless they were meant to collide."

"You and I collided."

"That was meant to happen."

"I doubt your wife would say the same."

It was at the gynecologist that I saw her—both of them actually. But I saw her first, before I even noticed that Quinn was next to her. Lily was not thin. This surprised me. I imagined her slinky and smooth-moving with long brown hair and dark eyes. I had expected her to be hard edges and fierce looks, exuding wit and brilliance, a wry expression on her lips, a hard-earned hourglass figure.

I was admiring the brightness about this woman, a smug private grin. I stared at her, and I waited for that tick to go off in her head, that subconscious twitching that causes a person to think *What?* making them look up to see who is staring at them. I never imagined Lily as this: a woman with streaked blond hair, pulled back loosely in a black hair tie, loose tendrils around a face that was flat and smooth and round, delicate. She was not beautiful in the conventional sense—her nose was crooked and her eyes somewhat dull and small—but her pouty mouth and gentle look gave her a reassuring appeal. She wore faded jeans, an oatmeal-colored sweater, and heavy black boots. She was plump; a body that was all curve, inviting and healthy. She looked like she had just rolled out of bed, a charming tousled mess. She didn't look like a lawyer. She looked artistic, motherly, soft-spoken.

When I finally looked at whose hand she was clutching, I thought it wasn't Lily. I thought it was another lover of Quinn's, somebody else on the side of his already busy side. But then a nurse in pink scrubs came out, holding a chart and calling for Lily. Lily stood up, leaned over to whisper something in Quinn's ear, and then followed the young nurse back to the examining rooms.

For the first time I felt guilty about the affair. Lily was out of sight, they didn't have kids, and I had talked myself out of the belief that I was doing anything wrong. I felt guilty because she looked nothing like I had imagined, because she looked happy, because she looked like she had no idea I had created a triangle in her marriage. It seemed that there was no excuse for the love I had marched into and reveled in. I now saw this woman and couldn't actually hate her, and the shield that protected me from the consequences of my choices—our choices—was removed. The geometry: I was a woman, unmarried, in love with a man, married, and the woman who knew nothing (or who knew everything and still held on). The three of us were tethered on a frayed rope hanging from a mountainside, two of us with bloody fingers gripping the rock and praying there'd be no fall.

Quinn stood up. He looked at me and tilted his head toward the door, walking out. I followed him and we stood in the dark. A full September moon glowed. A couple walked past us and the wife, a young round Asian heavily pregnant, was crying, her hand on her belly, talking harshly to her husband in another language. With her other hand she held his tightly.

"I wonder what they're fighting about," I said to Quinn after they passed.

"It could be anything," he said.

Quinn stood with his feet slightly apart, hands behind his back.

"She's pregnant, isn't she?"

I asked him with a calm and clinical resolve. The vulnerability of going to the gynecologist is unnerving—so you place your mind in a clinical space, detached and practical. You are naked, and yet you are not; you have selected what portions of yourself will be seen.

"Yes, it's apparent that she is," he said. "The question is, what on earth was she muttering about? Do you think she was speaking in Chinese? Korean? Maybe Thai?"

Intertwined with my love for him, I believed he was possessed.

"That's not who I'm talking about."

I turned to walk up the steps, focused on going back to my seat and waiting, wondering how quickly I could get back there. *The shortest distance between two points is a straight line.* I had to go undress and lie back on a table and let somebody determine the health of my reproductive organs. I knew how to detach. I had been practicing for hours before arriving. This was the best possible place to run into Quinn with his wife. If it were the Sweet Potato Bakery or Quick Time Dry Cleaners, seeing them together would have caused great panic. There is no detachment in the mundane activities of our lives. People see the prescriptions you pick up, the kind of cereal you buy, the magazines you page through. But a doctor's office is a place where your guard is up. *You are fine,* you tell yourself repeatedly. *You are dying,* you think behind that mantra. You detach so much that eventually you are not the person in the waiting room who will have to take off her clothes, lie back, and find out if the news is good or bad.

"Anjou," he called out to me, his voice light and jovial.

"What do you want, Quinn?" I asked, exhausted, upset, but ultimately relieved. Finally I knew who she was.

"Did you look at the moon?"

"No," I said, purposely not looking up.

"You should," he said. His head was tilted back. "Look up. Look now."

I started to walk up the stairs again. I didn't want to see anything else. His wife who might or might not be pregnant was inside and with a doctor and vulnerable. I was not pregnant. I was not his wife.

"Anjou," he called again. "Is it a sailor's moon or a summer moon or a winter's moon? Why do they always name the moons?"

"It's a harvest moon," I said, finally looking up to the sky. "The full moon nearest the September equinox."

"What will be harvested from this moon?"

"I don't know, Quinn."

"Hopefully something good. Hopefully."

"Yes," I said. I almost felt good.

"I want to take that harvest moon and stitch it over your heart," he said, his back to me, hands in his pocket.

"Is she pregnant?" I asked again, with a shaking voice, all the while knowing I would go home that evening and write that very line he had said to me—about the harvest moon and my heart—on a slip of paper and put it in the wooden candy box engraved with the words *Wildwood Chocolates,* where I kept all of my slips of paper with small things people have said to me. I had many slips of Quinn's words. At that moment under the moon I hated him, but I cherished everything he told me.

"We don't know yet," he said, still looking up.

Grace and I only met that once, a coincidence that only Quinn could have been aware of, at one of Quinn's mixed happy hours, a few weeks before Halloween. I rarely went to these happy hours. Quinn and I believed that we did not have to conduct our relationship joined at the hip. We spoke for less than three minutes. She was drinking an Amstel Light and I remember thinking this: She has great breasts, but her jeans are outdated. My initial sizing up of a person is always physical; it is shallow and immature, but this is not a personal flaw I'm interested in remedying. We spoke of the impending turning back of the clocks to end Daylight Savings Time. I asked her about the Halloween party that was coming up, the one that the Doctors and Poets Group, as Quinn referred to them, was throwing in a conference room on a Friday evening. I asked her what she was going to dress up as. Quinn wanted to go as Prince John, the hidden son of King George V, who was kept secret from the world because he was "not quite right" and died when he was only thirteen years old. Quinn wanted to wear a child's sailor suit and speak with a British accent and act that way—"not quite right."

10

TWO OUT OF THREE

I EXPECTED THREE WIDOWS at Quinn's memorial service: Lily, the first and most deserving of the title, then me, then Grace, just barely claiming rights. It is an odd business, the reality of a person no longer being yours or just beginning to be yours, and then that person dying. I was at the end of the relationship, Grace at the beginning. Only Lily knew the depths of the beginning, middle, end, and everything in the long trail thereafter. I had written my questions for Grace on a piece of letterhead from Wida's Hotel & Seafood Restaurant.

- *What song did you think of when you thought about Quinn?*

- *When was the last time the two of you made love?*

- *Did you love him more than he loved you, or did he love you more than you loved him? (Note: If she can't answer this question, remind her that there is always an answer to this question.)*

- *Do you remember what you two talked about that morning before he went to catch the train?*

- *Did you think it would be forever?*

On the long drive to Mt. Gretna, where Quinn's service was held, Kip attempted to determine my mental status. Stella had offered to stay through the week and for Quinn's memorial service. I persuaded her to go home and to let Kip take care of me. She didn't push the issue. We both knew without saying that I needed comfort from somebody who had also loved Quinn.

I had refused the bevy of tranquilizers Kip had offered from his medicine cabinet. He was driving us in his beat-up Karmann Ghia, a heap of Volkswagen machinery that needed a new muffler. No airbags, a heater that sporadically worked, and a death wish with Kip's lead foot on the gas.

"Are you sure you're okay?"

"No," I said.

"So you're not okay?"

"No, I'm not," I said, staring out the side window, farms and silos and cows in brown grass zooming by.

"You look okay," he said, speeding past a Mack truck.

"I am trying to keep up appearances."

"Christ, Anjou, just say something."

"I have nothing to say, Kip. I want everybody else to talk."

I clutched the Wida's list and tried to figure out how to get Grace alone. I wasn't quite convinced I'd actually ask her the questions. I move slowly.

"You're not okay, I can tell."

"You're repeating yourself, Kip. Please stop."

"I'm just worried."

"Don't worry about me. Worry about Quinn. He's the one going to hell."

Kip said nothing else, but he yelled at me with every cigarette I smoked, telling me I was going to kick the bucket before him at this rate, that lung cancer is a nasty, nasty way to die and he could attest to this, having watched his uncle and his father pass on this way.

Quinn's memorial service was at his parents' summer home, set on a lake in the Lebanon Valley in Mount Gretna. It's a woodsy conglomerate of summer homes—big cedar houses with large porches and quirky little cottages painted pink or purple or green with overgrown gardens and stray cats, turkey buzzards flying overhead. Mount Gretna was settled by the Methodists in the 1800s, and every summer Vacation Bible School camps descend on the area. The settlement thrives in the warm months, every house filled to the brim with families and children who swim and canoe in the lake and cook out at a canopied picnic area that was called the Men's Club at the turn of the century. A large placard still hangs from the ceiling that reads *No Women Allowed.*

His parents' cedar-shingled house, large and drafty, was brimming with people. It was a rush of thrill to see people smiling and talking with the very type of passion the deceased once had. Quinn's siblings were everywhere, and their names blended into one. I thought of all of them as a collective Nicole. I didn't know how to break in, to touch a shoulder, to pull one of them aside, to say *I'm sorry* and *How could this happen?* and *Did you know that I loved your brother from start to finish and still now?* and *Where is Grace? Have you met Grace? What about Grace?* Lily looked wonderful. She was across the room in the mix of Quinn's parents and siblings. She was much thinner than when I had seen her years before. Her hair was no longer blond but a short bob of chestnut with streaks of caramel in wisps around her face. I knew it was her—the soft jaw and the small feet and the way she tightly held the hand of a tall suited man who stood next to her, both of them wearing gold bands. She wore a gray fitted dress, hugging tight across her hips and legs, narrowing around her knees, and pointy black shoes with inches of thin heel. She moved through the crowd, in command almost. Kip held my hand as I followed her movements. I waited; she'd feel it soon, the pull of my stare. As if I had called her name, her hand slid from her husband and a hand slid off the shoulder of Quinn's sister and she was crossing through the crowd and she came up to me, not introducing herself but instead taking my hands and pulling me close to her. She put a hand behind my head—behind my head—and pressed her mouth against my cheek in a slow sorrowful kiss. I felt close to breaking right there, in the muffled mania and buzz of a roomful of mourners. Her hand slid to my shoulder and down my arm and I swallowed everything as she looked me in the eyes without saying a word.

Turning to Kip, shaking his hand, she said, "My name is Lily."

"I'm Kip. I'm so very sorry. Quinn was a good man," Kip said, words that seemed downright impossible and invariably true.

A person is not the sum of their mistakes, Anjou, Kip had said to me on the ride to Mount Gretna. I had told him he hadn't yet met my father.

"Where's the urn? And where's Grace?"

Lily and Kip looked at each other, and then at me.

"This is awkward," I said. "And I'm sorry. I loved Quinn but I need to know things. I don't want to talk about how I feel. I just want to know things."

"You are right, everything is awkward, Anjou," Lily said, taking my hand. "There is no urn because Quinn's ashes were spread on the lake at dawn."

"Was Grace there?"

"No," Lily said, looking to Kip for help.

"I know this is inappropriate. I know. I will go talk to Quinn's parents and his sisters—I can't remember all of their names. I will do all of those kind things, those right things. But I need to know about Quinn's ashes, and I need to know about Grace. You understand this, don't you?"

I was shaking, and Lily's body was a sympathetic patience.

"Anjou, Grace was not there. It was just Quinn's parents and his sisters."

"Were you there?"

"No, I wasn't."

"Why not? Quinn said that you two would always be connected. That there were certain things about you two that would never break."

"His parents asked me, but I thought it was best not to."

"I don't understand. You two were not breakable."

"Anjou, Quinn and I loved each other, but we were breakable. He didn't want to think we were because it made it easier for him to be the person he was. He loved me, and I know he loved you— he told me, even after you two were together for a while—"

"You two talked?"

"Occasionally. He would call me."

"Why? Why would he call you?"

"He would call me when he was scared."

"What was he scared about?"

"You. The price of loving. How to be settled. He couldn't do it with me. He wanted to do it with you."

"He couldn't. He went to Grace."

"I know."

"How do you know?"

"He told me, Anjou. He called me a few weeks before he left you. He was very confused."

"What did you tell him?"

"I told him to stay put, to wait until the storm settled."

"When did you find out about me—when you were married to Quinn, I mean—when did you know?"

"I knew you long before you knew I did."

"Did you know what I looked like?"

"Of course."

"You saw me?"

"Yes."

"Where? When?" I asked.

"It doesn't matter."

"But it does, Lily. It does."

I wanted to know about a slice of my history that she had quietly observed.

"Anjou, I'm not mad at you anymore. It doesn't matter when I saw you."

"It's a private memory," I said, nodding in understanding.

"Yes."

"I wanted him dead, Lily. I prayed to God for it. I really did. I believe in God, and I believe He answers prayers and I prayed hard that he would die."

"You'd better stop praying so much," Lily said, laughing at the weight of my comment, and Kip smiled at her. He took my hand.

"I just needed to know that Grace wasn't there when they spread the ashes," I said, in the middle again. Kip had one hand, Lily the other.

"She wasn't."

"I need to ask her some questions. I only have five. Lily, I had more, but I brought five. I need you to be with me when I ask her things. I brought the questions with me," I said, letting go of her hand and digging into my purse.

I handed her the questions, feeling lightheaded. All the people I knew in Quinn's life were in the periphery and I saw the stares— the look when people want to come up to you and say something but they don't want to interrupt what you are already doing. Kip stayed close by my side ready to catch me. I was close to falling. I had run eight miles that morning, not eaten for two days, and smoked thirty-five cigarettes in less than twenty-four hours.

"These are good questions, Anjou," she said after reading them and without a hint of patronizing me handed them back to me.

"Why don't we go get a drink? We can go see Quinn's parents, and I know his sisters want to see you. They were asking me when you would be here. They've been calling you for days," she said.

"Is Grace here now?" I asked.

"No," Lily said, still holding my hand.

I heard Quinn's mother in the background, a big belly laugh, a guffaw that spanned the rooms. I knew she was heartbroken but warmed by all of these people here. I saw the people of Quinn's life, his coworkers and his secretary and his friends from the Humanities Department, his college roommate, Leo. The department secretary, Jill, wanted to come talk to me. She kept looking up at me and then back down at the floor and then at the young man who was with her. Bernie the psychiatrist and Mark from the Department of Mathematics and some of Quinn's students, even, whose faces I did not recognize but whom I would know from their voices that had called on the phone at all hours. So many of these people had called me. Neighbors had left casseroles. People had reached out, and I had ignored them all.

"Will she be here later?" I asked Lily.

"No, I don't think so."

"You talked to her?"

"Yes."

"She should be here," I said.

"Well, I think she would feel better if she had come."

"No, you see, Lily, she should be here because the three of us should all be here together. Technically she's a widow. She should be here with us. We all know the same story, you know?"

Kip and I were floating in a stolen canoe on Lake Gretna. The sun had set, and the reception following Quinn's service was still going strong. From the lake you could see the glow of light from Quinn's parents' house and hear the door open and shut repeatedly as friends and relatives came and went, stood outside to smoke, took long strolls through the settlement. I had purposely sat in the back during the service in the living room, chairs and couches everywhere filled with exhausted and exalted and sad family and friends. I didn't want to share my love or my loss with Quinn's deepest connections, with his very blood. I was scared that it would slip away if I handed it over, that it would be blunted if I took on anybody else's. I knew this was selfish, but it wasn't about to change my behavior. I had managed not to make a scene, but I had repeatedly asked Quinn's Great-Aunt Maria, who was seated next to me during the eulogies, if she liked to listen to Quinn's words. She kept saying *What? What, honey?* and I kept whispering the same question. Quinn's sister Nicole had asked me to speak—she had left several messages for me about it—but I hadn't prepared anything. Quinn was mine, and I didn't want to share our memories. When Lily spoke, everybody laughed at her anecdotes, the way she showed the bright, warm, captivating side of him, the generosity, and the darker and more unreliable side. She delicately handled the hypocritical, complex, oxymoronic way of Quinn—the way we all are, really.

The memorial service was not upsetting. Moments of breathtaking grief, utter disbelief, and a cold-crush emptiness happened in places where cranky parents and rushing commuters and tireless teenagers convened—at stores and establishments, at places where cash registers rang and tract lighting prevailed. I tried to say the right things to Quinn's parents, but mostly listened instead. His mother's fluctuation between hysterical laughter and hysteria was an event to be witnessed, not to be partaken of. Kip stayed close by my side as I tried to talk with Quinn's friends, his siblings, his second cousin AnnThomas, two names fused together to make one. I kept asking AnnThomas if she ever just went by Ann, that surely Quinn must have said something to her about such a name. She stared at me strangely and tried to walk away, but I pursued her relentlessly across the room, hailing her as if she was a cab, calling, *AnnThomas, AnnThomas, what did Quinn think of your name?*

That was when Kip found my jacket and led me outside. We sat at a picnic table in the *No Women Allowed* pavilion and after I smoked four cigarettes, Kip announced that we should go canoeing. We were in the depths of February, bone-cracking cold, but there was no wind and both of us were already numb. He pointed to the string of canoes across the narrow street, which led down an embankment to the lake.

"The canoes are not for public use."

"How do you know?"

"Because last summer Quinn and I had to get keys from his parents to get their canoe. They're locked on a chain down there."

"Oh," Kip said.

"I can go ask his mom for a key."

"I don't think this is the appropriate time, Anjou."

"I suppose not," I said, staring up at the stars, finding the Little Dipper, convinced that Quinn could trump death, that he could still think and wrestle with words up there in heaven.

"Let's go see if we can steal one," he said, taking my hand and leading me across the street.

Kip found the long chain that was tethered to each canoe, hoping one would not be tightly locked.

"Got one," he finally said.

Kip dragged the canoe into the lake and helped me in.

"Sucks without a moon," I said as Kip paddled us toward the middle of the lake.

"When did you write those questions for Grace?"

"The day he died. At the Shore. I used the hotel stationery. Did you see?"

"I saw," he said, his voice coated with a deep worry.

"I just don't want to talk anymore. It doesn't matter how I *feel*."

"What are you feeling?"

"I just told you I didn't want to talk about feelings."

"Indulge me," he said, and his tone reminded me that he loved Quinn, too, and that talking about Quinn would soothe him.

"I believe that he is dead. It's true and complete. I wish I had the book he was holding when he was hit. I wish I had touched his shoulder when he left me that night. I loved his shoulders. He knew I loved him. He knew that. I'm not worried about that. I wish

I had a note of his, something recent, telling me to pick up his dry cleaning. Did you ever see his handwriting? It was these big block letters, perfectly aligned across the page. It was strict, but playful."

I lit my nineteenth cigarette for the day.

"And I wish he loved only me when he died."

I put my right hand into the cold water.

"I think Quinn would be okay with being dead," I said to Kip.

"He doesn't have much of a choice, does he?"

"No, I'm serious. He used to always say my God quest was because I wasn't comfortable with my own mortality. He said he'd support my God endeavors but didn't need them for himself."

"I think St. Peter is still going to let him inside the pearly gates," Kip said.

"You think?"

"Oh, absolutely. He'll charm his way in and have angel's wings in no time."

"I can tell you what he likes about being dead."

"Yeah? What?"

"Well, he'd definitely like that he died young. He knew how beautiful he was and he knew it so much that he put on this subtle affect of not knowing. And Quinn would think it was romantic— and tragic—to die young. Not that he was that young, but he was young. He'd be happy that he had a quick death. He'd say himself that he earned a slow painful death long ago, but he'd be pretty psyched he went out in a car accident instead of something like brain cancer or a stroke or Alzheimer's. He would never want to get old *and* sick."

"That's quite a list."

"He'd also be glad that he died without children. He said he thought the legacy should die with him."

"What legacy?"

"Who knows. He would just say 'the legacy.'"

The slow float was soothing, and as a lone car or two passed down the road dividing the settlement from the lake, a swipe of headlights moved across the water. We stayed in the canoe for an hour, finally making our way back to Quinn's parents' house. I sat in the car while Kip said good-byes for both of us. Lily gave Kip a small note to give to me. *Anjou, please call me. I'd like for us to talk.*

On the ride home, we stopped at a Cracker Barrel on the Pennsylvania Turnpike. The restaurant was large and empty, and everything—carpet, booths, tables, waitresses' uniforms—was brown. I ordered a cheddar cheese omelet and hash browns. Kip ate them for me after he finished his banana pancakes. I excused myself to go to the bathroom.

I walked into the ladies' room. Half of the long cylinder bulbs overhead were burned out, and there was a jagged quality to the light that nauseated me. I went to the handicap stall. The door wouldn't shut properly and the floor was a mass of dull yellow tiles. I don't like public bathrooms: I won't touch a door handle without a paper towel, I pee standing up, I flush the toilet using the heel of my shoe. After I wash my hands, I use my forearm to release towels, and I use those towels to turn off the faucets. I am able to use a public bathroom without touching a single surface. But I put my back against the wall and slid to the floor and got out my cell phone and dialed my father's number. It rang twice and I hung up. I called again, and the moment he picked it up, before he could talk, I hung up. I called one more time, and on the second ring he picked up. He said *Anjou.* He repeated himself, *Anjou,* in a long sad voice, an old voice. (*Quinn will never be this old,* I thought. *He will not answer any more questions.* The questions had started coming to me, in that sweet-still time of waking up and not knowing what day it is or where you are or what is actually the mechanics of your life.

There in Wida's Hotel, with a warm body next to mine, Stella, my life song, asleep, still and unstirred, it was there that I had questions for Quinn: *When did you first start loving me? How long after you left do you think you'd have kept loving me? I know you won't come back but I have to ask anyway, will you come back? Will you listen to me? Will you let me tell you why you should stay?*)

I shook my head at my father—and he couldn't see this, of course—and for the third time he said *Anjou* and so I hung up. A woman walked into the bathroom and briskly entered the first stall. She was wearing a worn pair of British rider boots.

"Hello," I yelled, and I saw her feet shuffle quickly.

"Hello," I bellowed again.

"Well, hello," a girl laughed. I could hear her pee.

"Hey, stranger in boots," I called out. "Do you love your father?"

I heard the toilet flush and watched her boots as she stepped out of the stall.

"Are you okay?" her voice echoed.

She bent down and I leaned down from my sitting position, and in the space between the floor and the bottom of the door our eyes met. She was young, with eyes lined with charcoal and long curls of burnt-sienna hair.

"You okay?" she asked.

"Are you going to answer my question?"

"Will you come out of the stall?"

"Don't answer my question with a question," I said.

The girl laughed with a long youthful cackle. She wasn't worried that I was a serial killer or strung-out junkie. Cracker Barrel is a place for the overweight and the lower-middle-class and weary travelers. I thought to myself that she probably borrowed books on tape from the Books on Tape Library that's in every Cracker Barrel restaurant. She probably never remembered to drop them off at the next Cracker Barrel she was in. It's an honor system and she wanted to stick to the system, but she couldn't seem to manage to. I knew this about her because I wanted to believe that she was kind. She might just have been young. My cell phone started to ring. It was my father's phone number on the incoming screen.

"Do you love your father?" I asked.

She slid down to a sitting position on the floor. She wore black tights and a pea-green corduroy skirt. I couldn't see any farther up from my spot on the floor. The way she sat was sloppy and easy—and the way she was willing to talk, taking her time—I decided she was nineteen years old.

"Most of the time I do," she finally said.

"When don't you?"

"About 10 percent of the time."

This wasn't the kind of answer I was going for. I wanted the nature of the times she didn't love him, not the statistics, but it was a good start. The cell phone was still ringing.

"You gonna get that?" she asked.

"No. It's okay. It's my dad."

✐

One week after Quinn's ashes were scattered in Mt. Gretna, I asked my boss, Frances, for a leave of absence.

"If you want to apply for a leave, you're going to have to write an eighteen-hundred-word explanation of what you plan to do on your leave," Frances said.

"May I write that my boyfriend left me and died so I'm going to go swim in a grotto?"

I took the calculator from her desk and did the math while she stared at me with her mouth agape.

"If I write that 120 times," I said, looking up at her, "if I write *My boyfriend left me and died so I'm going to go swim in a grotto* 120 times, that will equal an eighteen-hundred-word essay."

Frances never smiled. The one time I heard her laugh, I was so shocked by the uncommon sound that I thought a strange bird had flown into her office. She was my boss, and she took this very seriously, as she should: I analyzed other people's creative financing for the sole purpose of landing them in the court system, getting them to pay retribution, sending them to jail, or all of these. Her job was not to make me like her.

"Anjou, you have experienced a major loss. I know this. I am extremely sorry," she said, her restraint always more telling than her words. "But the matter at hand is this: Your request has to be approved by me before it goes on to human resources."

"Fine," I said.

"Have you thought about filing for a medical leave of absence—mental health?"

"Yes, I thought about it," I said. "The problem is that I'm very healthy, mentally speaking. You can confirm this with my psychiatrist, David. He doesn't need to give me drugs, but I'm willing to pay more for a psychiatrist—they have the M.D., they know the biology of our lives—than for a psychologist. I'm just shocked. And upset. But there's nothing wrong with my brain or psyche or psychological well-being, per se. If I were to file on the mental health card, I'd be expected to seek treatment and human resources would have to keep track of all diagnoses and pharmacotherapeutics and prognostic indicators. I don't plan to show up to see David every day while I'm on leave."

"Well, then, what are you going to do on this leave of absence?" Frances asked, taking in my missive, leaning back in her massive chair, arms crossed.

"I already told you. I am going to swim in a grotto," I said flatly.

"Swim?" she asked, trying to digest my words.

"Swim. In a grotto, specifically."

"You can't get a leave of absence so you can swim, Anjou. I'm sorry about Quinn. I mean that. I really am. I don't know what to say to help you, but I want to help you."

I reached into my purse and took out a cigarette. I crossed my legs and lit the stick and leaned back.

"You can't do that," she said, her voice a staggering cough.

"Do what?" I said, exhaling.

"Smoke. You can't smoke."

"Oh, but I can," I said, waving my cigarette at her slowly like a pendulum, then taking a long drag.

She stood up, looking like a frightened child.

"Perhaps we should end this meeting now. You should go home, get some sleep, and we can talk about all of this tomorrow," she said, eyeing the movement of my cigarette.

"I'm not tired, Frances."

"Excuse me?"

"You said I should get some sleep. I'm not tired."

"Anjou."

"Maybe you are, tired, you know. Maybe you're just projecting how you feel."

"Anjou."

"Why do you keep saying my name?"

Each word was released like an individual sentence. I looked at my right hand. It was in the air, my index finger thrust out. I wanted to cry suddenly, knowing Quinn would be very, very proud of me. He constantly pushed me to be more assertive, embrace the possibilities of being aggressive. He said his favorite thing about

Stella was her no-nonsense ability to tackle any topic head-on. Two months after he moved in with me, she had him on the phone, grilling him about why he had pursued me when he was married. Quinn answered her directly—he told her that sometimes you meet somebody and everything else in your world must stop. When he got off the phone he said my sister was one brave lady. I told him I was brave, too. He laughed at me. And when I started to cry, he came up to me and squeezed me like a vice, saying *Honey, the bravest thing you ever did was to get mixed up with me.* I felt worse, like a coward, and I cried harder.

I don't remember the exact sequence of events. I remember standing up. I remember saying *Fuck you, you stone-cold cow.* I said this nine times. I said a run-of-the-mill *Fuck you* eight times. I also said *shithead* and *asshole*, eleven times each. My voice was raised, security was called. I do remember wondering if swimming in the bluest of blue waters felt something like this, all swallowed up and honest. I don't remember most of my drive home, if I had rolled down the windows or listened to my radio. I know I smoked. I think I cried. I do remember one moment: thinking about that instant of Quinn's—when he was hit, just when his body flew upward and the sound of the people behind him finally made sense, if he thought it was a joke, if he started to rhyme words as his copy of Proust went airborne, creating a poem from that moment before he died.

Kip came over that night. It was after midnight and every light in my house was on. I was lying on my couch reading catalogs—a soothing unobtrusive act—and Lurch scuttled across the floor when he heard Kip on the porch. He let himself in and I met him in the hallway, where he stood holding a bottle of margarita mix, a bottle of tequila, and three limes.

"Got salt?" he asked with a spacious grin.

Kip threw ingredients into my blender and yelled at me over the whirring, doing his best to conduct an intelligent conversation with the shrill of crushing ice.

"Did you go to work today?"

"I guess you could say so," I shouted.

"You either went or didn't."

"I went. But I got fired. Sort of."

"Is that like being sort of pregnant?" Kip asked after he turned the blender off.

"Sort of."

"I think I can probably guess what happened," he said.

"Stella said I shouldn't make any big decisions right now."

"Stella's a very pragmatic woman."

"So you agree with her?" I said, my voice spiking up, trying not to sound defensive.

"Actually I don't. Don't get me wrong. That sister of yours is one straight-shooting, no-bullshit, smart lady. And I like her. I like her a lot. If she wasn't married I'd probably try to make her my wife. And you know that I gave up on marriage after the fourth divorce. Yeah, sure, there are books and psychologists and suggestions and lots of pathetic clichés about how to handle grief. And people say the most ridiculously stupid things to you in an attempt to make you feel better when really they're just trying to come up with something to shield them from the possibility that this could happen to them, but quite frankly, every person has to carry on in whatever the hell way they choose."

"Kip," I said after a long pause, "Today I can't stop thinking of Quinn in only one way, only as a complete prick."

"It's okay to think that. That's just what you think today."

"But he was a prick."

"Yes, he was. I'm not going to argue that point. But he was a lovable prick."

"And stupid," I said. "Getting hit by a car. What a fuckup."

"Definitely a fuckup. But Lurch loved him. That's always a good sign."

"Why is it that when a person dies, everybody says only good things about the person?"

"Those are the rules," Kip said.

"The rules suck."

Twenty-eight days after Quinn died and I lost my job, I saw an advertisement in the paper that was meant for me, no coincidence. I had willed this one.

United States Government seeking part-time enumerators for the 2000 Census. Call 1-877-429-6478. Experience not required.

The roll call of the nation. I was hired by Thadius Benton, who looked like he was fifty but was probably in his late thirties. He was born old; you could see it in his skinny frame and pinched brow and knobby knees that kept hitting the underside of his desk. He asked remarkably few questions after reviewing the standardized test all applicants are given as well as my résumé. He was not interested in my career aspirations or failures. My tests and résumé said everything—I was overqualified. I was a numbers person. I'd be his most competent hire. I was a professional and even-keeled, at least on the surface.

"You'll go through orientation, but the basics—as you've read in the introductory materials during your test—are that you will be going to homes that did not return a completed Census form by the April 1 deadline. You'll interview any of the adult members of the home, preferably the homeowner or person whose name is on the lease, asking them a series of questions about the household occupants, names and ages, type of house, stuff like that. We're using the Short Form, so nothing about salary." He held up his copy of *The United States Census Manual*, gnarled and frayed.

"I'm going to give you one of these to read tonight. You'll get oriented tomorrow and get started April 7. You don't work in the middle of the day—most people aren't home of course. You hit the field around 4 P.M. and usually finish up about 8:30. Then you drive here to Cynwyd and drop off your completed forms."

He held the manual over his heart, like a preacher about to holler warnings of fire and brimstone.

"Bear in mind that people can be sensitive—hostile at times—about the Census process. They believe that the government has no right to know pertinent information such as whether or not there are three or thirty people living in their house. People can and will bring emotions to this process. So you need to be prepared—it can get a bit uncomfortable at times."

"I'll keep all of that in mind," I said, not feeling particularly worried. Only the overbred bluebloods had the propensity to be loose cannons. "Can I enumerate in Glyn Neath?"

"Well, you live there so we can't assign you there. It can be uncomfortable for both the enumerator and the people you gather information from if you live immediately next door. Even with the Short Form."

"Please? My car is on the fritz."

"Isn't that how you got here today?"

"Yes, but it's fritzy."

Thadius stared at me a moment—he was mentally rifling through his rule book and he was also weighing the cost-benefit ratio of assigning me to my own town. He knew I could bring in more completed Census forms than any of the senior citizens or bored housewives lined up behind me. He looked at a map, seeing where I live and the assignment areas in my town.

"I suppose I can give you the north side of Glyn Neath. Don't tell anybody, please. I'm not one to break rules, but I am one to make exceptions. Now, do you have any friends or acquaintances in that area?"

11

SOMPTON AVENUE

121 South Sompton Avenue

"HAVE YOU EVER WISHED SOMEBODY YOU LOVE WOULD DIE?"

Mitzi Lancing has finally stopped talking.

When she first answered her door, I knew she was a talker. I developed a detection system within the first few days of enumerating. It's a taste—tart like a lemon drop, welcome, but difficult to swallow. She stood in her doorway, holding a cup of coffee, speaking with me for a full fifteen minutes before I even asked the first question from the Census form. Mitzi Lancing is extraordinarily tan, but without the creased and leathery mask of retirees who spend their winters in Boca Raton. *Brazil, honey,* she said when she caught me staring at her taut and wrinkle-free edges. *Don't ever get your face done in the States. Go to Brazil. Ever see the girls there? Their work is so good you can't even tell they had work.*

"I just need to ask a few questions."

"I sold candy, you know," she replies.

"I won't need to ask you about your occupation, ma'am, but—"

"Don't call me ma'am," she says. "I paid way too much money to be anything but a miss. Actually I'm not a miss, because I'm married. How does that work anyway?"

"I'm not too sure, but I'll be happy to call you Miss Lancing."

"Works for me."

"How many people—"

"I told you I sold candy, didn't I?"

"Yes, but—"

"I sold it for thirty-nine years—thirty-nine years of candy, go figure. You think I'd be fat, but I hate sweets. Never touch the stuff. I had a little shop in the Public Ledger Building, right near the lobby. It's right near Independence Hall. *Ladies' Home Journal* used to be there. Ever been there?"

"Yes."

"Hershey bars and circus peanuts and Zagnut bars and Three Musketeers. Licorice, too. Lots of licorice. Lots of my ladies hated chocolate—said it gave them pimples and migraines. My sister Gretchen worked at the *Ladies' Home Journal* back in my early years there. She was secretary. Worked for the editor-in-chief. She said he was a real skirt chaser. Gretchen said that once when she was cleaning out his desk she found a pink lace bra and a gun. Can you imagine that? A pink lace bra and a gun. Who was he, I said to her, Jimmy Hoffa?"

"I wonder if she knew my mother," I say. "My mother worked at the *Ladies' Home Journal.* Decades ago."

"Well, I'd ask my sister, but she's dead."

"So is my mom."

She stared at me solemnly.

"It was a long time ago," I say.

"Never stops smarting, though, does it?"

"Nope."

This prelude makes me confident.

"So," I say with a deep breath, "I need the names and ages of all residents who live here more than four days a week every week."

"We can start with me," she says, taking a large gulp from her coffee. "Mitzi Lancing. I'm sixty-four years old but I look fifty-four now, eh? Anyway, sixty-four. Social Security here I come."

"Anybody else?"

"My husband, Walter Lancing. He's sixty-seven. Our eldest son—he's a Walter, too—who is thirty-eight."

"Okay, anybody else?"

"That's more than enough."

I ask her the remaining linear, simple questions to round out the basics of her life. I sign the form, *Anjou Lovett, 4/26/00,* and hand her the clipboard for her signature.

"Have you ever wished somebody you love would die?" I ask.

She drops the clipboard, steps backward, and slams the door in my face. This is my fault. I probably phrased the question wrong so that it came off as insensitive, which it wasn't, not to me. I walk down the porch stairs, trying to figure out how I will rephrase this question so I can ask it of somebody else. I need to know if that secret wish, like the one I had about Quinn—and it was a wish, it wasn't just anger—happens with other people and when. I am going to call my father soon today. I am going to call him, my German-lineage father, from Sompton Avenue, a British-named street in a Welsh-named town. With Quinn and my father, I am always off the map.

The door opens and Mitzi calls out to me, *Hey you, Hey you.*

"I should call your boss, you know. I should report you," she says with a wagging finger and a look of rage on her face.

"I know," I say. I realize that I have left the clipboard in the spot where it landed on her porch. She is still holding her cup of coffee, and her right foot is on top of the clipboard, but she doesn't notice. If she did, she would pick it up and hurl it at me.

"You have no right to ask those questions. Just who the hell do you think you are?"

A couple with their child in a stroller and a black Labrador at their side are walking across the street, and they are watching us. They look alarmed, but they keep walking.

"I'm sorry," I say.

"No, you're not, Ms. Census Lady. You are not sorry. You would not ask that question if you were sorry. Now get your ass up here. I'll answer your question. Come on, now," she demands.

I don't want an answer anymore, but I have made this bed. I walk up to her and she grabs the shoulder of my sweater and pulls me into her house. I catch a fleeting glimpse of a man at the top of the hallway stairs. Her house is immaculate, if a bit dated in decoration. There is an extraordinary amount of orange and red—upholstery and carpets and picture frames and wall colors. *This is an October morning,* I think.

"My son is living with us for complicated reasons that you don't know and that you don't need to know," she hisses. "But I do not want him here and I hate how he talks to his father—but I can't stop him, and I cannot kick him out because he will certainly not make it in this world without us. We are stuck with him and although I love him—I am his mother—well, this year it has happened twice—that thought in my head—both times after he talked to his father, saying things no father should hear. And my husband, you see, he is an honorable man, honorable. Do people your age even know what that is? Do you? He has served our country and he serves God and he has served me for our entire marriage. He has never deserved anything like this. My son is not well, do you understand? Do you understand?"

"Yes," I say, although I have no idea what she means. I just know that she has no choices. Out of the corner of my left eye I see the man who must be her son, thin and disheveled, now sitting on the top step of the staircase. He is watching me and his mother. She knows he's there, but she does not turn around.

"He doesn't know what he says," she continues. "He cannot truly understand what he does. But you do. You do, miss. Don't you?"

I cannot say anything, because I am starting to cry.

"That's right, you cry. 'Cause you do know better. Lady, it ain't always easy to be graceful with the cards we've been dealt, is it? So remember that when you ask somebody a question like that. Now get the hell out of my house," she says.

Her son is rubbing his knees with the palms of his hands. He has begun to hum, loudly. I stand for a moment longer than I should because I know this song and it is on the tip of my tongue and I want to know what is running through this man's head. I feel close to evil. He waves to me.

Mitzi pushes me out her door and slams it behind me. I wonder if she will call Thadius, if she is relieved by her confession, if I have made her pain worse, if I should walk the six blocks right now to St. Theresa's and open the middle of the trinity of red doors, find the confession box, kneel, and tell the priest everything that he is waiting to hear. I pick up the clipboard from the porch. I brush off the grit and go down the stairs. I want that tip-of-the-tongue feeling to disappear, for the title of what the man is humming to come to me. I keep waiting. I want to remember the song.

I am driving to Chinatown to meet my father for dinner tonight. Thadius will fire me soon. I need to get busy. My father and I both love old houses—I remember him telling my mother when I was a child that suburbia and tract housing were the scourge of our society but that he loved her enough to position her close to a PTA board and baby oak trees. I bought an old house, I collect old postcards, and I hold fast to old memories and decisions. I have branded myself with history, a hot iron on my soul, and I wonder now, talking to my neighbors, if this is necessarily the best way to live my life.

I called my dad last night, after talking with Mitzi Lancing.

"Dad, it's me," I said.

"Anjou," he said, an excitement to his voice despite my flat and weathered tone.

"Can we meet?"

"Of course. Where shall I meet you? When? I mean, well—"

"Tomorrow. I'll come into the city."

"Good, yes, good. You can come to my house. I can make us dinner," he offered, his voice shaking.

"Why don't we go out to eat? We can meet in Chinatown. There's a Vietnamese place on 9th and Race. I can't pronounce the name of the place. I call it Chooch. It's got a big window with a neon train going across it," I said, softening my voice, wanting to cry. I was in my kitchen and Lurch was asleep in the living room.

"On 9th and Race?"

"Yeah. Chooch on 9th and Race."

"The name is Chooch? Chooch?" he said.

He sounded confused, but I could tell—just by that word *Chooch,* the way he said it with forced confidence—that he didn't want me to know. My father is far from senile, but he is older, much older; he's edging toward that last part of his life. Having lost one parent, you are acutely aware of the other one, for better or for worse, talking to them or not. For a moment I felt guilty, because maybe I wanted answers and nothing more, because my father sounded lonely, a sound I was not expecting.

"Because of the train. The big neon sign of the train. Choo-choo train," I said. "Tomorrow at 9 o'clock. Is that okay? That'll give me enough time to get into the city after work."

"Perfect. Tomorrow. Nine. 9th and Race. At the Chooch."

Not *the Chooch,* I thought, just *Chooch.* This was a trait of my mother's, to add an article—a *the* or *an*—before a proper noun. I told Quinn about this quirk of my mother's, about how it used to annoy me. He accused me of being too picky, that once we really grow up and realize the uncertainty of this world, it is natural to try to make everything more solid, that the use of an article introduces the importance of the word.

My Volkswagen Beetle, a 1970 Super Beetle, is Crayola red-orange color, and it has a modified stick-shift gear system. It's an automatic that you have to shift the gears for, but you don't have a clutch. Quinn told me it was an unreliable and unsafe car, but he begged me to drive it anytime we went somewhere. I rarely drive into the city. I almost always take the train, but I want to be able to flee tonight. The radio is blaring out a scratchy reception: Steely Dan is singing "Deacon Blues" and in that instant I am saddled with a memory from the faded-ink list of memories I have of my father: It is 1977 and I am in the car with him. He is driving the two of us in his gray stick-shift Pontiac Tempest to get ice cream. It is nighttime, no moon, the Big Dipper visible from every window. Our father has just come home after a two-month stay at Maggie's; it was his seventh homecoming, and I was twelve years old. We had already gone out to dinner at Minella's Diner, but then later at home my father wanted ice cream, insisted that I come along for the ride, and, not wanting to cause a problem—Stella and my mother looking too relieved—I acquiesced, quietly seething. Instead of going to the 7-Eleven, we took the ten-minute drive to a small strip mall with a deli, a dry cleaner, and a Carvel Ice Cream Store. My father wanted Carvel ice cream sandwiches, thick disc-shaped sandwiches, the cookie portion brittle and chocolaty. He wanted ice cream for the unspoken celebration of his return. I was in the car, my father driving especially fast so the ice cream sandwiches wouldn't melt, Steely Dan singing.

I crawl like a viper, through these suburban streets.

"I love this song," I said to nobody in particular, in that getting-my-voice-in-the-air way. I certainly didn't care what my father thought. He was a movie character, traveling through the scenes in my life, talking, pretending, but missing in so many frames.

"This station knows how to kill a song," my father offered, tapping on the steering wheel nonetheless to the song's beat.

"It's a popular song. Every station is going to kill it," I said.

"They don't go killing any Glenn Miller songs," he said, winking at me.

"They can't kill Glenn Miller. He's already dead," I said, my cheek pressed up against the window, trying to get all of the Big Dipper in view at once. The ice cream sandwiches were in a white paper bag, cold on my lap.

"You can put the ice cream on the floor, peaches," my father said, looking over, turning the music up.

"It's fine here," I said, still looking at the sky.

"But your legs are going to get cold. What will your mother say if I bring back a frozen daughter?"

The world is not that small. The cliché is wrong. For twelve years after college I went into the city to my job, to find cheaters and liars and the numbers that simply would not add up. I walked through every section of the city: Society Hill; Old City; the red-brick sidewalks of Pine and Spruce and Lombard Streets; the neighborhoods of South Philadelphia, Queens Village and University City and Bella Vista. And all of the squares—Rittenhouse Square and Washington Square and Franklin Square. I sat on every bar stool and in every restaurant during those twelve years. And I never saw my father, never caught a fleeting glimpse, not even a confused moment when I thought I saw him. He lived in Center City, on the cusp of Society Hill, six blocks from where I worked. I found him in the phone book. I walked by the house every Friday after work for two years. It's a small and narrow trinity row home, tiny abodes featuring one room on each floor, an architectural triumvirate—rooms for the Father, the Son, and the Holy Spirit. Maybe we breathed the same air during all of those years, crossed paths, one of us with our head turned the other way or attention caught by a conversation or a pretty face or an obsessive thought. I am certain of this: Both of us worked very hard to avoid such a moment. We could control it. It was a choice both of us made.

My father is standing outside of Chooch and upon seeing him I feel tears come to my eyes. I do not want this, so I recite the Grotto poem in my head. He does not try to hug me because he can read what I'm open to. But he holds the door for me as we walk in. The restaurant is cramped and too bright and cheap looking: metal-scratching chairs and ugly white-tiled floors. But the food is inconceivably good and that is why I have brought my father here.

We sip our waters from filmy plastic cups, and I order us vermicelli noodle dishes with pork and chicken, grilled squid on broken rice, papaya salad, and crispy spring rolls, telling the waitress that we'll be sharing everything.

"Family style," my father says with a smile.

My father has never eaten Vietnamese food before, despite his fascination with that war, and he asks me if I've ever been to Vietnam. I tell him no, but that Quinn had gone there several times. My father gives me a quiet nod, and it feels good to mention Quinn without another person uttering consolation or looking uncomfortable. This is sort of like being with Kip.

I want to ask more than the ten items on the list: I want to know what he and Maggie did on weekends. I want to know if she died in the hospital or in their home. I want to know how good it felt to be loved twice at once. The Vietnamese patrons are chain-smoking and gesticulating wildly, the Polish construction workers dusty and tangy-smelling, sitting at the table next to us, drinking vodka and slurping their noodle soup loudly as they argue in their thick and cutting language.

"Let's eat first, okay?" he says, reading my mind that we should ease into this.

He points to the fish tank near the register, big and bubbling with murky water and a large blue-and-gold fish looking irritated and moving slowly. My father gets up from his chair and walks to the tank, hunching over. I walk over and he tells me about the fish.

"How do you know so much about tropical fish?"

This was not my intended first question.

"I used to snorkel in Grand Cayman every February. With Maggie."

"Oh," I say. I want to ask how Maggie died. Stella knows, but I never asked and, at this point, she'll let me come to things on my own.

"It scared me the first time I snorkeled. You go from this regular world to a different one. It is so shocking, all of these colors and fish and plant life—and really, you could stand up if you wanted— the whole thing scared me half to death."

I am looking at him now with a small smile.

"It was sort of funny, but I screamed. A grown man, screaming underwater. I made Maggie hold my hand the first ten minutes or so."

"Strange," I say.

"It was very strange."

"Did you see anything like that when you swam in the Grotto with Mom?"

"No. Nothing like it. But we wouldn't have wanted to see anything anyway."

I turn around and see that our waitress is putting dishes on the table. She is a thin and quick-moving Vietnamese girl with her hair cut in a jagged array of wisps and strands, all bony legs.

"Our food is here, Dad."

He straightens up and leads me back to the table, his hand touching the small of my back. I have not eaten in two days. I have run fourteen miles in these two days and smoked eighteen cigarettes. My father talks throughout the meal—interjecting his rambling sentences with praise for the food, for my choosing the Chooch—I still can't bear to correct him, and actually don't want to because it makes me think of my mother. I finally recognize him while eating, a buoyancy to his demeanor, and I wait for him to rhyme. We are picking at all of the dishes randomly, steam rising in small curls off the plates. He is clumsy with his chopsticks and I take his hand and show him how to hold them so he can get a better grip.

"My house is a hundred-and-sixty-eight years old. The original beam is in the basement—it's where my cat, Kisa, sleeps."

"I like that name," I say.

"It's Russian for cat."

"Your house sounds charming," I say, the kind of thing I would say on a first date. You're there at the movies and you're not saying anything to each other—for almost two hours throughout the movie—but you are in close physical proximity with that person, and this is good, because you can start to be comfortable simply in that person's presence.

"I saw your house," I confess.

"I'm glad you've seen it," he says with a warm grin, alleviating any sort of shame for spying on him. "When did see it?"

"A lot of times. For years. I'd go look."

"That's good. I'm very glad. I hope you can come inside some time."

My face flatlines. *Slow down.* He sees this.

"Would you believe it was slave quarters in the 1800s? Rather unsavory neighborhood then, full of prostitutes and the like," he says, twirling his noodles clumsily, trying to slurp them up. "In the 1900s the house was actually used as an ice cream factory."

"How did you find out all of that?"

"Oddly enough, from the great-niece of my next-door neighbor Harry. She's getting her Ph.D. in architectural history. From Penn, I think. She studied all of these archived documents about our neighborhood and happened upon records of my house."

"What a coincidence," I say.

"No such thing as coincidence," he says.

"Why do you think that?"

"The past is always available somewhere, and it has a will to move things forward. It comes to your doorstep at some point, no matter what—that creates the supposed coincidence."

He shakes his head a little and tells me about his retirement, how he is taking violin lessons, about his day trips to Atlantic City with his neighbor Harry (*I stop at sixty bucks—whether that's losing or winning it*). He tells me about his heart: the pills, what it's like to wake up after they've sawed your chest open—the magnitude of this—the fear when the pain sets in. We continue to eat off the same plates and we agree how stupid I am for smoking, even temporarily.

"Stella worries about you," he says, after telling me that she has told him about my recent habit.

"Stella has been worrying about me since she was five years old."

"It's very backward, you know. This relationship you have."

"It's like that poem," I say. "From when we were kids."

"What poem is that?"

I look at him cockeyed, surprised that a poem would slip his memory.

"One bright day in the middle of the night, two dead boys got up to fight. Back to back they faced each other. Drew their swords and shot each other. A deaf policeman heard this noise. He came and shot those two dead boys—"

"If you don't believe my story is true," my father interrupts. "Ask the blind man, he saw, too."

"I knew you would remember."

"Of course. I taught you that rhyme."

"You did not," I say.

"Yes, I did."

"When? I don't remember."

"You were very young. About six years old. I taught you when you were learning to read."

"That's not possible. I remember everything."

"I taught you in notes, so that you would memorize it slowly. I would write a line of the poem on a piece of paper and put it in the front pocket of your coat. Every week you would get another line of the poem."

"Why don't I remember this?"

"Maybe you blocked the memory. When the poem was done, you cried for weeks, waiting for the next line."

"Why didn't you do that with another poem?"

"I did, but you wanted more of that first poem. You wanted the dead boys' poem, that's what you called it."

"Why didn't you make up lines for the poem?"

"I don't know, Anjou," he says quietly. "It just didn't seem fair."

The waitress comes back and clears the table, asking in a faint voice if we'd like tea. We both nod at her. I take the questions out of my back pocket and place them on the table, face down. And then my father does the same exact thing—he goes to his jacket pocket and takes a piece of paper out, putting it face down on the table. I can see that it is folded and worn.

"I have a list," he says.

"What?" I say, swallowing a rush of the past two months, a rush of Quinn and the way he was more in my world dead than alive, of my neighbors letting me in their homes, of Stella, who should be here, moderating and mediating our fumbling. I want to cry, because I cannot be that much like him.

"It's okay," my father says.

"No, it's not," I say.

I remember his handwriting distinctly. He writes in a tight cursive that slants backward slightly. He is left-handed, and his script always looked like such a laborious task.

"We're ready for this," he says calmly.

"Did Stella say something to you, about how I keep lists?"

"No, your mother told me about some of it, some of it I remember. The movie phone calls—we all remember that. But your mother said you hoarded all of the notes she left you, and even the ones she left Stella. When I was with Maggie, she would send letters to my office about how you girls were."

"Why in God's name would she do you any favors when you kept leaving?" I say, although I am grateful for my father's honesty.

"The accountability for our choices was twofold," my father says.

We are in the water.

"Is that your way of shifting blame?"

"No. It probably sounds like it."

"It does," I say.

"I know about the Orkney Islands in Scotland. She told me," my father says. "She told me you wrote a list of all of the island names—there were two hundred of them, but you were having trouble finding the name of every single one, because the *Encyclopaedia Brittanica* only named the big ones."

"I used to say I'd go there for my honeymoon," I say, smiling through tears I can't control. "I wanted to go to Muckle Green Holm the most."

"Why did you want to go there?"

"Because I liked the name. I imagined it would be cold and very romantic."

"An interesting observation for a twelve-year-old."

We both smile, and I blow my nose on a used and greasy napkin. The Polish men are still drinking vodka, their plates cleared long ago. The level in the bottle is lowering but they are steady, far from drunk. They are looking at us like we are one of them—talking in a language in a room full of strangers with words nobody could begin to understand.

"What's on your list?" I ask my father.

"Answers."

"To what?"

"To the questions I imagine you have."

"That's what's on my list."

"Questions?"

"Yup."

"This should be a good start," he says.

"You know what Stella would say?"

"No, what?"

"She would say that people don't actually talk like this, like we're talking right now."

"But they do," he says, his hands crossed on the table.

"Who goes first?"

"That's up to you, Anjou."

⌒⁄⌒

These are my father's answers:

1. *I don't know.*
2. *Because I didn't know how to keep love from going wrong.*
3. *I hope you will.*
4. *I can't choose.*
5. *I still miss her.*
6. *Whatever—however—whenever you want.*
7. *I'm sorry.*
8. *I hope I would. I hope.*

9. *Because I didn't just lose your mother that day, and I couldn't breathe because of it.*
10. *I can't.*

Most of these answers would have been easy enough to get from Stella. But I have always been a late bloomer, and a reluctant recipient of information that I'm not too sure I really want. Stella knows that my ability to forgive—or even just consider or reach toward it—is not a linear *I'm sorry, You're forgiven* act. For Stella it has always been that way—pragmatism shrouds many of her decisions. This does not preclude the complexity of her love for me or her husband and child or our father—Jack—it's just her way.

These are my questions for my father.

1. *What did it feel like when Mom died?*
2. *Did you love Maggie more than Mom?*
3. *Have you ever called either of us and hung up, just to hear our voice? Or looked us up in the phone book and driven to our houses and parked a few blocks away and watched us from afar, just to see?*
4. *What is your favorite poem?*
5. *Do you still go to church?*
6. *What do you want from me?*
7. *Are you lonely?*
8. *Knowing what you know now, would you have done things differently?*
9. *Why did you leave after Mom died?*
10. *Are you sorry?*

Our lists are for the most part useless, but the fact that my father brought one isn't. At first only our eyes go back and forth, across a question or an answer.

"I would have thought we'd have a match with number four."

"We do," my father says.

"But you don't have a poem on your list."

He points to answer four.

"I can't choose."

"You never could."

I stare at him, and he is brave enough to hold my gaze with nary a pleading for forgiveness or an expression of sadness.

"Can you choose one now? Right now."

"Probably not."

He wraps his hands around the small tea cup, looking off at the big fish in the tank.

"I blame you for everything," I say.

He waits a few moments, to see if I will say more.

"You can blame me for a lot," he says. "And I'm sorry for more than I could ever tell you. I will never be able to fix this. But you cannot blame me for your life."

We sit there for a while as he watches me cry. After a while I stop, and I ask him to choose just one poem that he loves and he finally settles on one—"Hurried Love" by Gavin Ewart. I ask him if he would please write the poem on a piece of loose-leaf paper and mail it to me, that after I read it I will then mail it to Stella, that she should see how those words travel and she'll want to know that they meant something to him. Stella meets so many of my needs in an unending way. She tells me that I meet hers in an equally thoughtful way.

"Do you think question 9 might have a match?" I ask.

Why did you leave after Mom died?

"Nine's a hard one, Anjou." My father takes a long pause, scanning the room as if going from shore to waters, question 9 the walk.

"The day before your mother died, she called me at work to tell me she was pregnant."

There would have been more to see, I immediately think. There would have been something magnificent after Stella, the second and more powerful child who crashed into this world with beauty and grace and aplomb. She built the momentum of my parents' love and I later confirmed this with her, that she too thought the next child would have reached unsurpassed heights.

"That is so sad. That is so sad, Jack."

I am crying again, warmed in the smallness of Chooch, and my father watches me closely.

"That is so fucking sad," I say, shaking my head.

Our parents would have loved that child the most. Parents choose favorites; this doesn't mean any other child is less loved, but there is a unique quality of love that they bestow on one child. I was my mother's favorite, and Stella was my father's favorite—we all knew this instinctively, and it was perfectly acceptable. That baby would have been favored by both of my parents—leaving Stella and me to fend for ourselves on our already burgeoning fraternal twinness.

He pushes the list closer to me. *9. Because I didn't just lose your mother that day, and I couldn't breathe because of it.*

"You couldn't breathe?"

"I made a very grave mistake—an unforgivable, unspeakable one—in walking out on you and your sister. I couldn't take care of you two. I couldn't take the full responsibility—of the guilt, of how your mother and I waged our marriage, risked our love and yours and your sister's. And I will always—always—feel responsible for your mother's death."

"Why?"

"Because when the accident happened she was driving to the city to buy lemon meringue pie. For me."

"Why didn't she take the train?"

"She had told me she was going to drive it that day, while you girls were at school, that she needed to spread her wings because if that baby was a boy he'd need a stronger mom."

I stare at him for a while. He is sorry, but I don't forgive him. I don't know if I ever will.

"How did she tell you that she was pregnant? What did she say?"

"She called me at work and said, *Jack, three's a charm.*"

Words of my mother's I never knew existed, more important than my father's failures.

"That's how she said it?"

"*Three's a charm.* I came home that night."

"This is so fucking sad that I feel like I should leave right now. I think I should leave."

"Don't leave. Please."

"Does Stella know any of this?"

"No."

"Why not?"

"Because if I told her, I was scared I'd lose her."

"So you kept it a secret? If there's one thing you and Mom managed to do right it was not making your fucked-up choices a secret."

"The day your sister came to me, she was very emotional, very upset, and she had a lot of questions."

"I'm sure it was quite the Q-and-A pit," I say with a snort.

"It was. It scared Bruce half to death. But he held on, sat there for her and let her rip. Here she was, at my house, launching into this demand that I tell her how to be married in the right way, that even though I had fucked up my own marriage—those were her words—that she needed to know how to try to do this. Maggie sat next to Bruce and watched the whole thing."

"Stella hates secrets."

"I decided I'd rather live with the guilt of not telling her than have my conscience absolved—barely—and not have her."

"Selfish." I say. "And risky."

"Yes."

The tightness of his brow brings to light that this is stressing him out. I care about this fact, his anxiety, the stress on his face—his heart is bad, he fucked up royally, but Stella has taught me about compassion and I haven't found it but I know it must be somewhere nearby. My father scratches the back of his head, and he has begun to shake. I am still taking in the vulnerability of him, how it has shifted each time I see him. How he has said he is sorry, but not for everything. How real he is being—seeing the problem for what it was, what was done, who was to blame, and how much we can spread that blame across the expanse of our lives. Stella is right. He is Jack.

"Did you want this baby?" I ask.

"Yes. We started to try when we were at the Grotto."

"I wonder what it was, if it was a girl or a boy."

"Your mother thought it was a boy. She said we had enough women in the family."

"What were you going to name it?"

"We didn't get that far."

"What about now, Jack?" I ask, not with spite or anger, and my father has begun to cry. "What do you think you would have named him?"

We are in my car. My father is in the passenger seat, stroking the vinyl, which is white and so worn that chunks of yellow-brown foam peek through tears on the side. I want to tell him that I understand the importance of old things, but I don't want to say everything now. This is the third meeting with my father, and I am certain that there will be a fourth. I am already imagining one where Stella is there, too. There is nothing warm or comforting in these thoughts; my father left us, repeatedly, but he was there from the beginning of my life and my mother is more dead than I realized and I will not get out of this world without loving Quinn until the end.

I have a new list for my father, and I am going to mail it to him. When we met at Chooch, I explained to him how everything has more meaning when you can hold it in your hands, that the sense of touch should not be removed from our exchanges in life.

"Okay, read it off to me," Stella says.

We are on the phone the day after Chooch, and I tell her that two important questions were answered, that I had forgiven nobody, that I would see him again. I tell her that I will start addressing certain issues with him via the United States Postal Service, that there is great comfort in the government having a hand in all of this.

"That's the stupidest thing I've ever heard in my life, Anjou," Stella says with a warm giggle.

I am not offended. She just gives it to me straight. Who wouldn't want that from somebody who is your unofficial twin?

"Not really. They're like the silent mediator," I say.

"No, darling, they're like snail mail."

"It's more powerful on a piece of paper. It's harder to get rid of. He can't just not listen or press *Delete*."

"I think you have his attention as it stands."

"I agree, but I want him to think about everything I have to say."

"Fair enough, kid."

I can see her nodding her head up and down.

"It has a title," I say.

"Of course it does," she says.

"Listen, Stella, I won't read it to you if you're going to make fun of—"

"I meant that in a good way. Jack puts titles on everything."

"He does?"

"Yup. He sends me notes, and he always titles them."

"He mails you things."

"Yes."

"Why didn't you tell me?"

"You made it clear long ago that you didn't want me to bring up Jack. For the most part I respected that."

"Well, you could have told me that. Especially now. Since I started calling him and all."

"No, I couldn't. I can't read your mind about what you want to hear or not hear. I love you, but contrary to popular belief, sometimes I have to let you find your own way."

"How does he title the notes to you?"

"He writes the dates on the upper right-hand corner and then below it he'll write *Mail, Volume 1, Issue 1,* and so forth. Like each note is a new issue."

"Why does he do that?"

"I don't know. I never asked him."

"You should," I say.

"Maybe you should," she replies.

"I already gave him a list of questions."

"I know."

"You do?"

"Yeah, he told me. Did you think he would meet with you and not tell me about it? Anjou, I have a relationship with Jack. I have for a long time. He tells me things, lots of things. He shares his life with me. The minute you started calling me, he has told me everything that happens."

"Everything?"

The baby is my first secret ever from Stella. For now I hold this tight to me and I do so because I want to protect my baby sister from knowing anything else about our parents that will make her sad, something that eventually she will be told, by me or by Jack, but for now I want to protect her—if only for a brief time.

"No, not everything. He didn't tell me what questions you had for him. He only told me that you brought a list, and that he brought one, too."

"I don't know how to do this, Stella. I wonder if questions are the answers."

"Can I tell you what I think?"

"As if I have a choice?"

"Seriously, on this one, I will not make you listen to me."

"Okay, go ahead," I say, trusting her more than ever.

"I think you are going to get answers by sitting across a table from him again and again, from taking walks with him, from letting Lurch get to know him, from finding peace with Quinn, from going to his house and letting him show you his cat asleep on the beam."

"I don't forgive him, Stella. I am not like you. We do not get through our lives the same way."

"Thank God for that. You probably wouldn't want to do it my way. Trust me."

I believe my sister. She struggles with how she executes her choices as much as I do—she, too, is not special.

"I promise you that if you keep an open mind, you'll get more answers than you knew were possible. Now, let's get back to your list of seven items. I like that you made a list, really, I do."

"It's called 'Seven Things You Didn't See.'"

"That's a good title."

"At least it doesn't rhyme."

"This is true," Stella says and we both laugh.

"In no particular order, item 1: *A conversation on Route 81 on my way back to school after Christmas vacation in my senior year of college. The snow was so bad that everybody pulled off the roads but we kept driving. Aunt Vicky's car ran out of windshield-wiper fluid and the muddy snow kept smearing up the windshield but we kept driving. Every mile Stella and I would get out and wipe down the windshield with Windex that was in the backseat.*"

"That's number 1?"

"Yeah, that was an important one. I was having so much fun in the car, but I was also scared shitless."

"That's a good one, Anjou," my sister says with a gentle tone.

"Number 2: *Telling me what you thought of my ability to play the cello when I was fourteen years old.*"

"I already told you that. So did Mom. You sucked."

"Dad missed it, though. I quit before he got home. He should have had a say. If he'd said I wasn't too bad, then it would have been a toss-up, really. Two versus two. With just the three of us, I lost."

"Are these all childhood memories?"
"No. They get more substantive."
"I was hoping they would."
"I'll skip to Number 7."
"Okay."
"Number 7: *Quinn.*"

12

HOLYWELL AVENUE

I AM NOT SURPRISED TO SEE Thadius at my door because two days
ago I asked Mitzi Lancing the wrong question. I have asked plenty
of wrong questions in these past three weeks, but the question for
Mitzi felt particularly wrong.

"You're terminated, Anjou."

I am immediately crestfallen, because I was about to start enumerating on Portmeirion Lane. It is April 29 and I had promised
myself I would call Grace and actually say something when I was
done enumerating Portmeirion Lane.

"I didn't want you back in the field before we spoke. Listen, I
received two phone calls last night from some residents on
Knighton Avenue that you interviewed. The residents were quite
upset."

"You want to come in?" I offer.

"You don't seem surprised."

"I'm not," I say, opening the door and motioning him in. Thadius walks in and immediately freezes when he sees Lurch.

"I'm not really a dog person," he says, backing up.

"That's okay. Lurch isn't really a people dog."

Thadius gives me a strange look, and I lead him into the kitchen. Lurch didn't bark in his standard frenzy when the doorbell rang. Lurch is at the end of the hall growling, but it's not a mean-spirited growl, and I explain this to Thadius.

"It's my fault, really. I should have known better," he says. "Should have known when Jessica St. James called. Should have pulled you from the field then."

"I'm sorry, Thadius."

"I don't get it. You seem so, well, so level-headed."

"I am," I say, and this is logical to me, here in this season between Quinn and the Grotto.

"I gotta tell you, I have had a lot of problems with enumerators—forging Census forms, asking residents out on dates, but asking inappropriate—and deeply personal—questions that are certainly not on the Census form, well, this is a first."

"A lot of people didn't mind it."

"I guess so. I'm surprised I didn't receive more calls. Why were you asking people such strange questions?"

"The questions weren't strange."

"They sounded pretty strange to me. Helen Calloway said you asked her what it felt like when her mother died."

"She wanted personal questions. She did, Thadius. I'm not lying. She came right out and asked me for them," I said.

"Even if she asked you for these types of questions, you shouldn't have done it."

"Who else called?"

"Simon Heller."

"Oh," I say, remembering how flabbergasted I had made him.

"He said you asked him what one decision he's made in his life that he most regrets."

Simon laughed at me, then asked me to repeat myself—not quite believing what I had just said. So I repeated myself, and then he just stood there for a few seconds, shaking his head at me. Then he said, *Oh for Christ's sake I cannot believe they let nutcases like you out of their cages.* He didn't even slam the door on me, didn't even seem that mad—more amused than anything.

"Why are you doing this?"

"I'm looking for answers, Thadius."

I like that Thadius is curious, that he may understand—possibly—that turning to strangers can sometimes be helpful. I seem to shoot at about fifty-fifty here in Glyn Neath. I don't need to tell him about Quinn, or my father. These men were starting and ending points for the same circle.

"I want answers about love. About pain. About regret and loyalty and poetry."

"Have you ever thought about opening up a philosophy book? Or the Bible? How about a therapist?"

"A book won't have the answers."

"Why aren't you asking the people in your life—your family?"

"I want a fresh perspective. I already know exactly what my sister, Stella, will say. My mother is dead. I hadn't spoken to my father in seventeen years—"

"Seventeen?"

"Seventeen. But I am speaking to him again. I actually gave him all of my questions, in a list."

"A list?" he asks, and the domino effect of confusion picks up speed.

"How else can you keep track of things?"

"Anjou, you are a piece of work."

"No, I'm not. I just appreciate the obvious. I figured if I asked strangers about all of this stuff, it would be easier to ask my father. And Grace."

"Who's Grace?" Thadius says.

"She's the woman Quinn loved."

"Who's Quinn?"

"The man I loved."

Thadius nods his head up and down, studying me.

"I've gotten a few answers. And this town is like my neighbors—alive, Thadius."

Kip said Glyn Neath is like a set of parents, a nurturing mother and narrow-minded father. The people who live here are the children—some are unruly, some follow directions, some are black sheep. *I've always been the unruly child, and for a long time you followed directions. But now you earned yourself a black-sheep sticker,* he said to me.

"I could probably get a good answer from you," I say with easy confidence. I feel more capable than I have in years.

"Now. Well. I don't think so," he says, flustered. "And besides, it would probably get me in trouble to in any way contribute to this mess you've stirred up here. I've got a lot to clean up, you know."

"I'm sorry about that. Really, I am."

"No, you're not."

"Okay, fine, I'm not that sorry, but I know you want to answer a question. You just fired me, Thadius. You can say anything you want to me now."

"I had to fire you."

"I know that. I'm not mad at you. I expected it sooner. To be honest, I thought Veronica England would have done me in. She was on Knighton Avenue, too."

"What did you ask her?"

"I asked her if she had ever cheated on her husband."

"You did not," Thadius says, jerking up, eyes widening. I wish he lived here in Glyn Neath. Kip would definitely like him. Kip would tell him that he needs to update his wardrobe, too, but he'd do it the right way—over beers.

"Yes, I did. I wanted to dispel my own notion that men are the natural cheaters in relationships."

"Well?"

"She cheated."

"She told you she cheated on her husband?"

"No. She bitch-slapped me. Right hand against my left cheek and then against right cheek. Like something out of the movies."

Thadius bangs his hand on the table and we both laugh.

"God, I'm glad I fired you."

"You should be. I needed to be stopped," I say, relieved that somebody has inadvertently forced me to stop procrastinating. Because I know that no matter what street I walk down in my own neighborhood, I need to go to Holywell Avenue soon.

"How does that tell you that she cheated on her husband?"

"Because it wasn't a *How dare you?* slap. It wasn't like the question itself offended her. It was that her truth erupted. That's how I knew."

Thadius scratches the back of his head intensely and stands up. Lurch stands up, too, watching him.

"So, what's your question?" he asks.

He looks relieved already.

"Who broke your heart?"

"Sheila. My ex-wife," he says without pause.

I nod, an invitation for him to continue. Thadius knows how safe it is. My dog will not bite him, the Gatorade I poured for him is not poisoned, the cigarette I lit is not as necessary as it was three weeks ago. Thirty-seven left, and then back to clean living.

And Thadius talks—about his wife, who was an engineer and then decided to be a revolutionary, so she got her Ph.D. in Russian and decided she didn't want to be married anymore.

"She said that marriage didn't suit her, philosophically. That it was starting to feel too soft for the adopted Russian in her. She said it was also about the math, two technically doesn't make one, even though she'd long ago given up on the sciences."

"Did you know that Wendy's Frosties are made of potatoes?" I ask Kip, finishing off my third gin-and-tonic.

It is 3:00 in the morning. Kip and I are outside on the second-floor deck of his house making a healthy dent in a bottle of Blue Sapphire gin. There is a lunar quality to these middle-of-the-night hours, as if we are moving in slow motion through space. People should recognize the power and the benefits of insomnia, how night stillness is like a spiritual vision.

"I think you're drunk, Anjou. A Wendy's Frostie is a dairy product. I ought to know. I eat at least three of them a week."

"I swear. Potatoes."

"Who told you this crock of shit?"

"Some guy from my Census orientation class. He was one of those vegan types."

"Don't ever believe a word a vegan tells you," Kip says, pointing his ruddy finger at me. "Anybody that has eliminated everything but sawdust and tofu from their diet starts to lose the capacity to think clearly."

"He seemed to really know what he was talking about."

"Ketones, Anjou. Ketones! That's what happens when you're deprived of real food. You start burning ketones because you have no carbohydrates and crazy shit happens. You get bad breath. You get irritable. You get dizzy. You lose the capacity to think clearly. Just like with the Hare Krishnas."

"Kip, listen to me," I say, pointing my finger back at him, "anything is possible. They put men on the moon. They can operate on a baby's heart while it's still inside the womb. They can decipher the language of dolphins. So what makes you think they can't make ice cream out of potatoes?"

"Because all of those other things make sense. But potatoes into ice cream? That, my dear, does not make sense."

"You know what actually does make sense?"

Kip looked at me with a poker face. He is a surveyor, a purveyor, feline in his tendency to observe.

"Hmmm," he says.

"I got my ass canned," I say.

Kip breaks into a loud laugh, slapping his thighs and waking Lurch, who was curled up by the door.

"Yup. That is definitely the first thing you've said tonight that makes sense."

"Why do you say that?"

"Christ, do I even need to answer that question?"

"That's my job, though."

"Huh?"

"That's my job. Asking questions."

"Right. Sure. And that, my dear, is what got you fired."

"I think I made a new friend out of it."

"That Wendy girl?"

"Well, her, too. I'm supposed to go shopping with her next week. But Thadius, the guy who was my supervisor, he's coming over for dinner one night next week. You need to join us."

"I do?"

"Yeah. He's sort of nerdy. You'll like him."

"Is this guy dating material?" Kip asks, and I love him for the very even way he asks me this. Quinn is dead, but Kip knows I will need to stop acting as if I am, eventually.

"No. Nothing like that."

"How old is he?"

"Forties? Hard to tell."

"Just what you need. Another middle-aged single male for a friend."

"Don't worry, you'll always be my favorite. But seriously, I've met two people during this job who I'll be social with. Stella will be proud. This is progress."

"I bet I can guess who got your ass canned."

"Go for it."

"Tina Buckley on Sompton Avenue," Kip says with a solid nod.

"I don't remember a Tina Buckley."

"She wears those cat's-eye glasses, thick black ones. She's about your age. Lives with her husband, a guy who's like ten years younger than her. She's like a marine—gets the job done before 6 A.M. or before you even have any idea she's getting that job done."

"Now I remember her," I say, impressed by Kip's accurate assessment of the very unflappable Tina Buckley.

"What did you ask her?"

"I asked her when she feels the most lonely."

"What did she say?"

"She asked me when I feel the most lonely."

"Seems fair."

"I guess, but I told her not to answer my question with a question."

"Christ, Anjou, you are losing it," Kip says, and I see a spread of concern across his face.

"I'm very focused right now, Kip," I say, and I feel tears coming to my eyes.

"I know you are."

"I need to know when other people feel lonely. This is important to me."

"I know, sweetheart. I know. It's a good question," Kip says and he puts his hand on my shoulder as I let everything go.

Kip loved Quinn wholeheartedly, and his tolerance of my method of grief has been admirable. Together he and Lurch have followed me on new routes through our neighborhood. About a week ago, Kip added a new item to his lawn: a street sign, *Yale Avenue,* paying homage to Quinn's alma mater. All of the streets in Mt. Gretna are named after colleges, and Quinn snuck out to steal it while I was in the middle of a conversation with Lily and Quinn's sister Celeste about Quinn's clothes and personal effects. I was telling them emphatically that nobody from Quinn's life except Kip can enter my house, that Quinn's ghost in there is mine, that Quinn would understand this request, that I would pack up everything and give it to Kip to drive to Lily's. I nailed a small shelf to the imposing oak tree in his front yard and set the street sign on it. Glyn Neath likes history—it will preserve it, keep it, and nod to all that it was.

⁂

Grace's house is a massive twin, three stories, big porche. It sits next to a fire station, and I wonder if that is alarming or soothing, how we rush to a disaster or save somebody from one. Her side of the twin is painted burnt orange, and she has an array of lights hanging from the roof of the porch. Unlike her neighbor, who has a modest wooden bench, Grace has an antique bumper car, red and silver and rusty, with the tall steel connector that reaches from the back bumper toward the ceiling. I immediately understand some aspect of Quinn's decision to love her.

I've called her fifty-one times, she lives only 1.6 miles from my house. I stand on her front lawn. It is May 24. May is perfect in Philadelphia, a month in which a string of days convinces you there is an Eden, with a cutting freshness of birth-death air, nirvana in a small backyard, all sounds stop because you will, too, you will stop in this moment of time that you are acutely aware of, vigilant to. It is one of those May days, in the middle of the day. I know Grace is here, because I can't imagine it any other way. I can't imagine that forcing this coincidence will go any other way. It is Tuesday afternoon. It is 2:30 P.M., an indefinable time that you know is there but you don't necessarily think of, a time Quinn always said is the best for making love. *The world is more interesting in the middle of the day, because it rests like a secret.* It is a time when little streets in quiet little towns are in a march of the black-and-white: Nothing or everything is happening at this time.

I have the list of questions for Grace. It seems the most sensible—the most reasonable—thing to do. I am being selfish—this entitlement, to expect her to tell me why she and Quinn chose each other. Stella would have done nothing, clung to dignity. Liz would have driven her car into Grace's living room window. Grace and I have both made selfish choices because of Quinn. I think she'll understand.

I have more questions that I think of now: What rooms did Quinn stand in or sit in or sleep in? What items of his do you have? Do you feel like a widow again? Whom did you call first when you heard that he had died? Do you believe in God? What do you think Quinn thought of at the moment he was hit—there in the air and swaying from life to death—what do you think he was thinking? Did you know him well enough to be able to imagine?

The world moves things for me today. I am standing on her porch about to knock on her door and she walks out from the side of the house. She is wearing gardening gloves. She stops in her tracks, and a look of surprise turns to ease.

"Anjou," she says, a small smile of relief on her face.

"What are you planting?" I ask.

I believe in small talk as a start. It works with my father.

"Annuals—geraniums, marigolds, petunias," she says.

"I'm here to ask questions," I say, and I instantly regret that I sound like an enumerator.

"Of course," she says, walking up to me at the porch, taking off her gloves. There is something I like about her immediately. She doesn't try to shake my hand or say anything nice. She barely looks me in the eye, but not rudely so.

"Why don't we go inside?" she offers.

She has dirt on her face, her knees, but her hands look so soft. The gray in her hair, the gray I was very aware of the first time I saw her in the bar, is gone. Her hair is shiny brown, and it is pulled back in a loose ponytail. It makes her wrinkles show more, but her face is comfortable in this age. I can understand why Quinn loved even just this face. I know nothing about her, but I know how Quinn saw the world. A settled-in look was the perfect counterpart to his reckless restlessness. He once told me that he loved the way I saw the world—the need for quiet, the fixation on the mundane and the subtle, the awareness of but not the need to control the order of things. He told me that he knew he loved me when he consistently saw how much I was pleased by a bowl of ice cream—that this level of simplicity in a well-educated person, a simplicity without self-awareness, was something he craved and admired. Quinn loved me in part, much to my confusion, because of how much I loved ice cream.

"Can we stay out here? Can we sit on your porch?" I ask.

"Of course," she says.

"He was in your house and I can't be in the house, because his ghost is there, at least for me, and the triangle of the three of us will scare me. You were never in my house, were you?"

"No, no. Never," she says quickly.

"Good."

I sit down on the uppermost stair to the porch. She will be sitting closer to me than she probably wants, but she is like her very name and she moves to the step and sits beside me. I hate that I would probably like her. I wanted her to be a scientist in the most literal sense, dismissive of data and observations and empirical evidence if they cannot reproduce themselves under the same conditions repeatedly, if they don't make for a reliable result. The list is in my pocket, but I'm on my own.

"What rooms in your house was Quinn in?"

"What rooms?"

"Yes, what rooms? Is it okay to ask you these questions?"

"Yes, of course."

"I know I don't have a right to know. But I want to know."

She nods at me.

"He was in my kitchen, the living room, my bedroom, the upstairs and downstairs bathrooms," she says.

"What about your son's room?"

"Even I don't go in there," she says with a small smile.

"Did he meet your son?"

"No. He's up north in college."

"That's all the rooms?"

"Well, the basement, too."

"To fix something?"

"Sort of. He thought he could fix my dryer. He tried."

"I told him he'd get himself killed playing with wires. But he found a dumber way to get himself killed," I say.

Kip is right, people don't become saints when they die, they are who they were, and Quinn could be pretty stupid at times. Walking and reading in the middle of an intersection was stupid. Tragic, but stupid. And he was duplicitous, outwardly and strikingly so, but I think he was not very different than the rest of us. His faults were just less hidden.

"What things of his did you have? Personal things. Books. Notes. Pictures. Anything like that. Anything he gave to you. Do you have his Delta Airlines weekend bag?"

"I don't have anything like that—no bag or anything."

"But he came here? The night he left? The night he left my house?"

"No," she says, shaking her head.

"He didn't come to stay here with you?"

"No. He asked if he could, but I wouldn't let him."

"Why not?"

"Because I didn't love him."

⟋⟍

We are inside her house now. If she didn't love Quinn, the triangle was not complete. It feels safe to me now. I am glad she did not love him. This is petty, I know, but I want this ridiculous claim, that I was the last person to love him.

"Why didn't you love him?"

We are sharing a bottle of wine and her windows are open. A cat sits on the floor in the corner by her cabinets and stares at me. Quinn hated cats, with a passion. He was quite vocal about this, about this small and insignificant thing. Cats! I know even more now that he loved her.

"Because I didn't trust him. I was in a very good marriage for a very long time. I know about trust, how important it is."

"Why was it a good marriage?"

"Well, the depth of friendship my husband and I shared was unlike anything I've ever known—far more important than the romantic passion those first few years of our marriage. I didn't even really love my husband until several years after we married."

"You didn't?"

"No," she says. "I cared about him immensely and I couldn't imagine spending my life with anybody else, but I didn't love him at first."

"Then why did you marry him?"

"Because he told me that we would get married. And I believed him."

"What was your husband's name?" I ask.

"His name was Alex. Alexander, but everybody called him Alex. He was from Germany. He was tall and very warm and he smiled a lot, completely unlike my stereotype of Germans, especially German scientists. He was a cell biologist," she says with a wide and comfortable smile.

"Do you think you would have loved Quinn, eventually?"

"Yes. I think so," she says with resignation, and Quinn is in the room.

"You would have," I say and I begin to cry. I put my face in my hands and cry for a long time and Grace does not reach for me.

≈

I have been at Grace's house for a very long time. It is late in the night but I have no idea what time it is. Grace doesn't keep clocks in the house. She says she refuses to be in a rush.

"This annoys my friends, and my son—I'm late a lot, or too early—but I don't want to know what time it is. The sun and the moon keep me abreast of things."

"Now I know why you scientists hung out with Quinn and all of the poets."

"A lot of us in the College of Medicine take great solace in words."

"And each other," I say.

"Yes, and each other," she says, looking me in the eye.

We are on our second bottle of wine, and the room is full of smells. Grace is cooking. I sit and drink and smoke. She likes casseroles.

"My son calls me the one-dish wonder," she says with a proud grin.

"I like casseroles."

"This is a good one," she says, leafing through a discolored and swollen copy of *The Joy of Cooking*. "Sausage, sweet potato, and fruit casserole."

Loose with alcohol, I cringe.

"It sounds gross, but trust me, it's great."

She gets ingredients and pans and utensils, refusing any help from me and only coming over occasionally to have one of my cigarettes. She tells me that she wanted to be a chef before she went to medical school, that she excelled in the sciences but didn't want to commit her life to them, that she was in culinary school for a solid year before dropping out to study medicine, that she finally realized that there were as many dishes to make as there were diseases to figure out.

Aside from Kip, Grace is the only person I have felt so comfortable talking to about Quinn since he died. I know this is the first and the last time I will see her, and this is why I have stayed so long. She will let me know if I have overstayed my welcome. She is a doctor—and doctors, as Quinn always told me, get to the point. Grace has patiently waded through my plethora of questions specifically related to the book in Quinn's hands on the day—that moment—that he died.

"I really wish I had it," I say. "I want the last thing he touched."

"I can understand that."

"I wonder what happened to it," I say, troubled by my fixation on the stack of words he held and read before he died.

"It probably got thrown out by a street cleaner, or run over and torn into shreds. Maybe somebody even took it."

"It was Proust," I say.

"Maybe somebody very smart and very patient took it."

We both laugh, buzzed and warm with the ghost of Quinn between us. I am glad that Quinn loved her, instead of anybody else, after my love was not enough love (and I could never have given enough love, but this never compromised my love for him or changed his love for me). This is not graciousness on my part. I am glad because my sadness can be focused, because I don't have to compare myself to Grace. I don't have to think he didn't realize how good he had it with me. He did know how good he had it with me, but that was not what defined love for Quinn.

"Was there something of your husband's—of Alex's—that you wanted after he died? Something you couldn't have?"

"As strange as it may sound, I wanted to feel his breath. I just wanted to feel him put his face up against the side of my cheek and breathe, just a lean up against me, about to whisper something."

"That's a nice thought—I mean it's warm," I say.

"It comforts me," she says, nodding.

I want to know, but I will not ask her if the complexity of her pain has shifted with the years to something she can articulate.

"Where did Quinn stay during those three days after he left?" I finally ask.

"The MacIntosh Inn."

An impossible set of words to be spoken between us, bright and stark and common.

"The MacIntosh Inn? In Aberdeen Station?"

"Yes," she says, looking down.

"That's fucking depressing," I say, shaking my head in disbelief.

"It is," she says. "I wish I had let him stay here when he asked."

"I didn't mean it that way when I said it. I didn't mean to make you feel bad or like you should have—"

"It's okay, Anjou. I know you didn't mean it that way. I felt that, though. I felt that when he died."

"Quinn hated hotels. He had a class he taught and the acronym was HOTEL—"

"History of the English Language," she says, finishing my small memory.

"How do you know that?"

"Bernie told me. I asked him lots of questions after Quinn died. Bernie was a very good friend to Quinn."

"He called me, especially after I started calling you," I said.

"They were an interesting match. Him being a psychiatrist and—"

"And Quinn being crazy," I say, finishing her sentence this time, and we both laugh, sad tears down my face and the laugh crossing over.

"I hate that I have that memory now. It's worse than when you see the body of the deceased at a viewing and they're puffy and have on a lipstick color that they'd never wear. Very sad. The entire time I was with Quinn before he left Lily we never met in a hotel—not once. Not in the city, not in the suburbs. Never. Quinn liked to be surrounded by warm, old things."

"I know."

"That's why he loved my house so much. It has scratches and creases that I didn't make," I say. "Quinn refused to sleep anywhere that wasn't at least fifty years old. He said that sleeping in a new place was like sleeping in a crypt."

Grace gets up and pours us glasses of water.

"Why didn't you go to the service at Mt. Gretna?" I ask.

"It would have been unfair," she says with an easy shrug. "To everybody—to his family, to you and Lily, especially. I was a secret of Quinn's for several months. It had only been three days since the secret ended. It would have been appalling, in all ways, to show up there."

"I was hoping you would be there. I had the list of questions for you. I showed the list to Lily at the service."

"She told me."

"She did?"

"She was pretty worried about you."

"She called me. Fourteen times. I never called her back, either. All of these nice people calling to help, and I ignored them."

"Lily is an extraordinarily kind woman."

"Why are you being so nice to me?"

"I don't think I know what you mean," she says.

"I don't know. *Nice* isn't even the right word. You're being compassionate. Why are you being so compassionate to me? I've called you a lot. A whole lot. I've practically stalked you."

"Yes, you have called me a lot."

"Fifty-one times."

"You counted?"

"Yes."

"I understand how you feel, in a different but same way, I understand."

She gets up and begins to pull plates and silverware from drawers. I stand to help her set the table and I am wobbly on my feet, the wine and cigarettes and weeks of little food taking their toll. She motions for me to sit down.

"You said you didn't love Quinn?"

"I didn't. But I loved my husband. He died many years ago and when he did, I did some unthinkable things. More unforgivable than your behavior—no offense intended, because I know your pain is as real as mine was. But grief is warped. So I know how you feel."

"I'm sorry."

"For what?"

"For calling you so much and hanging up. For all the shit I ordered—the magazines and the chickens—all of that, the day he left me."

"Turduckens," she says, and she reaches across the table to take a cigarette from my pack.

"Turduckens," I repeat, lighting her cigarette.

"Nasty habit," she says offhandedly. "Haven't smoked in years."

"I'm going to Italy in four days. I'm quitting the day I leave."

"Sounds like a good plan," she says, nodding at me.

"What did you do when your husband died?"

"I lost the plot, as the Australians are wont to say."

"You lost the plot?"

"I fell apart, went nuts, did unspeakable things."

"Unspeakable?"

"Pretty much," she says.

Enumerating has taught me how to read tone and eye movement and the placement of hands. I am waiting for her.

"My husband, Alex, died on a September afternoon in 1992, just an ordinary day, really. I remember the leaves weren't colorful— we had too much rain early that month, and so all of the leaves were torn from the trees long before they could turn. I don't want to talk about how he died because that is not how I remember my husband—I don't focus on those details, just that he was no longer alive and in my life and the life of our son. Two days after he died, I woke up, packed a bag, and left our house, this house. Our son, Christopher, was upstairs, still asleep. He was ten years old at the time. I drove to the airport and purchased a one-way ticket to Paris. When I got to Paris—it's where we honeymooned, where I knew I had chosen right even though I didn't love him yet—I holed myself up in the same exact hotel room that we had stayed in, in the Latin Quarter, for an entire week. I did this because I wanted to be alone to think about Alex for a while. I didn't want everybody coming at me—everybody telling me how they felt and asking me how I feel and telling me what to do and distracting me from the very important task of remembering. I did not call home or send a fax or do anything to inform my panic-stricken family where I was. They knew I was in Paris—tracked my plane-ticket purchase on my credit card. But I paid in cash from thereon, so I was virtually untraceable. My brother was here at the house with Christopher. It was a huge mess. I came home to such a huge mess, a devastating mess that I had caused for everybody. It was the single worst and most selfish thing I have ever done. My son lost his father and I disappeared. And the worst part was that for a very, very long time, I wasn't sorry. My son forgave me, but I think he only did so because he was so damn scared I'd leave again. Sometimes I'm still not sorry."

She puts out her cigarette and gets up from the table.

"I told Quinn this."

She washes her hands and brings the casserole over to the table. She begins scooping carefully into the casserole—the sweet smell of fruit and salty sausage run together with potatoes. I am starving.

I leave for Capri tomorrow. Kip is driving me to the airport. I have invited my father over for a walk through Glyn Neath with Lurch and me. Lurch is a hard dog to love, which made it easy for me to love him. For the first three months after I adopted Lurch from the local animal shelter, I rarely tried to even pet him. Mostly I would just talk to him. He didn't understand the insides of my words, but he understood what carried them. He was skittish and nervous. But over time he began to nuzzle me, to slap his lean shank against my leg or nudge at my hand for affection. A new growl emerged, a deep and warbling crescendo of sound, his vocal cords throttling, sounding almost mournful.

Because my father likes mail, I wanted to do the usual—make him a set of cards out of vintage postcards—but I do not know him well enough to choose a theme from somebody else's history. So last Saturday I went into the city to take a picture of his trinity on Addison Street. I didn't tell him I was coming. I just showed up with the digital camera I bought so many weeks ago along with all of my other shiny new electronics. Kip was as perplexed as I with the camera's functions. I called Wendy, and she came over with her husband, Jeff. Jeff is as blunt and outspoken as Wendy and together they showed me the basics of digital photography. Wendy brought a dog toy for Lurch, with a note from her cats. Lurch was none too pleased at their arrival, so I kept him upstairs. It takes Lurch time, and he is not used to how new people have been coming in and out of our house.

My father's trinity has a long crack on the upper section, near the two bedroom windows that are original to the house, the glass wavy and distorted. At the two windows of the first floor are flower-planter boxes. There are white-and-fuchsia bleeding hearts, their delicate necks holding the heavy load. The front door is colonial blue and distressed, a heavy gold knocker near the top. I wondered what it was like inside. The day was bright. I didn't know if my father was inside at the time, but it didn't take me long to get a good picture. I made ten copies of the picture and mounted them on a beautiful cream-colored card stock. This is as much as I know about my father's life now and, although my specialty is vintage, this was the only choice I had. I will give them to him later today.

My father and I take Lurch on a walk on my favorite route through Glyn Neath. We head north on Cardiff Avenue for several blocks. This is the busiest street out of the borough. Then we take a left onto Tremadog, where we descend into a quieter more leafy section of the hamlet. Tremadog is hilly, and Lurch is perceptive of my father's need to walk more slowly than our usual pace. My father looks very slight in his jackets, and this is something I'm still getting used to. At the top of Tremadog we cross over St. David's Avenue and head into a section of town where the roads stop being straight, the houses get bigger. We walk all the way down Ruthin Avenue and pass the high school. We can hear the screams of girls practicing lacrosse and watch as the boys' track team circles around the spongy lanes.

We haven't been talking about much of anything. I've explained some of Lurch's habits on this walk, his favorite trees, the dreaded beagle on Penn Road that always gets him in a fury. I like who my father is—right now, at this time in his life—understated, thoughtful, honest, vulnerable and lonely, and willing. He does not try to fix things. I do not like who he was, which I know is still part of who he is now. I don't know if I love him, or if I will ever love him again. But in the here and now, in Glyn Neath, with my dog and a list of questions that I'm allowed to ask at any time, anywhere, in any way, well, this is enough for me.

Eventually we circle back toward my house, taking a short cut through a woodsy section of town that is neither park nor property. There is a footpath, and for a short three minutes you feel like you are in a forest.

"Can I talk about question 8? From my list," I say.

"You can talk about anything you want, Anjou."

"Okay, well, the question was, knowing what you know now, do you think you would have done things differently, with Mom?"

My father is now holding Lurch's leash. My father takes a while, finally looking up.

"I hope so, Anjou," he says, looking far above my head into the spread branches of a large oak tree.

"What about you?" he asks after a pause. "With Quinn. Would you have done things differently?"

When Quinn died I was certain of my answer—No, I wouldn't have done a single thing differently. He was that powerful a force. Most people wouldn't give love that kind of power, but nothing had ever given me the same type of aliveness—the infinite present tense—that Quinn gave me when he loved me. That stunning cryptic and difficult love from Quinn did not fade or disappear or go away. It is hard to believe I would sacrifice a steady, even love for something like what Quinn gave me.

"It's too soon to tell, Jack."

13

CAPRI

I AM STANDING AT MOLO BEVERELLO, the port in Naples. I can see Mt. Vesuvius in the distance, grandfather-like and brooding.

"It's like sky swimming," my father said to Stella.

I was twelve. He was sitting on the edge of Stella's bed, where, weary and feverish, she had been home from school for days with the flu. She always asked our father to tell her about the Grotto when she was sick.

"The Italians call it La Grotta Azzura," our father said, consonants trilling across his tongue with his exaggerated accent. "The Grotto has an underwater cavity where the sunlight comes up, illuminating the cave and turning the water a rocket-force, almost unearthly shade of bright blue."

"What if the sun isn't shining?" Stella asked.

"It always shines in Capri. Always. Even when it's cloudy. Even when it's raining."

"How blue is it?"

"Well, it's like swimming through the air above you. They say that centuries ago, so so so long ago, long long long before you were even an idea in the pea-sized brains of your mother and me, the local fishermen believed the Grotto was haunted with evil spirits."

"I love evil spirits," Stella said, pulling her blanket up further under her chin, thrilled and smiling.

"But I disagree with ancient history, my butter cupcake," he said. "Only good spirits could make water turn that color."

It is a day that has stretched on, to Rome, to Naples, and now here buying a ticket for a ferry to Capri. I could get there more quickly on a hydrofoil—an *aliscafo*. But I am certain I should take my time. Before I caught my train to Naples, when I was standing in Roma Termini with a collective rush of people and sounds and a man calling times and trains in a language I did not know, I purchased a postcard for my father—it's a cheesy postcard, most new ones are to me, a bright picture of the Coliseum—and I mailed it to him. I wrote, *I'm almost there.*

When the ferry arrives at Marina Grande in Capri, I walk across the dock and get in line to wait for a bus, the Autoservizio, to take me to the other side of the island, to Anacapri. There are more than just tourists in line; locals crowd into the queue, which is getting longer, and more informal. Without a hint of rudeness, friends and acquaintances see each other and the line changes: Some people step out of line and go toward the back and some people come right in front of you and take their place. Two locals start talking to me, telling me the bus is always late. A striking middle-aged woman wearing a black dress and high heels and an old man in a dark gray suit talk to me in their earnest and choppy English.

Sandwiched between them, I tell them I am going to Evangelina's Guest House. *Ah, yes yes yes.* Everybody knows Evangelina, I learn. I ask them the best way to get to Evangelina's and a discussion ensues. Words are floating and shifting and then their voices rise.

The small bus arrives. We probably won't fit. If Stella were here, she'd organize everybody, and she'd tell a few of these women to repack their suitcases or double up the items in their shopping bags, and there'd be room to spare. A man from the end of the line—in his fifties, with rheumy eyes and oily dark skin—rushes up to me. He takes my backpack and, before I can respond, butts to the front of the line and carries it onto the bus. From the window he is smiling at me widely and shaking his head up and down and motioning me to get on. The man and woman on either side of me are yelling now and the woman tugs at my arm to keep me moving as the bus fills.

Capri and Anacapri are separated by a solid force of nature— a limestone cliff. In 1874, a road was paved on this cliff, finally joining these distinctly different sections of the island. The bus drives up the narrow cliff, cutting back and forth like ribbon, without yellow lines or speed limits, and I hold my breath when we pass other vehicles on the outer portion of the cliff, the marina below. Bodies are pressed everywhere. German tourists, old ladies, Americans, local teenagers—a weaving death-defying drive up an impossibly steep cliff with nothing to keep us from careening over the side. I am still sandwiched between the bickering twosome. They look a bit friendlier, but are still negotiating. The man who butted in line to carry my backpack keeps smiling at me.

We reach the first stop in Anacapri at a busy intersection where cars and vehicles that are motorcycles with a small wall-like shield around them are clogged at every corner, pedestrians shopping and sitting outside in cafés and restaurants. The two-some continue the negotiations. I stand up, ready to grab my pack. But each arm is grabbed. A young Italian girl, probably in her late teens, shakes her head and smiles at me.

"They're figuring out what is best for you."

I am standing on a rickety grate at the bottom of slippery metal stairs that are built right into the cliff face. Inches above the sea, the waves are not rough, and lap at the bottoms of my feet. The Grotto is just a few hundred feet away, a jump and a short swim. I am still and three German ladies behind me start to whisper. I am holding things up. I can hear the Canadians in the distance. They were in front of me coming down the stairs and they have already swum away into the cave. I hear them shouting, but I can no longer see them.

The woman behind me taps me on the shoulder.

"Pardon?" she says delicately in an accent that could be any language. She puts her hands out, palms skyward, in a universal gesture—*What gives?* She's ready, and so are her friends. I leap forward and water that is colder than I expected envelops me. I swim to the cave, the voices of people getting closer, the ocean a different sound now—it goes back and forth. My arms are deep in the impossible blue, the sun still bright but in the horizon it is turning pink, moving down fast. In the cave, the blue hurts my eyes, so I float on my back. I am swallowed up, I am held, I am joined in these waters.

All of these strangers around me know how important it is to be quiet. They see something, too. The color of blue has silenced us all. It's time to just listen.